JESSICA THOMPSON

A Caterer's Guide to Valentines and Violence

BITTERSWEET
MYSTERIES

First published by Bittersweet Mysteries 2024

Copyright © 2024 by Jessica Thompson

All rights reserved. No part of this publication may be reproduced, stored or transmitted in any form or by any means, electronic, mechanical, photocopying, recording, scanning, or otherwise without written permission from the publisher. It is illegal to copy this book, post it to a website, or distribute it by any other means without permission.

This novel is entirely a work of fiction. The names, characters and incidents portrayed in it are the work of the author's imagination. Any resemblance to actual persons, living or dead, events or localities is entirely coincidental.

Jessica Thompson asserts the moral right to be identified as the author of this work.

Jessica Thompson has no responsibility for the persistence or accuracy of URLs for external or third-party Internet Websites referred to in this publication and does not guarantee that any content on such Websites is, or will remain, accurate or appropriate.

Designations used by companies to distinguish their products are often claimed as trademarks. All brand names and product names used in this book and on its cover are trade names, service marks, trademarks and registered trademarks of their respective owners. The publishers and the book are not associated with any product or vendor mentioned in this book. None of the companies referenced within the book have endorsed the book.

First edition

Editing by Jamie Bates

This book was professionally typeset on Reedsy.
Find out more at reedsy.com

For Nathan.
My Jake.

Contents

Acknowledgement	iv
Chapter 1	1
Zuppa Toscana (Tuscan-style soup)	14
Voluntary Statement	16
Chapter 2	17
Thai Glass Noodle Salad (Yum Woon Sen)	30
…	32
Chapter 3	33
Beefy Chow Fun	45
…	48
Chapter 4	49
Rigatoni fra Diavolo	55
Chapter 5	58
…	66
Chapter 6	67
Chapter 7	74
…	86
Chapter 8	87
Microwave Chocolate Mug Cake (egg-free)	97
Chapter 9	99
Chicken Tikka Masala for the Slow-Cooker	109
Chapter 10	113
…	121
Chapter 11	122

Maple Browned Butter Blondies with Craisins and White...	129
Chapter 12	131
...	141
Chapter 13	142
Mango Lassis	148
Chapter 14	149
Chapter 15	157
Crusty Dutch Oven Bread	165
Chapter 16	167
Savory Green Ebleskivers or Ebleskivers Florentine	176
Chapter 17	179
Chapter 18	188
Chapter 19	195
One-Pan Penne	207
...	209
Chapter 20	210
...	224
Chapter 21	225
Almond Meringue Nests	233
Passion Fruit Pastry Cream	235
Chapter 22	237
Strawberry Coulis	246
...	248
Chapter 23	249
...	257
Chapter 24	258
...	265
Chapter 25	266
Chapter 26	275
Chapter 27	280

Mapo Tofu	289
Chapter 28	292
Ants Climbing Trees (a Chinese noodle dish)	300
Chapter 29	302
Tom Kha (Thai Coconut Milk Soup)	309
Thank You!	311
About the Author	312
Also by Jessica Thompson	314

Acknowledgement

I feel like I've grown so much, but also like I still know nothing. I rely so much on the people around me and they all helped this book to come out.

Thank you to Jamie Bates, my editor, who always gives me the boosts, the editing, and the advice I need. Thank you to Jessica (J.R.) Lancaster, my author friend and branding professional, for holding my hand (virtually) and helping me pray through the ups and downs of writing and publishing. Thank you to Heidi O'Barr and the rest of the Messy Manuscript Society for being my listening ears, my alpha- and beta-readers, my support system, my classmates, and my friends.

Always a big thank you to my Heavenly Father and my family. I wouldn't be able to do any of this without their constant and invisible support.

Happy Valentine's Day! I love you all!

Chapter 1

"Hey, gorgeous!" Josh called as the door closed behind him.

"Hey, handsome!" Violet said, raking her highlighted, chocolate-brown hair under a Cupid's arrow headband. No matter how many times he told her, and no matter how platonic she knew it was, it always brightened her day. He knew it, and that's why he always did it. She again adjusted her headband which made it look like she'd been shot through the head with a heart-tipped arrow. Violet grinned. "You're late. And did you remember your receipts?"

"Only ten minutes—I'm getting better! I think you're a good influence on me," he said as he took off a black baseball cap, uncovering short ash-blond curls, and tossed down a wad of tangled strips of paper. "Thanks for always keeping track. You're the best. You know the IRS would be all over us if it were left to me." He called to Taylor as she joined them in the commercial kitchen from the long, curved hallway beyond, "Hey, rockstar!" His ever-so-slight Scottish accent appeared only in his inflection.

"She's the only one keeping the health department at bay too," Taylor said, giving Violet a grateful smile.

Josh squeezed Violet's shoulder and laughed at Taylor. "Nice headband. I thought you were serious when you said you would wear those devil horns from last Halloween."

Taylor gave him a sarcastic smile from under her headband which featured little hearts on springs that bobbled when she moved. They had all agreed to wear their solid black catering outfits, but with the addition of some fun accessories to match tonight's themed dinner. Violet knew that the Dining Out dinner was a formal event for the Army, but she thought the unit would appreciate their small effort to match the Valentine's Day motif. "Yeah, I wanted to, but I wouldn't do that to Violet or our new business. And where is your outfit's Valentine's twist?"

Both girls hovered while Josh bent to his bag. He spun around with his hands at his throat. "Ta-da!"

"Is that a clip-on?" Taylor said, laughing.

"Nice, right?" Josh said, leaning back on his heels to display his addition of a pre-tied necktie covered in tiny red hearts.

Violet grinned. "I think it's perfect. Thanks, y'all." She got back to chopping onions and spied Taylor rolling her eyes at Josh and sighing.

The tingle of onions in the air threatened to make Violet tear up as Josh looked between Taylor and Violet. He said, "Anyway ... are you two okay?"

"What do you mean?" Violet said, looking at Taylor in time to catch a stink-eye that she was shooting at Josh. Her bright blue eyes glared in sharp contrast to her dark skin and natural twist out, making her icy stare look extra chilling. Violet's eyes narrowed in response. "What's wrong?"

"Nothing," Taylor said, a little too quickly. "He means you. Is today a good day or a bad day? Need me to grab some Dove chocolates for you from the big bowl out there?"

Violet sighed. "Always, but ... I'm feeling ... medium.

CHAPTER 1

Knowing that I have to see Derek tonight is not helping. It's so strange. When he was deployed, all I could think about was seeing him again and wondering if his battalion would be back before Valentine's Day. And now, with all that's happened, I don't know ... I don't know how to feel when I see him. And he keeps calling me, but ... I don't know."

Taylor lunged and snatched Violet's hand, raising it to show Josh. "Oh no. Look!"

"Uh-oh," Josh said, frowning and letting his shoulders slump. "She's relapsed."

"I can't believe you're wearing it again," Taylor exclaimed and turned towards the cooler bag Josh had brought. "Fine. Do whatever you want. I'm starving."

Violet looked down at the big engagement ring, the object of their ridicule. It had been such a source of comfort to her the whole year and a half that her new fiancé had been deployed—it was hard to let it go. Her mouth opened and closed a few times, but she didn't have any defense that her two closest friends hadn't heard before.

"When your fiancé cheats on you, you're supposed to dump him. Hard," Taylor scolded and pinned up one side of her natural curls, then the other, revealing the undercut she hid beneath. She wrapped her apron around her waist twice. "You're supposed to scream, throw things, and never speak to him again. You are supposed to throw that giant rock in his face, or at least pawn it and spend the money on our new catering business. If all you do is take a step back, then ..."

As Taylor trailed off, Violet couldn't help but admire the diamond's sparkle under the bright lights. Despite Violet's insistence on something modest, her fiancé had wanted to give her a ring she could show off. The industrial lights illuminated every facet and mirrored them back in fractured prisms on the walls. The Pearl Stable did have great lighting, and it had even been in the running for Violet's reception—before her wedding planning had ground to a halt.

The Stable was nestled in the heart of the trendy part of San Antonio that had once been the sprawling Pearl Brewery. Back then it was the home of the draft horses but was now an elegant event venue. Each day, when Violet left her culinary school classes to walk home, she traced her path around the oval building. She admired its antique Texas limestone, curved walls, and intricately carved details. Every day it gave her something pleasant to daydream about on the way home. Or at least it used to.

"I know, Tay." Violet let one tear leak out of the corner of her eye before sweeping it aside, sniffing, washing her hands until they hurt, and returning to the infuriating pile of diced onion on her cutting board. She curled her fingers back into 'the bridge technique' that she had learned more than a year ago, but despite all her practice, she was still slow at rocking the knife through the vegetable. "You've told me a hundred times. If I don't give it enough time and space, then I won't know when to trust him again."

Her vision clouded with tears, so Violet gave up cutting onions as hopeless, washed her hands again, and took two steps sideways to the pile of receipts in the corner. She pulled out more slips of paper from a side pocket of her purse, flattened out the ones she'd received from Josh, lined them up exactly, folded them, and paperclipped them together in a manila folder.

"Tell me I'm wrong," Taylor said and up-nodded at Violet as she stood next to her, making it look like a challenge. Taylor was about five inches shorter than Violet's five feet ten inches, but she could look much more intimidating.

"You're not wrong." Violet blinked hard. Despite how frustrated she was, she took the time to label the folder, lined it up exactly in her accordion-style file holder, and carefully wiped her eyes on her long, pristine apron. She hated that this conversation was overshadowing their big night. This event could really help their business take off. "It's just... it's hard to let go. I've been with him since high school."

"Right," Taylor said, now nodding slowly.

"And I believe in forgiveness," Violet said, adjusting her headband a little farther back on her head. "Don't you?"

"Of course!" Taylor pulled Violet to some nearby stools and sat down knee-to-knee with her. A group of chatting and bustling women dressed in red, some of whom were Violet's friends, marched by the open kitchen door carrying clear plastic bins of pink and red decorations for tonight's event. Taylor went on. "And being so forgiving is one of your best qualities. Heaven knows we wouldn't be friends if you weren't so forgiving, considering how often I stick my foot in my mouth... But Vi, don't you think you can forgive someone without making the same mistake of trusting them again?"

"So one misstep and I should never have faith in that person again?" Violet folded her arms in an effort to hide the offending gem under her other arm.

"Sure, maybe. You could have faith in him again, eventually... when he's made it up to you. And you know it wasn't only one misstep. It was months. He misstepped over and over and over again. Knowing what he was doing. And lying. And—"

Violet slumped on her stool. "Did you know studies show

that a person can only listen to about twelve minutes of censure before their brain checks out? Besides, we talked about this. Being deployed isn't exactly a normal situation. It's ... high stress."

"Sure. And I'm sorry about the rant. You know I only lecture because I love you," Taylor said, reaching over and squeezing Violet's arm. "But a person has to earn back your faith! You ... Well, I worry about you. Okay? You have to learn who is worthy of your trust."

Violet finally looked into Taylor's ice-blue eyes that contrasted so starkly with her dark skin. Over the last year and a half of being in culinary school together and becoming best friends, she had still never had the nerve to ask if they were contacts or natural. But Violet had seen colored contacts and she suspected Taylor's eyes were the real thing. Either way, they were chilling and shot a jolt of pity that Violet felt in her core.

Violet flinched as her phone vibrated, then played "Since You Been Gone," the ringtone that Taylor had put on her phone about a month ago as motivation and encouragement.

"It's him. I should probably answer it." Violet glanced at her phone, then sighed and set her cumbersome headband on the table. "But don't worry, he's probably checking on how things are going for tonight. You know this has been months of work for him."

"Mm-kay," Taylor said, getting up and striding towards the cutting board with the onions. "Just remember that you're too busy carrying us to carry him too." She gave a cheesy grin. "So be careful!"

She stepped out of the kitchen and into a rounded hallway that hugged the outside wall of the oval building. "Hi, Derek."

CHAPTER 1

"Hey, babe," said a smooth baritone. Lieutenant Derek Valentine, Violet's not-so-ex-fiancé, had always been able to make her heart flip despite her best efforts. "How's it going?"

"Good," Violet said, keeping the mood professional. "Your caterers, Taylor, Josh, and I, are here. Most of our food is already prepped and ready to go for stir-frying or tossing. Everything's already been unloaded from the vans and I've collected all our receipts, but I can tell you more about that later. I saw the Sweethearts Club come in with decorations. Suzanne was holding this thing that was like—"

"I mean, how are *you*, babe?" he purred into the phone. "Are you wearing it for me and my big day, like you promised?"

"Did I promise?" Violet said, clearing her throat lightly and looking down at her hand again. She had to admit it was a gorgeous ring. Her resolve started to melt. "Well, I'm wearing it. But I'm wearing it because you told me a breakup was bad timing for your career. Not because you own Valentine's Day—no matter what your last name is. After tonight goes well, then please tell your commanding officer that we're taking a step back. Please let me take this time. So yeah, I'm wearing it for you-professionally, not for you-you. Not yet."

"Thanks, babycakes, and don't worry about it," Derek said with a smile in his voice. "What would I do without you?"

"Hmm," Violet almost giggled but stopped herself. She stood up straighter to project a professional air. As she heard Josh walking up behind her, she cupped her hands around the speaker and whispered, "I'll see you when you get here."

"Yeah, it should be about a half hour. I have to wrap up one more thing."

Violet hung up and shook her shoulders free of the tension that had crept in during the conversation. She breathed in the aroma of the sausage and potatoes in the Tuscan-style soup that Josh had brought for their team to have a quick dinner before the rush of the evening. She called to him when she heard him walk up behind her.

"Hey, handsome!" Violet said. In the past, they had only used this greeting when they first saw each other every day, but since her breakup a month ago, they had used this greeting any time Violet needed a little pick-me-up. "Smelling good!"

"Well, hello," a strange man's voice replied with a chuckle, making Violet jump and turn. "I would reciprocate, but I'm here in an official capacity. But I agree, whatever y'all are making smells wonderful."

Violet stumbled against the wall and felt her entire face burn with embarrassment when she saw a pair of blue eyes and a face of chiseled features she didn't recognize. She laughed lightly. "I'm sorry, I ... I thought you were someone else."

The tall man grinned back at her with amusement. "Well, sorry to disappoint." His broad shoulders shrugged and his short red buzzcut signaled that he was with the military, like most people involved with this event, but he was out of uniform. He wore a gray Army PT shirt and jeans, so Violet couldn't find his nametag or rank insignia. But she knew this wasn't Derek's boss, Captain Shoenthal.

"Uh, official?" Violet repeated. "Did you need something?"

"Actually..." he said and gave her a warm smile that favored his left cheek. Violet smiled back at him involuntarily. "I'm here to help prepare for this battalion Dining Out in any way I can. I asked your team in the kitchen and they gave me a weird look and said that I needed to come to ask you."

Violet felt her cheeks burn again as she pictured Taylor and

Josh looking him up and down, smiling, and making plans for Violet's love life.

"Um, we, um, the catering staff, is actually in good shape. As you can smell, most of the food is almost ready," Violet said, stammering.

"Yeah, are you making Thai food?" he asked with a joy in his eyes.

"Yes, nice... um, nice nose. I mean, I'm impressed you could tell from the smell. Especially mixed with other smells."

"Well, Thai restaurants are my favorite, so the smells of fish sauce and lime juice jumped out and grabbed me."

"Oh, are those hallmarks of Thai cuisine?" Violet asked.

"Yes, well, they are to me. I'm alright in the kitchen, but I have no formal training. I guessed you would know better than me" he said.

"Well, sometimes I feel like I'm all formal training and need to work on branching out. And ... we haven't covered that in culinary school yet," Violet said. She surprised herself by divulging so much to a stranger, but his warm yet piercing gaze drew her in. "I think I need to try Thai food next."

"Never been?" he said with raised eyebrows.

"No, just the stuff that Taylor makes. That's what you're smelling."

"So ... nothing I can help with?" he asked again.

Violet flexed her mouth down to chase away her silly grin. "Well, I bet the Sweethearts Club needs help with the decorations. They just got here and they always need a tall person to help them hang stuff. Usually, they ask me, so you'll be helping me if you're there ... helping them."

Violet guffawed, then cleared her throat and wondered why she was being so awkward.

"Roger that." He smiled again. "I guess ... thanks for helping me help them help you."

"Well, then ..." Violet chuckled. "You're welcome, good job, and thanks to you too."

"I wish I could keep talking to you, but I think I lost track of what we're talking about," he chuckled.

"Me too. I think we got lost in a mire of platitudes." Violet said as she grinned and tucked one side of her hair behind an ear.

"I'm Jake Whitehouse." He stuck out his hand for a shake.

"Hi," Violet said and hugged herself with one arm and took his rough, strong grip in hers, trying to keep her smile cordial instead of letting it spread over her whole face. "I'm Violet. Violet Davis."

"Nice to meet you, Violet." Jake had a twinkle in his eye as he went on. "Hey, could I ask, what are you doing tomorrow night? Maybe I could show you my favorite Thai pl—"

The doors to the main room of The Stable burst open, revealing the low, elaborate lighting fixtures and exposed beams of the ceiling, and Suzanne Shoenthal, the bubbly and dramatic head of the Sweethearts Club. As the wife of the captain, she had put herself in charge of decorating for tonight's party, as well as most other battalion events.

"There you are, Violet! We're saved!" Suzanne crowed and gestured wildly with her hands. "We need you on the ladder for these decorations."

As Violet's eyebrows furrowed and she thought of a nice way to explain that she was there as the caterer and not as a member of Suzanne's little army, Jake cut in.

"Welp, that's my cue," he said. "I'll catch up with you later. You can focus on the food. I got this."

CHAPTER 1

She suspected that comment was as much for Suzanne's benefit as it was for hers and it made one of Violet's eyebrows rise with curiosity about the man before she strode back to the kitchen to get to her work.

"Order up," Josh called as Violet sat down after washing her hands and taping up a knuckle that was starting to bleed from too much scrubbing. She slid into one of the folding chairs in the corner of the big professional kitchen. Josh liked any excuse to use the lingo from his old waitering jobs he had worked after dropping out of high school. He was only nineteen now, definitely Violet's youngest friend, so he must have come straight from waitering to culinary school instead of from a university as Violet and Taylor had. "As my dear ol' dad says, 'Stick in till you stick out.' Eat what you can in fifteen minutes, then it's back to work."

He jammed a bowl into Violet's hands, then sat down with his own at the prep table.

"So...?" Taylor called from her perch on the stainless steel counter and grinned at Violet. She was the same age as Violet's twenty-two, both having begun culinary school after college, but Taylor sounded older because of a raspy voice from a kicked cigarette habit. "Did you meet that guy? Who was he?"

"Jake-something," Violet said and let a smile play on her lips despite herself. "He did say that you two told him that he had to come to meet me. Am I right in suspecting that you didn't mean that entirely professionally?"

"Mmm," Taylor said, cocking her head and looking around the room in exaggerated innocence. "Maybe."

Speaking around a mouthful of kale and cannellini beans, Josh was at least honest. "He seemed like your brand of chill. I had to send him your way. You know, in case you don't work things out with Lieutenant Douche-bag."

"Shhhh!" Violet hissed as her eyes flew wide. "I realized that everyone can probably hear us talking in this echoing space. And we're not exactly being quiet. Jake in the next room, or Derek who is coming soon, might hear us! Or the whole Sweethearts Club! And ... since when am I chill?"

"You know, he's like the kind of chill that you could use more of in your life," Josh said.

"Yeah, he's the kind of guy I picture you being with. Not Derek," Taylor admitted, shrugging. "On the other hand, I hate to admit it, but I suppose Derek was nice enough to get us this job, and at this point, we need any and all help getting this business off the ground, unless we want to go back to the grueling conditions of those professional kitchens."

They all frowned at the floor. Violet flashed back to the short time she had spent in the culinary school's campus restaurant, Savor, and the food truck job she'd had in college. The heat, the swearing, the endless rush and stress, not to mention the grime and sweat and 'don't get caught' attitude towards health code violations in the truck that made her neuroses flare up and her scalp contract into a wince.

"You're right," Josh said, his Adam's apple bobbing. "Can't go back to being a peon in some kitchen. But we'll rise above, right?"

Taylor opened her mouth to say something but looked as though she thought better of it, then joined Violet in nodding.

Josh declared, "Right, bring it in."

The three set down their empty bowls and were melting into a group hug when the kitchen door flew open. Derek posed in the doorway in his full dress uniform, complete with every little ribbon he could get away with wearing, whipped

CHAPTER 1

off his aviator sunglasses, and said, "Hey, babe. Your waiting is over. Whoa! Who died?"

Zuppa Toscana (Tuscan-style soup)

Serves: 4-6

Total time - 30 minutes

I love to make this soup with whatever greens are available. I like kale for the texture, but I've used Swiss chard, fresh and frozen spinach, fennel fronds, pea greens, and even sweet potato leaves.

Ingredients:
- 1 lb. ground Italian sausage
- 1 garlic clove, minced
- ½ teaspoon red pepper flakes
- 4 small russet potatoes, cut into ½ inch cubes
- 1 (14 ounce) can of cannellini beans, with liquid (optional)
- 4 cups chicken stock
- 1 teaspoon dried basil
- 1 teaspoon dried parsley
- ½ teaspoon dried rosemary
- ¼ teaspoon dried oregano
- ¼ teaspoon ground black pepper

ZUPPA TOSCANA (TUSCAN-STYLE SOUP)

¼ teaspoon salt
⅛ teaspoon ground dried sage
1 big bunch of fresh kale, midribs removed, roughly chopped
1 cup whipping cream

1. In a large, heavy-bottomed stockpot, brown sausage over medium-high heat while breaking up and mixing around your sausage crumbles.
2. Add garlic and chile, mix and cook for about 30 seconds, then add potatoes, beans and their liquid, and stock.
3. Mix in basil, parsley, rosemary, oregano, pepper, salt, and sage. Bring up to a boil, cover your pot, turn heat down to low, and let simmer for 20 minutes.
4. Uncover pot, turn heat up to medium if not bubbling, and mix kale into the boiling soup. Cook for about 2 minutes, or until greens are softened but still bright green. Then turn off heat and stir in cream. Add salt and pepper to taste.
5. Serve immediately with bread sticks or salad.

Voluntary Statement

Please give detailed information including what happened, how and why if known, and names of other persons involved or present at the time.

Statement:

...

I did it.

I can't believe I did it but I did.

I didn't want to but I had to. Even while I was doing it, it didn't seem real. Like I was watching someone else kick him. I was somewhere outside of myself, telling myself to stop but I couldn't. I had to do it.

...

Chapter 2

"Violet! I need you!" said Eve, Violet's friend from the Sweethearts' Club, at the door after Derek left, creating a crinkling noise as she rushed to squeeze her full, lavender skirt through the door frame.

Eve's hands gripped at the butt of her dress as her friend, Heather, came in behind her and cried, "Do you have safety pins? Like, a lot of them?"

It was about one hour until show time and Violet surmised that Eve must have finished decorating the hall and was getting dressed for the Dining Out. Her round, dark face still had no makeup and her usual goddess braids were unadorned, so Violet guessed she had discovered the tear before getting too far into the process.

Heather was still in her red t-shirt and jeans, but her pale, china doll face was fully made up with evening amounts of pink, sparkling eye shadow. Her platinum blonde hair was twisted up into a perfectly messy chignon and she was still sticking bobby pins in, so Violet surmised that they had come from the bathroom where they had crossed paths.

Violet grabbed Eve's dark brown shoulders and spun her around. "Let me take a look." As Violet moved Eve's hands and long braids away, she saw a huge tear in the iridescent fabric extending from the bottom of the zipper.

"My boyfriend pulled it out of the closet this afternoon and it got stuck on something and must've torn. I thought I saw something wrong with the fabric through the bag on my way in, but I didn't think it was that bad, and…"

Violet's heart fell as Taylor spoke up from behind her. "No way, girl! There aren't enough safety pins in the world for that rip." Violet looked at the fraying edges and the obvious lining fabric glaring through and had to agree. Taylor leaned in and said, "But Violet, you live practically across the street from here. You got a sweater or something she could wear? That way you could grab some more hot pads for us too."

"Oh!" Violet exclaimed. "I can do better than that."

After making sure the kitchen was in good shape for her to be away for a few minutes, and after getting Eve to change back into her street clothes, the two women rushed out the door, past one block of buildings, and into Violet's apartment.

"I know you're a little thinner than me, but I have this stretchy maroon, crushed velvet dress that I was going to wear for Valentine's Day before … Well, I canceled my reservations and now I don't know if I'm even going to need it in a few days," Violet said, quickly retrieving it from her bedroom as Eve drifted towards the living room. "And it's not as formal as your other dress, but do you think this will work?"

As Violet trotted in with the dress draped over her arm, she found Eve standing in her empty living room, slowly rotating towards her with knit eyebrows.

"What happened?" Eve asked with a high, sad voice. "How long have you lived here? Or were you robbed or something?"

Violet looked around, her throat tightening. The apartment had no furniture except a mattress that sat directly on the

CHAPTER 2

floor. Her kitchen was fully equipped with quality knives and tools, but a card table and the long kitchen counters acted as the only surfaces where her team had prepped this catering job. Violet had told herself that she was a no-frills kind of girl anyway, but it hurt now, having someone over that didn't know the whole story.

"I haven't told anyone, but Derek and I kinda broke up. It was all his furniture." Violet tried to keep smiling, but she could feel her expression turn to cardboard. "At least it's really easy to keep clean now ... but we're not really telling people yet, so don't say anything, okay?"

"Oh, I'm so sorry. But what do you mean 'kinda broke up?'" Eve said, her confusion changing to pity as she came to give Violet a hug.

"Well, he wants to make it up to me and get back together, so he hasn't officially moved out. Like on paper. And you know how slow it is to get something changed with the Army. He's been crashing on a friend's couch."

As Eve moved back to a comfortable speaking distance, her eyes glistened with unshed tears. They had laughed and worked together at Sweethearts meetings and events, but Violet suddenly realized they were not all that close. Not close enough for Eve to have known the story or been to her apartment before now.

"Can I ask what happened? Did he do something stupid?"

Violet forced a laugh. "Well, I don't know if she's stupid, but ..."

Eve mustered a tight smile and said, "I feel you. My boyfriend, Pete, has made a couple mistakes too."

"A couple?" Violet said. She couldn't help but raise her eyebrows. "Like, it's happened more than once?"

"Yeah, well," Eve said, fidgeting. "Men are pigs, and all that, right? Too bad we can't stop loving them."

Violet could not think of anything to say as she wondered if she herself sounded like Eve did right now.

"So, the furniture was his? Where is it now?" Eve asked.

"Right after I found out, I was crying so much that I couldn't sleep. I had to do something, so I moved it all one night before I really thought about how empty the apartment would be without it." Violet opened the door to the spare bedroom to reveal the stacks of chairs, the TV sitting on the couch, and the disassembled dining room table.

"Oh, wow," Eve gasped.

"Yeah," Violet said, frowning. "Derek has said a lot about how hard it is to change housing in the military, but I don't know if I believe that. I mean, don't military officers move all the time?"

They exchanged an awkward smile.

"Anyway, I don't know if he's even tried because he's still begging me to keep his stuff here, to wait, to calm down, to let him make it up to me, all that. I guess I'm giving us both some time this way," Violet said.

"Well... I'm sorry... but thanks," Eve said before slipping the dress off of Violet's arm and closing herself in the bathroom, leaving Violet alone with the stacks of furniture.

Looking at this room made Violet's stomach and jaw clench. It was everything she didn't want to take the time to think about. Not only the mess of belongings, but all of it.

Had she forgiven Derek? She wanted to let go, but of what? Let go of the anger, the betrayal, the furniture, or let go of him altogether? Could she forgive him for sleeping with someone he had been deployed with? Had he really been about to tell her when she found those pictures on his phone?

Sometimes she wished she had never found those incriminating photos. Then everything would have stayed normal and under control.

The part of that train of thought that rang true was the idea of 'normal and under control.' That's what she wanted. That's the idea that made her face relax and her stomach's knots untie.

They made it through hard times before. She remembered reuniting with Derek after a year. He was a year older and had left for college a year before she could. Even though they were only about an hour apart, they had been in different worlds. They had missed each other terribly. That was another time they had something come between them, but they had been able to get back to normal and fall into step with each other like they had never been apart.

Violet wanted that again. She wanted it to be like he had never betrayed her. She wanted it to be easy again so she could have the freedom to focus on her new business and culinary school.

"Thank you so much, Violet! You are the absolute best!" Eve said behind her, snapping her out of her stupor.

Violet saw that her friend, who had bigger breasts and smaller hips, fit the stretchy burgundy dress perfectly. "Wow, that looks great! It might even look better on you than me."

"Well, you are amazing." Eve grinned. "Should we get back to work?"

"Yes." Violet said, swallowing hard and refocusing on the Dining Out gig that needed to go off without a hitch. "Definitely."

Violet and her crew had been hired to cater the formal

dinner for Derek's Army unit, where soldiers and their plus-ones would gather for an evening of camaraderie and fellowship. Called a Dining Out because it was held off base, the dinner had been Derek's pet project and he'd advocated to hire her new company. It was a dream contract: a gorgeous venue, a healthy budget, and plenty of time to plan a perfect menu. And someone else had been hired to tend the bar. The arrangement was perfect for Violet who didn't know the first thing about booze, but had been a near constant source of stress for Derek.

The bartender had stayed aloof whenever Derek had followed up with him over the last month, until last night when the situation had finally collapsed. The bartender had canceled, leaving Derek with no time to find another. Instead, he'd bought boxes of booze and planned to leave the bottles out for everyone to pour their own drinks.

Violet did not see that going well.

It was a formal event, marked by decorum and restraint, and tradition required a long list of toasts at the beginning of the event to almost anyone they could think of—the president, the United States, the Army, the officers, fallen soldiers, the planners of the event, and anyone else whom the officers wanted to honor. And for each toast there was only one right way to respond, as scripted in the event's program. Everything about the evening revolved around etiquette and 'being an officer and a gentleman' as Derek had put it. But how did an open bar, required drinking, and somber etiquette coexist in the same party?

Violet could at least ensure that the food would be beyond reproach and hopefully secure future catering gigs for her fledgling company.

CHAPTER 2

When Violet returned, the kitchen got quiet. Residual smiles clung to Taylor's and Josh's lips as they looked at Violet and awkwardly got back to work.

"What was that?" Violet said with a tiny, nervous laugh.

"Nothing," Taylor spouted.

"That's okay, y'all can talk about me some more later." Violet said, trying to say it as a joke but feeling as though it were anything but "okay."

The background chatter of arriving guests flooded in through the gates of the shady courtyard and continued down the receiving line flanking the elegantly curved entryway. Carrying through the open oak doors into a huge and ornate interior room, the social hum was finally overtaken by the clatter of pots and pans as the three friends worked on three noodle dishes for tonight's dinner with a swift fervor.

"It's not you," Josh said and shrugged with one shoulder as he came to the stove with his arms full of bottles and Tupperware containers. "We were talking about your little Achilles' heel, Derek."

"Bro, don't ..." Taylor widened her eyes at Josh.

Josh raised his hands in defense. "It's better than her thinking we were talking about her!"

Violet looked between them, realizing this was not the first time they had been laughing about, or maybe at, Derek.

"So, wait," Violet said as she shook the mason jar of Thai noodle salad dressing that she had made the day before. "Do you guys really dislike Derek that much?"

Taylor pulled her head out of the refrigerator and Josh added vegetable oil to two woks, then they looked at each other with grimaces and said in unison, "Chyeah!"

"I thought you guys were doing a loyalty routine because of

our break, or maybe teasing me," Violet said, straining cold noodles from the water they had been stored in and letting the water run down the giant stainless steel sink. "But y'all are serious?"

"Of course we're serious!" Josh called out, dumping an enormous container of the creamy tomato pasta sauce they had made the day before into a pot on the stove. "We don't know how you two were in high school, or college, but I've never seen him treat you right."

Violet swallowed hard as she tossed the vegetables, noodles, and cold salad dressing together.

"Sorry," Taylor said, frowning as she separated containers of prepped vegetables by the stages in which they would go into her stir-fried noodle dish. "We never wanted to say anything serious, in case you two worked it out, but from what I've seen he does not deserve you."

Violet again stayed quiet as she slipped the big bowl of cold noodle salad, or Yum Woon Sen, into the refrigerator.

She had never thought about it in terms of who deserved what. Her relationship with Derek had always been the easy choice. The obvious path. The person she had always pictured herself with. Ever since high school when she had practiced writing "Violet Valentine" on the backs of her spiral notebooks. Ever since he had been the football star who had first noticed the persnickety neat freak in the corner.

"Well, when he finishes showing me how sorry he is, then y'all are going to regret everything that you're saying right now," Violet said. She pictured herself standing next to Derek at her culinary school graduation and felt her face harden into a determined squint. They had done everything together, grown up together. "We are going to get back to normal, then the three of us can get back to finishing culinary school and getting this business going."

After a long, icy silence where Taylor took two abrupt breaths as if she was gearing up to say something, Josh finally said, "And what if he's not sorry?"

Violet whirled on him and he visibly flinched. She had nothing to say, but after seeing his reaction, she realized she didn't need to say anything. As Taylor rolled up the door of the pass-through window with a whoosh and a clang, Josh stood there shrinking under her fiery stare and finally ventured, "Well, I hope Derek is."

"You hope I am what?" Derek said, appearing in the pass-through window with a sparkling, clear glass that Violet lamentably knew wasn't just seltzer.

"Ready to start, of course, because we are!" Violet hollered with a little too much gusto.

"Oh good, that's why I was coming to check on my minions," Derek crooned.

Violet could actually hear Taylor's teeth grind together beside her.

"Um, I'll take out the first bowl of Yum Woon Sen, and is that Rigatoni fra Diavolo ready?" Violet asked.

Derek slid away saying, "Great, well, I'll go get the party started."

Violet found herself hoping that didn't mean more alcohol.

In the big hall, Violet brought out the last dish of noodles to the banquet table, slipped it into place, lit the warmer, then stopped to soak it all in. The long wooden beams of the ceiling spread out from a central point with graceful earthiness while sconces along the arched walls and lumbering dark chandeliers with silhouettes of running horses provided the dim lighting. Everyone was sitting at big round tables that looked like polka dots on the beige carpet as Violet moved up the staircase in the back of the room to a balcony that was not being used this evening. When asked, the whole room stood, their chairs scraping back behind them. Many of her friends from the Sweethearts Club, including Suzanne, the president, and Eve, who was also one of the nurses in this medical unit herself, were in the glittering crowd that stood listening and following along with the appropriate responses, to the captain on the stage. As he led the traditional toasts, Violet realized that this was Derek's boss—the commanding officer or CO, Captain Shoenthal, whom Derek had been so anxious to impress since he had been assigned to be his executive officer, or XO, upon returning from deployment.

"I propose a toast to the United States of America!" The CO said. He was a tall, broad-shouldered man of probably half-Asian descent with a dark buzz cut. He raised his full glass, then paused for the response.

"The United States of America," chorused the room, then everyone took a tiny sip from their raised glasses. Pete, Eve's boyfriend that Violet had only met once, said it the loudest and with the most gusto, his enthusiasm incongruent with the dark bags under his eyes and his pale cheeks.

"I propose a toast to the President of the United States," the CO said.

"The commander in chief," said the crowd, some taking a quick glance at their programs for the correct wording.

As the toasts went on, sharp movement at the front of the room caught Violet's eye. It was Derek.

Of course it's Derek, Violet thought. As much as she didn't want to admit it, it was probably time to address his drinking, which she had noticed and had been shrugging off ever since his return from deployment. *Wait,* the thought flashed through her mind, *I guess he's not my responsibility anymore. Or is he? Anyway, someone needs to address it.*

"Gunner, charge this!" Derek said and hiccuped after throwing back the rest of his glass.

No, no no! Hold it together for tonight! Violet silently pleaded as she felt her pulse quicken. She knew he had been anxious about tonight going well, since he had been in charge of doing a lot of the planning, but she had hoped that he wouldn't drink more than one or two to "ease his nerves" as he put it.

He was speaking loud enough for the entire room to hear, but no one at his table moved.

"Gunner!" Derek said a little louder, waving his empty glass. "Dude, remember my promotion? You are the junior member at our table. So you gonna charge this or what?"

The commanding officer leaned away from the mic, but it still caught his voice enough for Violet to hear him say, "Gunners are not used during the formal toasts. Now please…" He stood up straight and centered himself behind the microphone stand again. With a somber smile, he continued. "I propose a toast to our fallen comrades."

As the rest of the room silently took a sip, Derek called out louder than ever, "Fine! I'll get it myself then."

Violet, and most of the room, watched in silent horror as Derek emptied the last of the fancy bottle on his table into his glass and downed it. When he spotted her in the back of the room, he raised his glass in her direction. "Hey, babe! Be a doll and get us another bottle over here!"

Violet's face blazed and she covered her mouth as she shrank against the back wall of the hall. At least in this moment, she couldn't remember a time when she had ever been more embarrassed. She couldn't decide if she should run to the front and stop him from calling out, run out of the room, or crawl into a hole and die.

As she stood frozen to the spot, someone else moved in front of Derek's face. It was Rob, his best friend and the person whose couch he had been sleeping on for the last month. It was clear that he was trying to be a quiet voice of reason, but Derek pushed him out of the way.

"Mr. Vice, I have a point of order," Derek hollered.

Captain Shoenthal scolded, "Lieutenant First-Class Derek Valentine, this is not—"

"I advise the mess that a toast required by courtesy has not been proposed. To my girl right there! To Violet! Ain't she the best?"

The throbbing behind Violet's ears intensified and she felt like she might pass out. The edges of her vision blurred as she heard the captain declare, "Get him out of here!"

He must have decided that the men handling Derek were being too gentle because the captain pounced off the stage and half-dragged and half-escorted Derek to the back door. Without thinking, Violet followed them, past the kitchen and bathrooms, right up to the back door where the captain simply said, "Go home and sleep it off. We'll talk tomorrow."

The captain pressed him all the way outside, returning to the hallway alone and letting the door slam shut on Derek's protests. By that time, Violet had caught up to them and said the only thing she could think of. "I'm sor—"

Captain Shoenthal cut her off. "No, *I'm* sorry. Hey, soldier!"

Violet first thought that Captain Shoenthal was talking

to her, then realized that the last part had been directed to someone behind her. As the person stepped forward and around her towards the captain, Violet recognized Jake-something, whom she'd met earlier before he had put on his uniform.

"Some assistance, sir?" Jake asked.

Captain Shoenthal said, "Yes, you're the MP that was coming? Great. I need you to stand guard at the entrance to this hallway."

"Guard the back door," Jake said. "Yes, Captain."

"No," the captain snapped and got right up in Jake's face. "Did I say back door? No! I said the entrance to this hallway! If that swine can't lay off the sauce and is fool enough to come back here, then he can use the bathroom and hopefully apologize to his fiancée in the kitchen, but he is not allowed back in my event. Got that?"

"Yes, sir!" Jake barked. As soon as the captain had lowered the hand he had pointed at Violet and stomped away, Jake pulled his gaze off the fixed spot on the opposite wall. He looked into her eyes and Violet saw pity from yet another person. He glanced at her left ring finger, then back at her eyes with tight lips and a nod.

Violet's eyes burned, her cheeks burned, everything burned. She didn't know it was possible to be this embarrassed and still alive.

Thai Glass Noodle Salad (Yum Woon Sen)

Serves 4

Prep time - 20 minutes

This is a fresh and flavorful cold noodle dish. If you don't want the bad breath from raw garlic, you can omit it, but it will not be as tasty.

Ingredients:
 150 g cellophane noodles (also known as mung bean noodles or bean thread)
 2 tablespoons dried shrimp
 1 cup frozen shrimp, any size, thawed in refrigerator if you can plan ahead
 ½ pork chop or steak, cooked and sliced thin (use whatever you have)
 3 stalks green onion, roughly chopped
 ½ bell pepper, slices cut in half lengthwise
 1 tomato, slices cut in half lengthwise
 10 stems of cilantro, chopped

THAI GLASS NOODLE SALAD (YUM WOON SEN)

2 garlic cloves
1 Thai chile
2 tablespoons palm sugar, chopped
6 tablespoons lime juice
4 tablespoons fish sauce
½ cup roasted peanuts, roughly chopped

1. Soak noodles in hot water for about 5 minutes while you prepare other ingredients.
2. Cover dried shrimp in hot water and let rehydrate for about 5 minutes.
3. If your shrimp is frozen, pour hot water over them, then strain and dry with a towel as soon as all the ice is gone. If you were able to plan ahead and thaw them overnight in the fridge, pat dry on a towel.
4. Into a big salad bowl, throw your thawed shrimp, sliced meat, green onion, bell pepper, tomato, and cilantro.
5. Strain the shrimp that has been rehydrating and discard the stinky water.
6. Into a mortar and pestle or mini food chopper, blend up the rehydrated shrimp, garlic, chile, palm sugar, lime juice, and fish sauce until you have a chunky mash and the palm sugar has dissolved.
7. Pour your lime juice mash over the meats and veg in your big salad bowl like a salad dressing and toss to combine.
8. Strain the noodles, then toss those into the meat and veg and toss again to get the dressing all through the noodles.
9. As you serve, either in another bowl or as you finish tossing in the same bowl, aim to have the noodles closer to the bottom so they get to sit in the dressing for longer. Garnish with chopped peanuts and serve.

...

For so many reasons, I had to do it. For loyalty, for money, for family, for safety. Before I did it, I almost chickened out. I almost went right back inside and said no. I stood with my hand on the doorknob and I couldn't let go. I had a death grip on that door until I let that part of my brain, whatever part that is, just let go. My mind floated up and watched what I was doing from the outside. It's the only way I could do it. I had to force myself to.
...

Chapter 3

"Bro! That's harsh!" Josh said. His voice rose from behind a cloud of steam as he stir-fried another batch of chow fun noodles to refill the chafing dish in the ballroom.

"Yeah, well, it's a formal event, and he was an idiot during the most somber part," Violet said, deflating and plopping down on a stool. "I can't believe he pointed at me and said my name and everything. At least he didn't name me as the caterer for tonight. I was thinking, if you and Taylor are the only people going in and out of the ballroom, then maybe our business can recover from this."

As the clouds around Josh's face dissipated, he switched off the heat and grinned at Violet. "Nice try. You're just too embarrassed and don't want to have to show your face out there again."

"Okay, maybe," Violet said, popping the cork on a replacement bottle for Derek's former table.

"But she's not wrong, she's doing what she does best—planning and thinking about us!" Taylor interjected as she brought over a freshly washed insert for the chafing dish, drying it with a towel. "Being associated with that disaster, even if everyone knows Violet is not the same person as her fiancé, or ex-fiancé, or whatever … anyway it might damage our reliability in their minds."

Josh poured the browned noodles into the stainless steel rectangle as soon as Taylor had set it down and nodded. "Okay, so Vi, you're lying low until this blows over, and we are carrying stuff out, retrieving stuff, checking on the guests?"

"Yes, and I'll open bottles, make new batches if needed, start cutting the sheet cakes for dessert and loading those onto trays, and whatever else needs doing back here."

"I think you might need to take the trash out too," Taylor said, smiling innocently at Violet and winking at Josh as she disappeared through the swinging kitchen doors carrying the noodles.

Violet's whole body winced at the thought of a giant bag of garbage filled with the evening's food trimmings and plate scraps. She instinctively leaned away, thinking about it being so heavy that it might have to be carried close to her body, touching her, leaking rotting garbage juice onto her sneakers. Nobody ever made her take out the trash because of her neurotic aversion. She opened her mouth to protest before being cut off by Taylor singing, "You know, to go see that Special Agent Charming by the back door!"

The next round of kitchen tasks descended upon them in a flurry and all thoughts of garbage juice and embarrassment were swallowed up in a whirlwind of slicing and serving until Violet was interrupted by someone in a dress uniform coming through the swinging doors.

"I ... uh," slurred Captain Shoenthal, moving unsteadily and grabbing the island for support. "I think I need ... I mean do you ... have any coffee?"

"Yes, uh..." Violet said. She blinked a few times at a tray of mugs she'd prepared for the dessert course. "Yes, sir."

CHAPTER 3

As Violet poured him a cup, she marveled to herself that someone who was so dead-set against public drunkenness had gotten so smashed himself. She slid the mug across the countertop to the captain as he dropped onto a stool and dragged his hat down his face and into his lap.

"I guess I was more stressed about tonight than I realized." The captain gave a bleary smile and wobbled on his chair like a buoy out at sea. "I've pulled thirty-six-hour shifts on deployment, and I've still never been this tired." He took several big gulps and clunked the mug down again. "I guess I was always more built for combat than for civilian life. Give me a clear enemy and a gun over fancy dress and civilized conversation any day cuz I'm beat!"

Yeah, sure, tired—more like wasted, thought Violet with a frown.

She reached for the coffee pot and filled his mug again, feeling more like a bartender and confidant than a caterer and his employee's girlfriend.

The captain drained his mug again, then struggled to his feet. "Don't worry about that fiancé of yours," he said, his sleepy expression impossible to read. "I'll take care of him tomorrow. Or ... Monday."

Violet was left wondering what he meant by that as Captain Shoenthal leaned on the swinging kitchen door, then fell through it and tumbled to the ground. She went to help him up, wanting to help him get a ride home, or at least save him the embarrassment of being seen by the rest of the battalion, but he swatted at her when she looped her arm around his.

"Get off! Leave it alone!" Captain Shoenthal barked as he got to his feet.

Violet was looking for the words to argue with him, but was

cut off by Taylor running up to her and pushing her back into the kitchen.

"Hey!" Taylor said. "I thought you wanted to stay in the kitchen!" As Violet argued, Taylor understood, giving her one final push. "I'll help him. Shoo!"

When she realized that debating was fruitless, Violet went back to work. She finished slicing the Costco sheet cake and went to throw away the plastic clamshell container it had come in. She tossed it in the trash can and used the rectangular top to push down the pile of garbage from the top, but it didn't squish down as much as she had hoped. There was no denying it—it was time to take out the garbage.

With a groan, Violet reminded herself that she loved being a caterer and that this was a necessary part of the job. *Besides,* she thought, *taking out the garbage means it's not sitting around here. Taking it out is like cleaning. Phew, just like cleaning.*

She gathered up the top of the bag and tied it, realizing in the process that the barrel that the bag sat in had wheels. She didn't have to carry it against her body after all! She finished tying the bag and washed her hands until the skin on her knuckles was red and painful and glanced at the shining stainless steel cabinet over the sink. On a whim, she touched up her lipstick and swiped at the mascara smudges under her eyes, then rolled the garbage towards the back door.

She kept her eyes down and focused on the barrel as she navigated the back hallway, passing a silent men's bathroom and a chattering women's bathroom. Violet could see Jake-something in her peripheral vision. She didn't need to pass him since the door from the kitchen joined the hall behind his solitary vigil, but she could feel his eyes on her. She avoided eye contact as long as she could, but then he called to her.

CHAPTER 3

"Can I help you with that?"

"No, thanks. It has wheels, so I'm okay." Violet said, wavering. Her eyes fixed on the back door only steps away.

Jake jogged over anyway. "C'mon, lifting that out of the can will be really heavy if you do it alone, and I'm not doing anything anyway."

His words made memories of Violet's dad spring to the surface of her mind although he was hours away in Austin. Violet's heart lilted despite herself. Her father often silently helped and responded the same way when thanked. 'I wasn't doing anything anyway.'

She was especially glad that Jake was there to help when they exited the doors into the crisp night air and rolled up to the overflowing dumpster. Jake lifted the bag out of the can before she could, but it stuck and he ended up pulling up both the bag and the barrel.

Violet expected a "See?" or "I told you so!" But instead, Jake laughed and said, "Whoa! I guess it was tamped down too much. Y'all have been busy!" He held everything in the air for a moment as his hands held the bag and the bag held the barrel and the barrel was attached to its wheeled cart.

Violet lunged forward and pulled down on the wheels, the wood frame holding the wheels, the can, anything she could, but the bag wouldn't let go.

"Looks like we're in a sticky situation," Jake said, looking around the bag at her.

Violet shook her head and laughed. She wasn't sure why, but she stepped behind the bag to stop him from looking at her. She sighed and was sure that she was only able to giggle through this because he was there to help with the worst part of her job.

When she finally glanced up at him and saw that he still had a kind and amused gaze settled on her, Violet's throat tightened and she shoved down hard on the barrel. Suddenly, it broke free. The barrel clattered down and to one side as Jake swung the bag back and to the other. Violet wasn't so lucky. She stumbled forward and into Jake's shoulder. She fell against him but was immediately seized around the bicep and supported by Jake's free hand.

"You okay?" He chuckled.

Violet immediately thought of the garbage his hand had been touching and without thinking, said, "Ew!"

"Oh, sorry," Jake said quickly, releasing her.

"No ... sorry. It's ... the garbage. Not you. Um, thank you. Sorry!" Violet stuttered as she grabbed the empty barrel and rolled it back inside as fast as she could.

Safely in her kitchen again, Violet heaved a sigh as she washed her hands over and over. She mentally kicked herself for being so awkward around someone she had just met.

Ugh, what was that? she asked herself. *Why are you so weird about him? Because he's handsome, or because he was about to ask me out before he saw that I'm engaged? Or was engaged ... ugh, I don't know!*

Violet dried her hands, taped up another knuckle that was bleeding from being scrubbed raw during this dry winter, then whipped the blood-speckled towel down into a bucket she had brought for dirty rags.

"It's time!" Taylor said as she and Josh shot into the room and hoisted up the full trays of plates of sliced cake.

Knowing that meant that it was time for the dessert course, Violet said, "Right. More coffee," and loaded up the big industrial double coffee machine with new grounds. The big urn in the main room was full, but the first thing she had learned on her first catering job was that a group of people that had been drinking always drank more coffee than she expected.

While her back faced the door, Taylor and Josh left, unfortunately leaving Violet alone with her thoughts again. When the kitchen door swung open again and someone moved up behind her, she assumed it was already Taylor or Josh asking for more coffee. "Hold your dang horses! It'll take a minute. Take out more trays of cake, for now."

"Babe," a familiar yet unexpected voice said behind her. "I'm so sorry."

Violet spun in surprise, then her façade melted.

Derek was disheveled, his tie undone and hanging from his neck. His dress uniform pants had grass on them as if he had been sitting on the lawn and his face was red and sweaty. He wiped it with a paper towel.

The man was the picture of a desperate apology. Violet could hear the waver in his voice and felt her arms opening automatically for a hug she knew he needed. She tried not to think of how dirty he was and buried her face into his shoulder.

"I guess she forgives me," Derek crooned to no one in particular, while Violet retracted a little and wondered if she really had.

"What are you still doing here?" Violet said, sweeping her tangled feelings aside to get to the more important topic at hand. "The captain told you to go home!"

"No! You know I need this night to work out." Derek said as he straightened up and tied his bowtie. "I was hanging around to sober up so that I could come back. Now, help me out, babe.

Get me a cup of coffee and clean me up."

"Uh, me cleaning you up for a minute in the kitchen isn't going to fix this," Violet reeled.

"Fix what?" Derek shrugged and it infuriated Violet that he didn't see a problem with any of it.

"This..." Violet said and swept her hand in a circular motion in front of his bleary face, "that ..." she swung her arm out towards the big hall with the party, "yuck ..." She swept at the grass on his pants and found that his flank was wet and he had a drip of pastry cream on his knee. "Wait, what is this? Did you go out to dessert instead of going home?"

"What? What's wrong with going out to dessert? You know I love meringues," Derek said as he shrugged again and the motion made Violet want to reach out and staple his shoulders down. "It's right there at the side of the courtyard around this building."

"I know where it is!" Violet wasn't sure why she was arguing about the location of a meringue shop, but she also wasn't sure how to explain why it was not an appropriate time to go out for something fun and frivolous. "You just ... I mean, you say you care, but then you ... do something so ..."

Violet broke off when Taylor and Josh came in the door again with the empty cake trays.

"What is he doing here?" Josh hollered.

"That's what I'm trying to figure out, now ..." Violet said, holding up a hand to her friends and trying to talk to Derek again.

"Ooh, no. Not tonight. I've got half a mind to—" Taylor said as she fixed her icy stare on Derek and advanced.

"Leave us alone. You DO have half a mind," Derek snapped.

Taylor froze in her stride, raised her eyebrows, and slowly

CHAPTER 3

turned her stare on Violet expectantly.

"I'm sorry, let me ..." Violet said and felt her stomach drop through the floor. "I'm handling this, okay?"

She yanked on Derek's arm until he was out in the hallway to the back door before she spoke again. "You need to leave. Get an Uber back to Rob's house and sleep it off on his couch. That is the best thing you can do for the situation."

"But it's my job to—"

"No," Violet insisted. "If the captain sees you, he will throw you out again and be even more angry. You need to leave and let him cool off. You can call him and apologize in the morning. Get an Uber and—"

"I've been banned from Uber," Derek muttered.

Violet had to blink twice. Pushing aside the question of *What could you do that gets you banned from Uber*, she struggled to stay on topic. "Then call a cab, but you need to leave."

"How do you call a cab?" Derek asked.

"I don't know!" Violet squeaked with anxiety.

"Our place is cl–I mean, your place is close. Can I come back?" Derek said and attempted puppy-dog eyes. "Please?"

"Ugh," Violet grunted. She wasn't sure if she wanted to let him get his foot in the door, but there was no time to think about that now. "Fine, whatever, but only for now! Get out of here before you mess things up for both of us!"

As she handed him the key and pushed him out the back door again, she noticed Jake still standing guard at the point where this hallway joined the big showy, curved hallway beyond. His tight-lipped, civil smile answered her question, but she asked it anyway. "I guess you heard all that, huh?"

"Sorry, ma'am," Jake said in an official tone. "It's my job."

Violet wasn't sure she liked being called ma'am, but didn't

know if it was because it made her feel old or if she didn't like hearing it from this guy.

Before Violet had to think of a response, she heard a SSSNIKT from the door to the women's bathroom, and Eve's friend, Josilyn, whom Violet had never officially talked to, opened the door.

"Oh... hi," she said and swayed forward in the doorway, then rocked back as if she had been about to walk out until she saw that there was someone in the hallway. Tanned and glowing, her makeup was flawless but understated, while her hair and gown were both tight, yellow, and sparkly. "Do you have any ... supplies?" she said, glancing at Jake with shifty eyes. When he walked back to the mouth of the hall, perhaps twenty feet away, she whispered, "You know, pads or tampons? Or maybe some stain treater, or a blowdryer?"

When Violet said no with a puzzled expression, Eve's other work friend, Reese, came up behind her from the direction of the dining room. "Okay, we have quite the situation in here. Thanks anyway. I was able to find a couple of things in the dining room though."

Josilyn and Reese disappeared into the bathroom and Violet heard the same SSSNIKT again and realized that it was the deadbolt on the door to the bathroom. Whatever mess they were dealing with in there must be really bad if they were keeping the entire room locked against newcomers. Violet tried not to imagine the mess, or how they were attempting to clean it up, and instead resolved to ask Taylor for "supplies."

"Nope, sorry," Taylor said and shook her head. "I brought my small bag and it's not even close to time for me. But hey..." Taylor looked into Violet's eyes, her eyebrows high in the middle with concern. "How are you? Are you okay?"

CHAPTER 3

Violet knew that Taylor must really be asking about Derek.

"Yes, sorry about him," Violet said, looking down at her hands. "But he's gone now."

"Oh, that's good." Taylor laid a comforting hand on Violet's arm as Josh came in through the swinging door. "Well then, it's time for the bad news."

When Violet widened her eyes in question, Taylor shot her a glance and exaggeratedly pointed her face at the wheeled trash barrel next to them.

"What? Didn't I already take this one out?" Violet whined.

"This is a different one—the one from the ballroom, so it will be heavy with leftover food," Josh said, then shotgunned a cup of coffee.

"Well, can you help me?" Violet said, wincing.

"We have stuff we have to do out there!" Josh darted out the door.

"Sorry, honey," Taylor said, shaking her head and washing her hands. "I have to take that coffee out to the urn in the ballroom. It's already almost out. But I'm sure you can manage, even if you just put the bag next to the dumpster."

Violet had already guessed, but her suspicions were confirmed in the hallway, that Jake would again not let her take out the garbage alone.

He saw her and automatically walked up next to her, then wordlessly held the back door open for her.

"Thanks," she said, prompting a nod from him.

"Look..." Violet felt the need to explain as Jake, this time easily, lifted the bag from the barrel and threw the dripping bag on top of the pile jutting out of the top of the dumpster. "I wanted to explain that Derek isn't a bad guy. He's been drinking a bit since he got home from deployment, but he—"

"Uuuunnnnhhh ... haaaa-ugh ..."

Violet broke off when she heard the moaning. "What?"

"That wasn't me," Jake said, listening for the sound again.

"Aaaaaargh ... help ..." The small voice came again, but this time it was clearly coming from behind the dumpster.

Violet moved clockwise as Jake moved counterclockwise around the dumpster. When they met at a pile of big black bags that looked like they had fallen from the top of the trash heap, they both shrugged at each other.

"Help!" The call came louder this time, but it was still muffled and garbled.

Violet gasped as she recognized a tuxedo shoe poking up from behind one mound, its shiny black surface blending in too well.

At the same time, Jake lifted a large trash bag with each hand revealing the writhing form of a very bruised Captain Shoenthal grasping at a wet spot on his black uniform coat.

Beefy Chow Fun

Serves 6-8 people

Prep time - 20 minutes

Rice flake is made of the same ingredients as rice stick or rice noodles, but comes in pieces and looks more like small, translucent chips. If you can't find them, using a different wide rice noodle is great and almost the same.

Also, this recipe comes together super fast once you stir fry everything together, so have everything prepped and ready like you are on a cooking show.

For the marinade:
 ½ teaspoon baking soda
 1 tablespoon cornstarch
 2 tablespoons soy sauce
 1 tablespoon vegetable oil
 8 ounce steak, sliced super thin

For the noodles and sauce:
 8 ounces dry "rice flake" or wide rice noodles

2 tablespoons Shaoxing wine
1 teaspoon sesame oil
6 tablespoons soy sauce
1 tablespoon sugar
¼ teaspoon ground white pepper
3 tablespoons vegetable oil
3 cloves garlic, minced
2 tablespoons ginger, minced
4 green onions (split in half lengthwise and cut into 2-inch pieces)
8 ounces mung bean sprouts

1. Whisk together baking soda, cornstarch, soy sauce, oil, then stir in thinly sliced steak. Set aside and let marinate while you prep other ingredients.
2. Boil 3 or 4 quarts of water in a big pot and boil rice flakes/noodles for 5 minutes. Drain in a strainer, then submerge noodles in cold water until you're ready, but save that colander so you can use it again!
3. In a small bowl, stir together Shaoxing wine, sesame oil, soy sauce, sugar, and white pepper. Set next to the stove so it's ready for the stir frying stage.
4. Put a large wok or large, heavy-bottomed pan over high heat and add the 3 tablespoons of oil. While it heats up, strain your noodles out of the cold water, cuz it's about to go fast.
5. Place meat and its marinade into the hot pan, poking at the meat to get as much of it touching the pan and spread out as possible. After about 30 seconds, when it's browned, stir the meat, scraping up as much as you

can from the bottom of the pan. Spread it out in the pan again and allow to brown again. Stir again and move meat to the outer edges of the pan
6. Add garlic and ginger to the middle of the pan, fry for about 30 seconds, and add green onions. After another 30 seconds, add all the noodles and pour sauce mixture over the top.
7. Immediately start mixing sauce, meat, and noodles together. Your pan is still over high heat, so never stop stirring! Stir and scrape the bottom of the pan as the sauce is absorbed and cooked off. When the noodles are getting barely crusty on the edges, about 2-5 minutes, turn off the heat and mix in bean sprouts. Serve immediately and enjoy!

...

I had to or I might have been beat up. Or killed. Probably beat up, like he was.

But he was asking for it. It was really his fault. If I trace all the little rivers and creeks back to their source, it was his fault. He made me do it.

...

Chapter 4

"This is CID Special Agent Jake Whitehouse," Jake said into his phone, speaking quickly. "I need a bus at The Stable in the old Pearl Brewery."

As Jake went on, Violet's mind darted around in a panic. *So that was his last name,* she thought, then her mind quickly jumped. *Why was he here at this battalion's Dining Out? Oh, I really should help him up. Wait, is there a way to help him without crawling over garbage bags? Ew, ew, ew! I bet several rats are hiding right here, right now. There is no cure for Hantavirus, is there?* Head whirling, her breathing became faster and faster.

"Captain! Captain Shoenthal, we're going to help you. You're going to be okay," Agent Whitehouse said, one hand still holding the phone up to his ear as he kneeled on a trash bag and applied pressure to the wet spot on the captain's dress uniform jacket. When his hand came away crimson, he fished through his pocket, then turned to Violet. "Do you have anything? A towel or …"

With that, Violet snapped out of her trance, but her skin continued to crawl. She assumed she could not take over either the phone conversation or the first aid, but she whipped out the towel that hung from the back of her apron strings. "Here. What should I do?"

As he accepted the dish towel, Jake almost fumbled the phone that his shoulder was holding. "Um, I have a partner in there," Jake said and nodded at the building. "He's Special Agent Donnelly. Please tell him to lock down the building. No one can leave."

"I'm on it." Violet expelled a big breath of relief, eager to leave the garbage and blood.

"He should be by the front door," Jake called after her before she darted inside the door.

Violet sprinted through the hall, past the bathrooms and back door to the kitchen, through the elegantly beige, curved hallway, and up to a prematurely balding, dark-haired man of about thirty who sat in a folding chair by the front door. As she approached, the man looked up from his phone with a look that quickly transitioned from sleepy boredom to alert concern.

"Shut down the building!" Violet blurted out. "He said ... Jake said ... We found ... I ... Are you Donnelly?"

"Yes, ma'am. Okay, slow down." Special Agent Donnelly took a deep breath as he held Violet's gaze. "Are you alright? What happened?"

"Yes, but–but Special Agent ... Whitehouse and I found a man, er, we found Captain Shoenthal ... badly injured. He's calling an ambulance and helping, but ... he asked for you," Violet managed to blurt out as she heard sirens in the distance. "He said to shut down the building. Don't let anyone leave!"

Violet hurried back to the kitchen, where the commotion was starting to spread.

"Vi, why were you running? Are you okay?" Taylor asked, turning away from the creamy, tomato-sauced noodles that were the leftovers of their Rigatoni fra Diavolo.

"Why is everyone asking me that? Sorry, I mean, yeah. I'm fine, it's that ..." Violet said and took a shuddering breath as Josh came into the kitchen, picked up on the tone, and joined the conversation. "Jake, or Special Agent Whitehouse, and I found someone beat up by the dumpster. It was the Captain. It was Captain Shoenthal."

"Is he going to be okay?" Taylor asked.

Josh demanded, "What do you mean 'beat up'?"

"I ... he ... I don't know. He was bleeding pretty bad, like maybe he was stabbed or something. Right here." Violet put her hand low on the left side of her stomach. "He was also all bruised and sounded like he was in pain, and—"

"Oh, I'm so sorry. You seem pretty shaken up. Here," Taylor said, pulling Violet to a kitchen stool and pouring her a coffee from the coffee maker as it piddled to a stop.

"Please, no, I don't ..." Violet put up her hands as if to shield herself from the coffee mug that smelled something like burnt popcorn. "The last thing I need is more anxiety, and coffee makes me ..."

"Come on," Josh said to Taylor. "What she needs is something to calm her nerves. I'll go get you something a little stronger."

Josh was gone before Violet could argue with him. He jogged out the kitchen door, Violet presumed, to the bar. She was determined to refuse anything he brought back, as she didn't enjoy losing any degree of control over herself, but she was grateful for the caring gesture.

Amid the sounds of sirens stopping right outside, the indignation of the guests as they found out that they couldn't leave, and the two special agents shouting directions to the guests and then to uniformed MPs as they arrived, Taylor and Violet hovered in the kitchen and watched. They peeked out the windows as EMTs walked from the ambulance to the dumpster that hid Agent Whitehouse and Captain Shoenthal from view.

"Ugh," Taylor burst out. "I hate how they legally have to walk. Watching an ambulance driver walk is the worst!"

Violet gave her a sideways glance as they both continued to lean towards the window. Violet could tell from her tone that she had some experience in that department, but she could also tell it was a sensitive subject and that now was not the time to ask for details.

When several men and women in BDUs marched past their pass-through window, Violet and Taylor rushed to the other end of the kitchen in time to hear Special Agent Donnelly issue their marching orders. "Alright, we need to set up a perimeter around this building. No one goes in or out until Special Agent Whitehouse or I have interviewed them. Got it?"

"Yes, sir" shot out of each mouth with an astonishing staccato and energy.

As the dozen uniformed people dispersed, guests crowded into the hall to face Donnelly with a torrent of questions.

"What's going on?" and "What's happened?" and "Who's hurt?" and some swear words sank into a jumbled din as Donnelly quieted the crowd.

"Ladies and gentlemen!" he called out. "Ladies and gentlemen, there has been an incident and—"

"Ladies." Special Agent Whitehouse appeared suddenly at Violet's elbow, his slate gray-blue eyes looking intensely into hers. "May I beg the use of the sink?"

Violet and Taylor both stepped back from the sink they had

CHAPTER 4

been leaning over. "Yes, of course," they murmured.

"Thanks. And sorry, the men's bathroom is out of soap ... and I ... need to wash extra well."

Violet involuntarily inspected the man's hands and her breath caught in her chest. He reached for Violet's dish soap dispenser. Most of the blood had been washed off, but his nail beds and knuckles were still a little orange and a smear of coral marred one of the wet shirt cuffs that extended out of his coat sleeves.

Violet's scalp winced and a tingle shot down her right arm, but she wasn't sure if that was from the surprise of seeing Agent Whitehouse again or from seeing the blood. She took a lolloping breath as she caught the end of Donnelly's speech.

"So, if everyone can head back into the main ballroom ... yep, back to your seats ... Special Agent Whitehouse and I, or some of our MPs, will either call you into this receiving area or come talk to you one table at a time. Thanks, everyone, and sorry for the inconvenience."

"Thank you," Agent Whitehouse said. "And I'm sorry about that towel you gave me. Can I assume that you don't want it back?"

"No. Thanks for checking, but no." Violet gulped.

"Good, because I've bagged it up as evidence. At least until we know more."

"So you think this was criminal?" Taylor leaned over Violet to ask. "You think there will be charges and stuff?"

"Yes, ma'am," Agent Whitehouse said.

"Is he going to be okay? What did the EMTs say?" Violet said.

"They said that we found him in good time. That he hadn't been out there long. They couldn't tell me anything definite, but they sounded hopeful."

"Oh good," Taylor said as Violet let out a big sigh.

Agent Whitehouse continued. "Since I know you have a lot of work to do, and since you were there on the scene when he was found, let's handle your interview first, Miss Davis."

Violet agreed as she looked into the agent's face. It was still chiseled and handsome, but had none of the glowing warmth she remembered from when they'd first met. Or when they had laughed together around the garbage can.

She fell into step next to him. As they bumped into each other near the kitchen door, Violet's hand accidentally tapped his.

"Sorry," the agent said quickly.

"No, it was my fault," Violet said, but the zing down her spine betrayed her, and she found herself wondering where Derek was at this moment. It certainly didn't look good that the attack had happened right after the big scene in the ballroom and Derek's censure. Violet couldn't decide if she hoped that he was still here to support her and comfort her, or if she wished he was far away, escaping the suspicion and giving her some space.

Rigatoni fra Diavolo

Serves 6

Prep time - 50 minutes - 1 hour

This is a wonderful, creamy, tomato pasta sauce with a hint of heat!

Surprisingly, crappy pasta sauce is usually cheaper than plain tomato sauce, so you can substitute one bigger can of that for the tomato sauce or crushed tomatoes.

Ingredients:
  2 tablespoons olive oil
  1 bell pepper, seeded and sliced
  1 onion, peeled and sliced
  3 cloves garlic, peeled and finely diced
  1 lb. Italian sausage, loose or squeezed from casings
  ¼ teaspoon crushed red pepper flakes (you can add more or less according to taste)
  1 tablespoon minced fresh or 1 teaspoon dried parsley
  1 teaspoon minced fresh or ¼ teaspoon dried oregano
  1 teaspoon minced fresh or ¼ teaspoon dried rosemary

1 teaspoon minced fresh or ¼ teaspoon dried sage
½ teaspoon minced fresh or a pinch dried thyme
1 bay leaf
2 (15 ounce) cans tomato sauce or crushed tomatoes
1 lb. dried rigatoni noodles (or penne, ziti, or anything)
1 (2.25 ounce) can sliced ripe black olives, drained (optional)
1 tablespoon minced fresh or 1 teaspoon dried basil
½ cup heavy cream

Optional garnishes - more minced fresh herbs, grated Parmesan cheese

1. Add 1 tablespoon of oil to a heavy-bottomed pan that is deep enough to simmer a big batch of sauce in and has a lid. I use a wide, low, stainless steel casserole pan meant for the stove. Heat over medium low heat until oil spreads to cover the bottom of the pan. Add bell pepper and onion.
2. Cook, stirring occasionally, until onions are caramelized, about 20 minutes. If you need to save time, you can turn the heat up to medium or medium-high, stir more often, and cook until browned, more like 10 minutes, but they won't be as good.
3. When onions are done, push the contents of the pan out to the edges and add garlic to the middle so it comes in direct contact with the bottom of the pan. Cook for 30 seconds until very fragrant, then immediately mix with onions, move everything out to the sides of the pan again, and add sausage meat to the middle and turn heat to medium.
4. Cook meat, stirring and chopping up with a spatula, until

lightly browned and the bottom of the pan looks crusty, about 10 minutes. To the meat, add red pepper flakes, parsley, oregano, rosemary, sage, thyme, and bay leaf. Then pour tomato sauce over the top of the whole thing and stir together.
5. Mix together while scraping the entire bottom of the pan for about 5 minutes. When the sauce is bubbling, turn heat down to low, cover the pan with lid, and simmer for 15 to 20 minutes.
6. While you wait, boil dry noodles according to package directions. When al-dente, or firm-tender, drain noodles, sprinkle with the other tablespoon of oil, then stir to coat. Set noodles aside until you are ready for them.
7. After simmering your sauce, uncover and turn heat to low if it wasn't already there. Stir in drained olives and minced basil, turn off heat, remove bay leaf, then stir in cream.
8. Serve immediately over noodles, or add noodles to the pan and stir together before serving. Garnish with more herbs and Parmesan cheese.

Chapter 5

Violet and Agent Whitehouse sat facing each other in wooden chairs. Jake Whitehouse had a look of sad civility plastered on his face. He pressed his lips together in something like a smile, but his eyes were distant. Violet looked down the hall in hopes of Special Agent Donnelly's approach. She turned back in time to see Agent Whitehouse looking away from the engagement ring that she was spinning on her finger, and she immediately folded her arms to hide the sparkle that had probably caught his eye. When he stepped out of the room to chat with the officers outside the front door, she slipped the ring into her pocket.

Agent Whitehouse came back inside a moment later and they both heard the approaching footsteps of Agent Donnelly.

"Alright, now we can begin," Agent Whitehouse sighed.

"Yes, sorry to make you wait, Miss Davis," Donnelly said. "I had to check in with our boys at the back door. Several people have attempted to leave, and one guy almost snuck past them. Anyway, he can be next, but I won't keep you waiting any longer."

All three of them fidgeted in their chairs and tried to get comfortable in a situation that was anything but. Agent Donnelly brought out his phone and set it on a small table next to him. "Is it alright if I record our conversation? This may turn into an investigation."

"Um, sure. But investigation?" Violet felt her eyes go wide.

"We have to treat every incident like this as a crime that needs investigating until we know that it's not," Agent Whitehouse said, frowning. "Just standard procedure."

"Does that mean you think he will die?" Violet squeaked.

"I don't—" Agent Donnelly began, before being cut off.

"The EMTs were confident. I suppose anything is possible, but so far I meant probable assault charges."

"Oh." Violet felt the jagged edges of her anxiety smooth down, but she still had to swallow hard around a lump in her throat. She was about to thank him for his explanation when Donnelly broke in.

"But we really shouldn't say too much." Donnelly shot a glance at Whitehouse. "As of this moment, starting now, it's an active investigation."

"Right, okay," Violet said and folded her arms again to hug herself. Despite how her cheeks burned, her hands felt like she had been digging through an ice machine. The blustery night outside made the shadows of the trees claw at the windows and Violet shook as much as she used to before taking final exams in college.

"Alright, Miss Davis," Donnelly began again, shifting tones to sound more business-like. "What can you tell me about the scene when Captain Shoenthal was found tonight?"

"Okay, well ... Jake ... or Special Agent Whitehouse and I went out the back door ... of this building, the Pearl Stable ... or the Dining Out event tonight ... I'm sorry, I've never done this before."

Agent Whitehouse gave her a reassuring look. "You're doing

great. And you can shorten it to our last names if that helps you." He rubbed a hand over his mouth and leaned his elbow on his knee.

Violet went on. "Thanks, okay, well ... we went outside because I was taking a big, wheeled trash can out to the dumpster, and Agent, or Special Agent, or Whitehouse, was helping me. I think he might have picked up on the fact that I was ... nervous about it. I can't stand dirty stuff and garbage and dumpsters really ... they really freak me out."

Agent Whitehouse gave one slow nod with his lips sealed together in a tight line.

"So anyway, we got out there and I heard some grunting or moaning or something from behind the dumpster," Violet said. "We walked back there and I still didn't see anyone. But then the sound came again and ... right before Whitehouse picked up some of the trash bags, I noticed an Army dress shoe sticking out of the pile. It was hard to see in the dark, and because it kinda blended in with the trash bags, but then, you know, Whitehouse lifted two bags and there he was."

"Who was it?" Donnelly prodded. "For the record."

"It was Captain Shoenthal." Violet swallowed hard.

"And how did he look?" Donnelly asked.

"He was all beat up. He could barely talk or move, so I thought he was in a lot of pain. Mostly I was thinking about how dirty he must be after sitting in all that garbage, but he had bruises on his face, and his hands were clutching at a wet spot on his jacket. It wasn't until after Whitehouse got in the pile and helped him that I realized it was blood. That's when I realized he must have been stabbed or something since the blood wasn't coming from his nose or something like that."

"Alright, did you see anyone else while you were back there?"

"Right then? No, only Whitehouse and me," Violet answered.

"No one else was by the dumpster or the back door?"

"No."

"How about inside?" Donnelly said.

"Well, there were lots of people inside."

"Was anyone near the back door as you exited?"

"No. No one was any closer than the bathroom," Violet said.

"How about the rest of the evening?"

Violet thought hard, then answered. "Well, the girls in the bathroom said they were going in and out of the party. Actually, they might have stayed in there. I'm not sure. I gather they were in there for a while. The only one of them that I saw come from the party was Reese. Um, I think her full name is Teresa. She's one of the nurses. She was the Latina girl in the red cocktail dress with curls over one shoulder."

"Was anyone acting strangely tonight?"

"Yeah, um, actually Captain Shoenthal was." Violet bit her lip, not sure if that was the kind of thing the investigators wanted to hear about the victim.

Whitehouse slid his hand down to his chin. "How was he acting? What was strange about his behavior?"

"Well, he was ... I guess you need me to be honest, so here it goes," Violet said, coming to a decision. "He was drunk. He was stumbling and slurring and ... he even fell over. He came into the kitchen to ask for coffee as I was setting up for the dessert course and ... frankly, I couldn't believe he was drunk and disorderly after he had given Derek such a hard time about it."

"And that's your fiancé? Derek?" Donnelly asked and made a note on a small notepad.

Violet gulped. "Yes, um, kind of. Lieutenant Derek Valentine. He did a lot of the planning for this Dining Out. He was nervous about it, so I think he had a bit too much to drink, you know, to calm down before the dinner even started."

Violet debated mentioning that Derek had been showing signs of alcoholism ever since he had returned from deployment two months ago, but she decided it wasn't the time or place.

"After he was escorted out of the party," Whitehouse said, "he came to see you, correct?"

"Yes, he came back to have me clean him up because he wanted to go back into the party. It was really important for his career that tonight went well," Violet said.

"Did he go back into the party?" Donnelly asked.

"No!" Violet was taken aback. "I didn't let him. I said he needed to sleep it off, let the captain cool off, and that he was too ... well, dirty."

Donnelly considered this. "Did he say where he was between the time he was escorted out and when he came back to see you."

"Yes, he went to get dessert."

"He got dessert?" Whitehouse's eyebrows shot up.

"Yeah, I thought it was ... I don't know, silly, too." Violet tried to smile away the crinkle in Whitehouse's forehead, but he continued to look concerned.

"Did he say where he was going after that?" Donnelly said.

"I wanted him to go back to Rob's—Lieutenant Costa's—apartment, where he's been sleeping since we kinda ... anyway, he had no way to get there, so I think he was going to our apartment. Our old apartment. My apartment."

Violet swallowed hard against her dry throat as Whitehouse's gaze bored into her, watching her over the fist that now covered his mouth.

When no one said anything, Violet rushed on. "We took a step back about a month ago. From ... our relationship. That apartment is still his address on his paperwork, but he's been sleeping on a friend's couch. Anyway, what is now *my* apartment is only about two blocks away from here, so he went there."

"Do you know if he ever got there?" Donnelly asked and made another note.

"No, I don't know."

Whitehouse asked, "Do you have a security system? Digital doorbell, security camera? Did he call you, anything like that that we could check?"

Violet winced and said, "I think the apartment complex has a camera in the interior hallway, but that only helps if he went to the front door. He used to go in and out of the back door. Mostly."

"And you haven't seen him back here?" Donnelly said.

"No."

"How about his mood? Was he angry about being thrown out?"

"Wait, you think Derek ... no, he wasn't angry!" Violet exclaimed as she was blasted in the face with realization. She felt like she had opened a hot oven door. Were the investigators looking at Derek as the main suspect for the attack on the captain? "He was ... disappointed, I guess. But he wasn't depressed or in a rage or anything like that. He's not that kind of a drunk."

"So you think he's a drunk?" Whitehouse asked behind his hand.

"No! Well, maybe. No, I mean, he doesn't get like that. When he gets drunk he gets even more ... smug. He's already a very confident guy, especially around Valentine's Day, so when he's had a few he thinks he's even more charming, and he thinks he's hilarious. And he thinks he owns Valentine's Day because of his last name. He uses it as the perfect time to charm people into giving him things, like free dessert or getting out of speeding tickets, stuff like that. Maybe he would have tried something like that on the captain, to get a promotion or forgive him or something, but that's it. Even when he's been drinking. When he's drunk he's clumsy and messy, and yeah, smug."

"Has he ever gotten violent in the past? Inebriated or not?" Donnelly asked.

"No, you don't understand," Violet said, rising to her feet and rubbing her forehead. "He's not violent. Especially not when he's been drinking. He can barely walk straight or take anything seriously, let alone throw a punch. And by the looks of the captain, it would have had to be someone who could throw several punches. A person that was determined and targeting him. Someone who took their time to make him suffer."

"We do understand," Donnelly said and tapped the air with the end of his pen. "Please have a seat. We have to make sure we are covering all our bases. But we can move on."

"Okay, sorry." Violet exhaled her tension with a controlled breath and slid back down into her chair. "This is stressful, and tonight was already not exactly easy."

"We understand. Sorry about this." Whitehouse said, then zeroed in on Violet with his intense blue eyes, but questioned Donnelly. "Are we done?"

CHAPTER 5

"I need to ask you a couple more questions based on this recent development at the back door." Donnelly answered Whitehouse's question but spoke to Violet.

Violet's heart sank. She covered her eyes with a hand, convinced that Derek had come back and come into the building, yelling at one of the officers, or doing something else stupid to make his situation worse.

"About the individual we caught trying to sneak out past the perimeter and away from our questions," Donnelly said, clearing his throat.

Violet's mind seized up like bad chocolate. She dropped her hand and raised her eyebrows. "Sneak out?"

Donnelly leaned forward. "Miss Davis, how much do you know about your business partner, Joshua McLennan?"

...

My mom would be so ashamed of me. Or would she be proud of me? I'm not sure. No, she'd be ashamed of me. Up until now she has been proud of me, but when all this comes out, then she might never want to see me again. I just hope she doesn't blame herself.

...

Chapter 6

"Josh?" Violet reeled back in her chair. "He's just a kid. Why?"

Donnelly nodded. "I mean to say that he was the individual who tried to sneak away and almost succeeded by pretending to go to the men's room, then bolting when my boys were distracted with another guest trying to leave."

"He what? Ugh!" Violet huffed and rolled her eyes. "He's pretty impulsive and I know he's been arrested before, but he's a good guy. He's had a rough life, you know?"

"Have you ever seen him become violent? Maybe he was trying to get away because he is guilty," Donnelly said.

"Maybe he was running away because he was scared," Violet said, folding her arms and squinting at them.

"Maybe." Whitehouse searched her face. "But as we said, we have to cover everything and everyone."

"You're right," Violet said, then unfolded her arms and let them fall in her lap. "I can appreciate that. You can't know who it was or wasn't until you take a look at them. You're … doing your job."

"Thank you," Whitehouse muttered as he leaned to retrieve a clipboard from the small table next to his partner. "We're almost done. Could you please give us your name, number, and address here? Then we'll let you get back to it and pull in the next person."

"Is it going to be Josh?" Violet asked as she wrote her information.

Whitehouse looked at Donnelly who offered an almost imperceptible nod.

"Yeah, probably," Whitehouse leaned in and said barely above a whisper.

"Take it easy on him, okay?" Violet said with pleading in her eyes as she leaned forward to match him. "He's scared of cops. He'll try to act rebellious and cool, but really he's afraid."

Whitehouse sat back. "Don't worry."

Violet followed his lead and let a hint of a smile into her eyes as she said, "I will be in that kitchen listening to every word you say, mister."

"Well, you're not supposed to be listening, but I suppose I can't stop you in a setting like this. So … yes, ma'am," Whitehouse said, his tone relaxing into his easy manner from earlier. The way the agent had leaned in and looked into her eyes made her heart flutter, but now it dropped like a stone as his eyes hardened to a searching stare. "I'll do just enough to find out the truth."

As Violet and Taylor watched through the pass-through window down the hall, Violet pocketed the business card that Whitehouse had given her "in case she thought of anything else." Josh was brought into the entryway by Agent Whitehouse, deposited in a seat barely out of sight, and was warned about the phone that was recording their conversation. They watched the profiles of Whitehouse and Donnelly as the conversation ramped up.

CHAPTER 6

"Joshua McLennan. Can I call you Josh?" Donnelly said.

"Fine," Josh said, and Violet imagined him folding his arms as a protective barrier.

"Josh, I'm going to get right to the point, given the circumstances." Donnelly did his best to stare keenly at Josh. "Were you trying to leave the premises a few minutes ago?"

"No." Josh sounded sulky.

Donnelly paused. "Were you trying to get past the guards who were posted at the back door?"

"No," Josh almost grunted.

"So you didn't convince my guys that you were going to use the restroom and then try to run outside and past the uniformed officers when their backs were turned?" Donnelly pressed.

Violet heard the wooden chair creak, indicating that Josh was fidgeting.

"I think you were trying to get away. I think you were trying to get past the perimeter we put up. The only thing I don't know is why." Donnelly leaned forward in his chair as Whitehouse snuck a glance down the hall. From where he sat he could barely see the pass-through window and he accidentally made eye contact with Violet, then quickly turned away.

"Okay, I guess I was," Josh mumbled.

"Alright, can you tell me why you were in such a rush to get out of here?" Whitehouse said.

"Because of this!" Josh cried and threw out his arms, making them visible to Violet, and gesturing at the two investigators. "Having to do this. Talk about everything. Watching what I say and still having the cops twist everything I say around on me."

"Sorry if you've had a bad experience in the past," Whitehouse said. "But we only want to find out what happened. We only want to help Captain Shoenthal. I can promise you that we're not out to get you."

Josh said nothing.

"We want to know more about what happened tonight," said Whitehouse.

After a pause, Donnelly returned to his questions. "Did you go outside the back door at all tonight?"

"Nope," Josh said.

"How about the men's room? Did you go in there?"

"Nope."

"Into the back hallway?"

"No, this guy knows I didn't," Josh said, extending an arm enough for Violet to see him pointing to Agent Whitehouse. "He knows I went between the kitchen and the dining room the whole time."

Donnelly glanced at Whitehouse, who nodded his assent.

Josh went on. "I got here about an hour before the event, and I didn't leave the building, go pee, take out the trash, nothing. I didn't even get close to that back hallway."

"Alright." Donnelly nodded. "How about other people? Did you see anyone by the back door? Going in or going out?"

"People were going to the bathroom, but that's all I saw."

"How about people acting strangely?"

"Oh yeah, there was a lot of that." Josh chuckled.

"Like who?" Donnelly asked.

"Violet said that Shoenthal was acting weird, but I didn't see that. I heard about it from her," Josh said.

"Well, who did you see acting strangely?" Whitehouse prodded.

CHAPTER 6

"Taylor." Josh shot out the name, surprising Violet. "I didn't think she knew that guy, the captain, but I saw her talking to him for a long time while she was supposed to be collecting plates."

Violet glanced at Taylor out of the corner of her eye, but Taylor bent towards the pass-through window, frozen with wide, glassy eyes.

"What were they talking about?" Donnelly said.

"I don't know—I couldn't hear them, but Taylor was nodding a lot, smiling, and taking notes on a small piece of paper or napkin or something."

"How did you feel about that?" Whitehouse asked, looking sly.

"Nothing, I mean, I didn't feel anything about that."

Whitehouse said, "You weren't jealous, professionally or … otherwise?"

"Nope, you got it all wrong," Josh said, his voice sounding confident for the first time. "Those ladies are great, but it's not like that—with either of them. I have a girlfriend, who is my age I might add, plus Violet is engaged, well, sort of, and Taylor is not my type and I am not hers. We're cool. It works out perfectly."

"What do you mean she's 'sort of engaged?' She's engaged to Lieutenant Valentine, right?" Donnelly asked, with a glance at Whitehouse.

Josh was all too happy to expose Derek's misdeeds. "Well, she got engaged to that idiot because he was her high school and college boyfriend and he was leaving on deployment, but when he came back she found out he had been cheating on her the whole time with a female officer he was deployed with. They 'took a step back,' as she puts it, but he wants to get back together. I don't think she knows what she wants at this point. If you ask me, she can't let go of the idea of him. Plus she's in denial and hates change."

Tears stung Violet's eyes. His comments had cut deep. Even if she knew that Josh didn't like Derek, it still hurt to hear it this way. At least she knew how he really felt. He never would have been so honest if he knew that she was listening.

"Alright, let's get back to people who were acting strangely tonight. Was there anyone else?" Donnelly tapped his pen lightly on his small notebook

"Yeah, Derek, actually," Josh blurted. "But you know all about that since you were here. Plus the girls in the bathroom were having some kind of wardrobe malfunction. I suspect it was Violet's friend having trouble with her dress again like she had before the party. Different dress though."

"But about Lieutenant Derek Valentine..." Whitehouse said. "Did you see him get angry at all?"

"Nope," Josh said.

"Did you see him come back to the building?" Donnelly asked.

"Sure, but I think he came to see Violet."

"How did you feel about him getting thrown out of the party? Or trying to come back?" Donnelly said.

Josh snorted. "Fine, I mean I already knew he was an idiot, so..."

Donnelly eyed him. "Were you worried it would hurt your company or your reputation? Since he hired you and since he is romantically involved with your business partner?"

"I guess I was a bit concerned for Violet because she can't wrap her mind around the fact that Derek is only concerned with himself," Josh said, then paused. "And I was worried that Taylor might slap Derek at one point and get us all into trouble. But to be honest with you lads, I am not too worried about my reputation as it relates to this catering company that we started. I actually won't be here much longer. I've already got another job lined up and I'll be leaving in a couple of months."

Violet gasped, squeaking with a stabbing feeling of betrayal.

"Oh crap," Josh said, much lower and more somber than before. "Was that Violet? Has she heard everything I've been saying?"

Chapter 7

"I can't believe this! I can't believe you!" Violet groused once they were all three back in the kitchen. "How could you do this?"

Josh moped. "Sorry, Violet. I got a great opportunity. My uncle is starting a place and he wants me to be head chef! Isn't that amazing?"

"Sure, but…" Violet sputtered. "But we committed to this company all together. We'll have to buy you out or something. You're leaving us high and dry!"

Josh looked over at Taylor who was being uncharacteristically quiet, then back at Violet. He said, "So I was supposed to leave my uncle high and dry? I was supposed to miss out on having my own kitchen?"

"I thought you hated commercial kitchens!" Violet cried, flinging her arms up and out. "Why would you go back?"

"No, that was you. I hated being a peon in a commercial kitchen. I could not stand the years ahead of me of working my way up, even with a culinary degree, but now I won't have to. I'm being handed my dream on a silver platter. I've never had a break like this! I thought you'd be able to be happy for me when I finally told you."

"And when were you going to tell me? How long have you

known? When were you going to say something? Were you just going to disappear? Don't you know that we'll need time to get together a loan to buy you out?"

"I was ... waiting," Josh said, then stared at Taylor again. "Waiting for you two to talk first."

"Bro, it's not the time." Taylor put a hand to her stomach. She leaned forward as if sick about something.

Violet's eyes darted between Josh and Taylor. "What is it? You two have been weird about something all day. What? You're not going to throw up, are you? I might pass out if you do. That's the last thing I need right now." She felt a pang of regret for sounding so harsh, but she brushed it off and told herself Taylor deserved it.

"No, no ... It's nothing. We can talk later. I ..." Taylor said, rocking back and forth with her hands on her knees.

"It can't wait any longer, Tay," Josh said in a commanding voice. "I told you, you should have told her a week ago. Now it can't wait any longer."

"What?" Violet said, rounding on Taylor.

"No, c'mon. We're almost done cleaning up. How about Josh and I finish and you go back to your apartment and make sure that Derek hasn't swallowed his tongue or something." Taylor looked into Violet's eyes, then came to her, clasped her hands in hers, and whispered, "We can finish all of this tomorrow."

Violet calmed down and decided to have mercy on Taylor. She was obviously suffering and Violet didn't want to be the cause of that. Taylor had a point. They could sort things out in the morning.

Josh called out, "Taylor is leaving too!"

Violet felt her face match Taylor's as she watched it contort into a dejected frown. "Is that true?" Violet said, her voice cracking.

"My dad got me an interview to be a food critic, and I got the job."

"Is that why you went home last week?"

Taylor dissolved into tears. "That's when I signed the papers and found an apartment."

Violet's mouth fell open. These details made it so real and immediate that there was nothing left to say. "I guess that's it then."

"That only leaves you," said a deep voice from the doorway. Violet was rattled until she saw that Agent Whitehouse stood and beckoned for Taylor to come with him. "Could you please come with us, miss?"

Violet didn't hear a word of Taylor's interview. Her hopes and dreams crumbled around her and the realization was a crushing weight. She had envisioned herself graduating and running an established catering job with her friends. Gone. She'd imagined herself being able to pay off her student debt and saving up for a nicer place. Gone. She wondered if that also meant that the picture-perfect Christmas card life she had dreamed up for her and Derek was gone too.

"Did you hear that?" Josh said as he turned away from the pass-through window. "This is where you were standing during my interview, wasn't it?"

"Um, yeah, but no," Violet said and shook her head. "I-I'm not listening."

Josh said nothing but leaned toward the opening and waved for Violet to join him.

Taylor's voice still wavered from their argument. She sat in the same chair that Josh had been in and, like him, was just barely out of their view. "Yeah, I was talking to him about a potential job. But I guess that's all off if he's in the hospital."

"And what was the nature of the job?" Donnelly asked.

Taylor sighed. "Well, I guess Josh and Violet are already mad at me, so ... alright, it was a private catering job. I was trying to keep it quiet since it was a small job, not big enough to share with my business partners, but ... oh well. Now I get to be a traitor and a deserter."

Whitehouse glanced down the hall at Violet again, confirming that she was now there and listening. He said, "And what kind of private catering job?"

"He wanted dinner cooked for him and his wife at their home on Valentine's Day. I will be leaving for my new job soon, but I will still be here and I don't have any plans for Sunday, so I accepted. Then we were talking about details, you know, food allergies, cuisines, preferences, logistics, all of that."

"And you said he began acting weird. How so?" Whitehouse asked.

"Yeah, really suddenly. I don't know what happened," Taylor said, then grabbed at her curls and swept them farther back and out of her face. "It was going well, but then suddenly he started slurring his words and wobbled on his feet. It was like he was drunk, but he hadn't been ten seconds before."

"Hmm, alright," Donnelly said. "What happened in those ten seconds?"

"Nothing," she said. "He was perfectly coherent, then suddenly he wasn't."

"Did he drink a lot? Take a shot?" Donnelly asked.

"No, I mean, just his water."

"Okay, did he eat anything?"

"No," Taylor said.

"Did anyone touch him? Maybe walk up behind him?" Whitehouse interjected.

"No, not that I saw."

Whitehouse asked, "Are you sure his water was water?"

"I don't know, I guess I couldn't be sure," Taylor said.

Donnelly tapped his pen. "Did it look funny? Smell funny? Did he smell like alcohol? Maybe his breath?"

Taylor thought for a second. "No, but I guess I wasn't paying attention."

Donnelly paused for a long time, scribbling in his notebook.

Whitehouse leaned in. "Should we do a tox screen? Blood alcohol level? Check for foreign substances?"

"Oh yeah,"—Donnelly nodded—"definitely."

"Can I go now?" Taylor scratched at the undercut in her hairdo. "My partners were already mad at me, and now I've probably made it worse. The least I can do is get back in there to clean up. Am I done here?"

"Sure, but you said you were going to leave the area soon?" Whitehouse said.

"Yeah, why?"

"Well, at the risk of sounding cliché, please don't leave town. Not yet anyway."

As Violet, Josh, and Taylor finished packing up their stuff, Agents Whitehouse and Donnelly were finishing up too. Most of the interviews had been the standard rigmarole to find out each person's name, rank if they had one, why they were at the party, if they knew the captain personally, plus their contact information, but the last interview of the night morphed into something intriguing.

CHAPTER 7

Suzanne and her army had finished taking down the decorations, and she was now sitting in the stiff wooden chair in the entryway that had acted as something like an office and interrogation room for the investigators.

"So, Mrs. Shoenthal..." Donnelly sighed as she scooted her chair closer to the investigators and into Violet's view. "Did I hear that you were able to go see your husband in the hospital?"

"Yes, sir," Suzanne said, fidgeting. "I stayed until he was out of surgery, then I came back here to finish cleaning with my girls."

"The Sweethearts Club?" Donnelly said.

"Yes, the wives, fiancées, and sometimes girlfriends of the soldiers. I'm the president."

"And Captain Shoenthal is already out of surgery?" Whitehouse put in. "That was fast, wasn't it?"

"Yes, they said it was one short stab, it didn't hit any major organs, and they were able to sew him up and give him a pint of blood."

"That's great news. So he's out of the woods?" Donnelly asked.

Suzanne faltered. "W-well, not quite. He lost a lot of blood, and he hasn't regained consciousness. Plus, it was the beating, or the blunt force trauma, that was worse. The doctors were optimistic, but I was shocked that he looked so bad. They said that his biggest danger now is infection, but he is also still bleeding internally."

"You didn't have to come back. Your club could have handled the decorations and we could have come to you for this interview," Whitehouse said. Violet watched him level intense eyes on his subject, watching for something.

"Oh no, that's alright." Suzanne declined as easily as if she were refusing a glass of water. "Our club's numbers are down, and a lot of the ladies are new, and I knew you hadn't wanted anyone to leave, so …"

"Well, thank you," Donnelly said with a big fake smile to match Suzanne's. "You saved us a trip. That's very thoughtful of you. I appreciate your consideration."

Violet was surprised by the joy shining out of Suzanne's face in response to the flattery. She had never seen Suzanne glow like that, but then she had never given her such a bold compliment. Violet noticed a sly smile spread across Whitehouse's face and a keen look of deep thought crossed Donnelly's face before he asked another question.

"Now, there are a few questions that I have to ask you—routine, of course."

"Of course." Suzanne gave Donnelly a coy smile. "Anything to help, Special Agent."

Donnelly kept his smile bright. "You own your own business, correct?"

"Yes, it's retail perfume," said Suzanne.

Violet had forgotten, but this rang a bell somewhere in the back of her mind. She now remembered that several of the nurses in the unit worked for her part-time, including Eve and Eve's friend Josilyn.

"How's business?" Donnelly said.

"Great!" Suzanne waved a hand to admire her long, pink, manicured nails. "I was even able to hire two more nurses from the unit to be my employees. And I secured a vendor in the Historic Market Square to sell my perfume there."

"So, how does that work when your family has to move duty stations?" Whitehouse asked.

CHAPTER 7

Suzanne laughed. "It's a bit tricky, but the business comes with me. I have to find new customers, and new employees—basically, start all over again. I have a couple of clients who keep buying from me after a move, but eventually they move on."

"New supply vendors too?" Whitehouse led.

Suzanne paused and looked between the investigators before she answered. "Honestly, no. I buy big batches of perfume online, rebottle it for retail, and sell it."

"That's got to be tough to find new customers and distributors though," Donnelly said. "So how would you feel about Captain Shoenthal securing his next promotion to major?"

"Oh, it'll be a dream come true," Suzanne said, keeping amorous eyes on Donnelly. "He has been passed up once already. His papers are in for a second time, so we're waiting and hoping. If he gets passed up this time, you know, it will be time to leave the Army. Captain to major is a transition where if you don't make it, they'll gently force you out. So, either he makes it and he'll have more control over picking his duty stations, or he'll be out and we can finally stay put."

"I guess either way could be good for business," said Donnelly.

"Yes, sir," Suzanne said, aiming another grin his way. Violet had never seen this particular smile from her. "I'm hoping I can stick around here. I have quite a nice setup with great employees."

"Speaking of them," Donnelly said and rubbed the stubble that was starting to appear on his chin. "Did you talk to them tonight?"

"No, sir," Suzanne said.

"All four of them were here tonight, correct?"

"Yes, sir." Suzanne held up a long, gem-studded nail for each name. "Eve, Heather, Josilyn, and Reese were all here at the party."

"Can you describe your movements during the party?"

"Yes, sir. After the receiving line out front, and after the setup before all that, of course, I was at the table the whole time."

"You never got up to go to the kitchen or the restroom?" Donnelly prompted.

"No, sir."

Donnelly made a note, then said, "Did you ever go outside, front or back?"

"No, sir."

"How about the people at your table? Can they confirm that you were there the whole time?"

"Yes, though several of them won't know because they weren't there the whole time."

"Did you get up to go to the buffet, or did your husband do that for you?" Whitehouse added.

Suzanne simpered, then said, "Well, I sprained my ankle a little bit during the setup. Do you remember that? You were there."

"Yes, ma'am," Whitehouse said, nodding. "When you tripped over that cord."

"Yes!" she squealed. "The one you were so kind about taping down to the floor afterward."

Whitehouse said nothing but offered a slow nod. Violet noticed he did not lap up the praise when he was complimented the way the other two did, but instead got adorably embarrassed.

Suzanne went on. "So anyway, my ankle was smarting a

bit, so I asked Randy, or Captain Shoenthal, to go up to the buffet and the bar for me. He was already walking around and chatting with everyone, so …"

As Donnelly shifted and took a breath, gearing up to ask another question, Suzanne cut in. "Wait! I did get up once. Now I remember. Randy wasn't back from all his schmoozing in time for the dessert course, so I crossed the room to get a piece of cake and a coffee."

"But you didn't leave the room?" Donnelly confirmed.

"No, sir."

"Can anyone attest to that?" Whitehouse asked.

Suzanne considered, then said, "Now, I don't know. I didn't look around at the people near me at the dessert table. But I suppose the people at my table, who were already eating dessert—without offering me anything, thank you very much—could tell you that I was only up for a couple of seconds."

Donnelly asked, "And your ankle was okay to handle crossing the room?"

"Yes, thank you. All that rest must have done the trick because it was almost totally better by the time I got up," Suzanne said with a grin.

"And how about now, do you need ice or anything?" Whitehouse asked, looking at her ankle.

Suzanne beamed. "No, thank you so much. No, it feels completely fine now."

After asking a few more questions that led nowhere and taking down her contact information, the investigators let Suzanne go. She waved a quick goodbye to Violet who, ladened down with bags and boxes, was taking her first trip of equipment out to Josh's van. When she stepped through the kitchen door and into the short hallway closest to the entryway, she heard the investigators conferring.

"Did you see what I saw?" Whitehouse spoke low to his partner.

"Mm-hmm, she wasn't exactly broken up about her husband being in the hospital," Donnelly answered.

"She even flirted with you a little," Whitehouse said. "Is that why you complimented her? To see her reaction?"

"Absolutely. One compliment can tell you a lot." Donnelly looked at Whitehouse and whispered, "As Special Agent Whitehouse or as regular ol' Jake."

Whitehouse looked puzzled and whispered back, "What do you mean?"

Violet suddenly got the feeling that she wasn't supposed to be hearing this conversation. If she'd been in the kitchen, she might not have been able to see or hear any of this. She retreated a few steps, determined to head back, but she couldn't quite make herself walk away.

"I mean one compliment can tell you a lot in your professional life ... or your personal life. Dude, I mean that girl, Violet," Donnelly said, still in a whisper. "If I had met her at a party or something, I'd be introducing you to your future wife."

"Don't do that, I mean..." Whitehouse said as Violet listened with rapt attention and silently shifted the boxes in her arms. "It's a really bad idea."

"Sure, she's technically a suspect, but it's not like she did it. And you can deny it all you want, but you told me, before any of this assault stuff, that you were going to ask her out."

"That was before I found out she was engaged, man. I think that ring must have been hidden when she was folding her arms because ... well, now I feel like an idiot. So don't say anything, okay?"

"Alright, alright but ... she's not really engaged. They took a step back. The way she talks about him, well, I'm not sure they're even dating anymore."

"I guess so, but, Don, it's not like I can ... This is the first case that I'm running. Well, the case that brought us here was, so I don't know about this assault case. Maybe it is mine, too, I don't know ..."

"I'm saying you can test the waters," Donnelly sang. "True, you can't date her while it's an open investigation, but this case won't last forever. Then ... maybe. Offer her a compliment and see what she does. Make something up."

"Oh, I won't have to," Whitehouse said sadly.

Violet's heart fluttered and she almost dropped the chafing dish cradled in her arms.

"There you go," Donnelly said in an excited whisper. "See if she is in a committed relationship. It'll be written all over her face when you compliment her, either way. Then you'll know."

Violet couldn't stand another moment of this conversation. Her face felt like it was on fire, and tingles shot down both arms. She kicked the swinging door, so the hushing sound would make it seem like she had just come out, and emerged from the tiny hallway with her arms full.

"Hi," Violet said around the lump in her throat, then kicked herself for not sounding more natural. "Um, am I allowed out to our van to start loading up?"

...

He even started our little arrangement. He recruited me when he found out that I needed money. He knew I was desperate. I couldn't say no. I could have lost what I already had since he was in a position of power. I had no choice but to join, to assimilate, to conspire, to aid and abet.

...

Chapter 8

Violet swung the back doors of the van closed, then gave them two loud thumps with a flat hand like she had seen in the movies. As the van's engine roared to life, a puff of exhaust drifted into Violet's face and she stepped away, waving away the offending stink. After all of their catering gear had been loaded up, Taylor had volunteered to clean the kitchen and had even promised to make it "like Violet-level clean." Violet had agreed with folded arms and tight lips. Josh backed up the van in a three-point turn until he pulled even with Violet who stood pinching her coat closed against the chill. He leaned out the driver's side window.

"C'mon, gorgeous, let me drive you home," Josh said for the second time that night.

"I have a lot to think about. I want to walk."

"Well, think at home," he said with a wry chuckle. "I can't let you walk home in the cold, in a sketchy area, at midnight. My mother would spin in her grave."

"What? This isn't a sketchy area!" Violet said, almost offended.

"This isn't," Josh said, pointing around them at the Pearl Stable, the building next to them that housed their culinary school, and the restaurants beyond that with their strung outdoor lights and simpering conversation. "But that is." He pointed behind her in the direction of her apartment, and she took in the dark parking lot under the freeway overpass, then a line of old, silent buildings held together with scaffolding and caution tape, awaiting refurbishment.

When she hesitated to answer, he sang, "And there are probably drunk guys peeing on walls, maybe even throwing up, whereas I cleaned out the cab in here—for you!"

"Okay, it's fine during the day, but I guess you're right." Violet walked around to the passenger door. "And I wanted to ask you something anyway."

"What is it?" Josh prompted as he rolled up his window and buckled his seatbelt.

"Why did you try to run? I mean, it's not like you to abandon your post or leave us to clean up, so why did you try to escape out the back door?"

Josh shrugged. "Weren't you listening in on the whole thing? I got out of there so I wouldn't get manipulated and trapped by those cops. I had to watch what I said and still, they twisted everything I said around on me."

"Hmm, yeah, I guess so," Violet agreed, but she kept her gaze on Josh as he pulled out of the parking lot.

He was uncharacteristically quiet during the short drive, but as he stopped at Violet's ground-floor apartment's back door, he said, "I'm sorry we're leaving."

"It hurts, but it's okay," Violet said barely above a whisper. "Or it *will* be okay. We'll ... figure it out."

"Thanks. Well," Josh said to the steering wheel, "you don't have to pay me. You don't have to buy me out. I'm the one skipping out on my commitment. And Taylor and I both know that you've been carrying the business side of things."

"No, you need that. I mean, it was all your savings!" Violet squealed.

"Exactly, so it's not like you have that much sitting around to buy me out. And I'm headed off to a good job. I can get by without it."

"Did you say your uncle's opening a restaurant?"

"Yeah, he wants to do Scottish food, but modern and sophisticated."

Violet hid her grimace and instead forced a smile. "Congrats on getting your own kitchen!"

"Thanks. It's what my mum always wanted, and what I've dreamed about since I was a kid," Josh said with a wistful smile.

Violet's smile turned genuine and she said again, "Congratulations. So it's your mom's brother?"

"Yyyyep. Never knew my dad's family, so ..." Josh trailed off. "But I'm a salaried employee, not an owner, so I'll have a good income right away."

"That's nice. But even if you can do without that money, I can't feel good about taking it," Violet said, looking down so that a tear from each eye bypassed her cheeks and fell onto her lap. "I'll think of something. Anyway, we'll talk tomorrow."

"You're the best," Josh lamented. "See you in class," he said before Violet closed the door and ascended the four steps up to her back door.

Violet was immediately annoyed that her back door was unlocked. She'd reached for the handle with one hand and fished around in the pocket of her peacoat with the other but abandoned the search for her keys when she felt the handle give under her grasp. She had been dreading coming home to a drunk Derek, but an unlocked door and him passed out on her bed in his underwear was worse than anything she had expected.

"Wake up!" Violet snapped as she flipped on the lights.

"Ugh, turn off the lights!" Derek moaned as he rolled to his stomach.

"I will when you get off my bed." Violet turned the lights on and off a few more times.

"Come on, where am I supposed to sleep?" Derek rose to an elbow, eyes still closed. He reached an arm out to her. "We've both had a hard night. Come join me."

It was true that Derek's warm embrace had solved many problems over the years. Many times she had crept into his familiar arms and before long, nothing seemed as bad. With an objective ogle at his defined abs and shoulder muscles, anyone could admit that he was hot. She immediately grew disappointed with herself that she had been tempted by anything that smelled like liquor and stale sweat.

"Derek! No!" Violet cried and slapped her purse down on the kitchen counter. "Get up. You can sleep on some of *your* furniture in *your* bedroom. Move two boxes off your couch, and then it'll be ready for you to pass out on it. Get up!"

"Alright, alright, I'm going," Derek groused.

Before he was even up the stairs, Violet was mixing herself up a treat she knew she needed on a night like tonight—a chocolate mug cake.

By the time the mug was out of the microwave and she was sprinkling chocolate chips on top, the sounds of Derek scuffling around upstairs had stopped. As she waited for the bloomed chocolate chips to melt, a stifling loneliness closed in around her and she wondered for the thousandth time what she should do about her situation with Derek.

CHAPTER 8

In high school, he had been much cooler than her and she had been thrilled to the point of delirium when he had asked her out. They had gone on like that, with him on a pedestal and her fawning over him, until he had left for college a year before her. They had tried to break up for that year, but it hadn't stuck, and she had followed him to the University of Texas, picking up where they had left off. As Violet sat eating her cake, she had to admit that those college years were when it had changed. There had been a slow, almost imperceptible shift, as Derek had stagnated and Violet had thrived.

He was in the Army ROTC and he was passing his classes with a bright future on paper. His looks matured from boyish good looks to devastatingly handsome with sexy swimmer's abs and a suave manner, but that was all. He still acted like the same Derek she had loved in high school. It was both comforting and disappointing. He was still the closed-minded kid that she then realized he had always been. He was still trying to be "cool" by making fun of people and never expanding his horizons. As Violet traveled and learned from mistakes, Derek just pointed and laughed.

Well, he's still young, Violet told herself. *He still has a lot of growing up to do, but that will come with age. And I can help with that.*

Another part of Violet's brain interrupted her plans for the future, as it did every time she got too comfortable over the last month. *But will it come with age? Is he growing up? Is it healthy to be with a man that you want to fix? If he was shallow enough to cheat on me while we were apart for a year and a half, then maybe not.*

Violet interrupted herself again. *We were apart for a long time. And it wasn't only the time and distance. It was deployment. It was high-stress.*

Was it? That niggling corner of her brain broke in again. *He was deployed with his unit to a hospital in Germany. He visited castles on weekends off. He drank beer in biergartens and he was never shot at. How high stress could it have been?*

He saw atrocities! Violet shook her head. *The worst injuries were sent to him and his hospital. Sure, they were already stabilized by then, but it was a concentration of the worst of the worst cases.*

It's not like he was a doctor or one of the nurses! the corner of her brain argued. *He was the officer over the unit of doctors and nurses. He was managing the people that were seeing the worst cases. He wasn't in the hospital performing surgery, helping them learn to walk again, or in therapy working through their PTSD. He was next door doing paperwork!*

She had not thought about that distinction before. Any time he talked about his deployment, which was very rare, he talked about the patients that were coming to the hospital where they were stationed. But how involved had he been with the nitty-gritty stuff of the everyday aftermath of the atrocities of war?

It doesn't matter, does it? The two sides of the argument converged into one question that sank to the bottom of her chest like a rock. *The part that matters is this—do I trust him?*

But the cohesive thought did not last long. Soon her mind spun off into other questions. *Well, do I trust anyone? Apparently, I shouldn't! Taylor and Josh are leaving. That's another type of betrayal, isn't it? We all committed when we launched this catering company and began working together!*

Is this normal? Should I get used to this? Is this just guys? Is this only imperfect humans? Are my expectations too high? Should I

CHAPTER 8

give up this idea of relying on people and settle for the reality of imperfect people?

At the same time, a memory from college caught up to her racing thoughts. When she had caught bronchitis during a particularly cold and wet Texas winter, he had nursed her back to health. He missed classes, made her tea, updated and reassured her parents, and kept track of when she needed to take her antibiotics. That was when she realized how great of a dad he would make someday.

The back and forth in her brain was exhausting. She leaned against the big stainless steel fridge and slid down until she sat on the tile floor that she had mopped that morning. She laid her head on the arm she perched on the top of her knees for a moment as she chewed.

Suddenly Violet jerked awake. She blinked hard at the oven clock that said 6:19 a.m. before realizing that she had been asleep for almost six hours. As she wondered what had awoken her, the sound came again.

"Military police! Open the door!" A familiar voice called from the front door over the sound of dull pounding.

Violet staggered to the front door and automatically looked out the peephole as her fingers unfastened the chain.

Special Agent Donnelly stood with several uniformed MPs in the fish-eyed view of the hallway outside. Violet wiped the drool off her cheek, kicking herself for not having brushed her teeth, and turned the deadbolt back when she heard the rapid thudding of someone behind her racing down the stairs.

Before she could register what was happening, she was opening the front door. Derek, still in his boxer briefs, was darting for the back door. Finding BDU camouflage whizzing past her face, she stepped back against the wall as the soldiers pushed into the apartment.

Oof! SLAP! Uh!

It all happened so fast that it took a moment for Violet to realize that the slap was Derek's bare body hitting the tile and he now lay flat on his back, moaning in pain. Whitehouse retracted his outstretched arm, evidently having laid in wait by the back door and clotheslining Derek when he tried to escape.

As Whitehouse gave Violet a pitying look, she realized what it looked like to have Derek in her apartment in his underwear.

Donnelly and the uniformed MPs continued past Violet and through the apartment and towards the back door to help, but Whitehouse was already clicking cuffs onto one of Derek's hands.

"There," Whitehouse said. "Now you can have your other hand for a minute. Don't try anything, just put on your pants so I can read you your rights."

"Violet!" Derek called out as he struggled to put on his tuxedo pants from the night before. "Violet, help me!"

"What—what is going on? Why are you here to arrest Derek?" Violet asked, shaking off the fog of sleep and the pain in her rear end from sitting on the tile for six hours.

Donnelly reached Derek and struggled to silence him, then he pulled out a piece of paper, unfolded it in front of Derek's face, and yelled over Derek's calls. "Lieutenant Derek Valentine, I have this warrant for your arrest. You are under arrest for the assault of Captain Shoenthal. You have the right to remain silent. Anything you say can and will be used against you in a court of law…"

"Violet! You know I didn't do this!" Derek pleaded.

CHAPTER 8

"This is crazy!" Violet squawked. "Derek didn't attack the captain! He couldn't have!"

Derek called out again as he struggled to his feet. "You gotta help me, Vi!"

"Me? Wha–what can I do? I can't…" Violet said and hugged a corner of the wall.

"Come see me! Promise me you'll come. I need to talk to you!"

Violet felt her breath quicken. Her mouth was open, but she didn't know what to say. *How is this happening? How can they think it was Derek?*

"Okay" was all Violet could say as Whitehouse looked at her, his mouth in that same flat line. Was that disappointment or resignation? She didn't know him well enough to know.

Derek's tux pants were on, but he had no shirt. Violet's hands shook as she retrieved a big t-shirt that used to be his from a hook in the bathroom next to her. She rummaged around in the now empty rooms of her brain for something to say, but there was both too much to say and not enough. She didn't want to have Derek and Agent Whitehouse looking at her and waiting for a response. But she also wanted to go on a tirade about how Derek was innocent, why he had been in her apartment, how nothing had happened with him last night, and maybe something about how they couldn't do this to her first thing in the morning in her own apartment.

Derek called again, "Promise me! Promise me that you'll come see me today. As soon as they let you!"

She ran over and wadded the shirt into his free hand. They shuffled his cuffs, letting him put on the t-shirt, then fastening his hands together behind his back.

"Uh, okay, I don't know how that will help, but… I promise,"

Violet said. "I'll come. Don't call me. Use your one phone call to get a lawyer."

"So practical." Derek smiled and leaned forward to kiss her, but was instead swept out the door by the investigators and other military police. Violet stood frozen and took a deep breath to calm her racing heart.

"Sorry," Whitehouse muttered before following them, but Violet made sure to avoid his gaze as she snapped her mouth closed and swallowed hard. "He'll probably be ready for his first visitor in about two hours,"

She didn't have a ready response for him and she squeezed her hands together to make them stop shaking. She wished she had something cutting to say. If only she had eyes like Taylor's, then she could freeze him to the spot with one look.

How could I have ever thought Agent Whitehouse was handsome? He's only seeing what he wants to see in Derek to solve his first case, she thought as she attempted an icy stare into Whitehouse's already mournful eyes.

After they left, she replayed the scene again and again in her mind. Her shock about the whole ordeal solidified into a hard anger, but it slipped through her fingers as the sadness in a certain agent's eyes melted it away.

Microwave Chocolate Mug Cake (egg-free)

Serves 1 or 2

Prep time - 3 minutes

Ingredients:
- ¼ cup all-purpose flour
- 2 tablespoons unsweetened Dutch cocoa powder
- ⅛ teaspoon baking powder
- ⅛ teaspoon salt
- ¼ cup honey
- ¼ cup milk
- 2 tablespoons vegetable oil
- ½ teaspoon vanilla extract
- Optional - a handful of chocolate chips for serving

1. In a microwave-safe big mug or medium bowl, use a fork to thoroughly mix together flour, cocoa, baking powder, and salt.

2. Pour honey into a microwave-safe measuring cup with milk, oil, and vanilla. Microwave for 30 seconds, then stir to combine.
3. Mix wet ingredients into dry ingredients with a fork until there are no dry pockets left.
4. Microwave for 1 minute 50 seconds or until the middle has risen and isn't jiggly.
5. As soon as the cake comes out of the microwave, sprinkle chocolate chips over the surface, if using, and leave it to sit and melt for 1 or 2 minutes before spreading and enjoying!

Chapter 9

By nine o'clock Violet felt enough like herself to be able to fake the rest. Since she had been forced to wait to see Derek, she went about her morning routine, trying to feel normal. She had flossed and brushed her teeth for more than three minutes, swished with mouthwash for exactly thirty seconds, exfoliated her face for exactly sixty seconds, and ran through a quick routine for her skin of toner, serum, and moisturizer. Plus she had wiped down her phone with a sanitizing wipe, run the sticky roller over her peacoat, and wiped off the little table in the dining room for no other reason than because it made her feel better. As a bonus point in her mind, she marinated the chicken and set the sauce bubbling away in a Crockpot for her team's favorite Chicken Tikka Masala.

She peeked out the living room windows and saw that the sun was burning off the chill from the night before. After hanging up her apron and grabbing her favorite maroon sweater, she stepped outside. Leaving behind the warm aroma of Indian spices, she breathed in the scent of rain and peach blossoms. Violet cherished that rare time of year in Texas when the sun was warm and the shade was cool. She knew that soon it would be unbearably hot, and two weeks earlier it had been unbearably cold, so before she walked into the parking garage, she faced upwards to soak in this manageable, bite-sized piece of warmth.

As she thumped the car door closed, Violet realized she had no idea where she was going. For perhaps the first time she could remember, she didn't have a planned route before she got in the car. Also for the first time, she needed to figure out how to visit someone in prison.

She pushed aside fears of the conditions she would find there and thought of logistics. Was he in jail or prison? How far away would she have to travel? Or was he still in the police station?

Violet took out the business card she had been given yesterday and spun it in her fingers over and over as she read and reread the name, 'Special Agent Jacob Whitehouse - CID.' Was this the kind of thing she should ask him? Was there anyone else she could ask?

While she knew that Agent Whitehouse was doing his job, it still irked Violet that he had gone so far as to arrest Derek. And in her apartment! How could he put Derek through that? Especially because he was so obviously innocent!

Now Derek would have this arrest on his record forever, wouldn't he? Violet wasn't sure if that's how it worked, but she knew it wasn't a good thing. Even if Derek was cleared, which he would be, some record of this arrest would remain on paperwork and in his coworkers' minds. It would stick to him like a 'kick me' sign on his back or a big stain on an otherwise pristinely white shirt.

Violet shuddered. She wanted to shrink back into her apartment, put the blankets over her head, and hide until all of this blew over, but she reminded herself that she had promised to go see Derek. In their long history together,

CHAPTER 9

Derek had saved her and sacrificed for her plenty of times—not that she was keeping score. He had come to pick her up when she'd had trouble with her decrepit college car. He had been her guinea pig and tasted some truly awful kitchen experiments of hers, like a spicy-chip-and-orange-chocolate sandwich cookie that he had needed to spit out. He had even cleaned her apartment for her, or attempted to, when she was down with a bout of bronchitis. She needed to do this for him. So she didn't have any other option: she would have to make the call

"Special Agent Whitehouse," he rattled off after a ring and a half.

"Yeah, uh, hi. This is Violet," she said. "Do you have a minute?"

"Yes, of course. Did you need to tell me something?"

Violet wished she had thought of some other pretext for calling. "No, sorry. I have questions for you."

"Go ahead."

"First of all, how's the captain? Is he going to be okay?"

"Mm-hmm. It looks like he is going to recover. It will take time. And we'll know more as time goes."

"Oh good," Violet said. "Also, I know people tease me because I'm persnickety, but tell me the truth: how dirty are prisons? Like will I need rubber gloves or a wipe for my hands at the end?"

"Uh, I guess just a wipe? It's not as bad as it looks on TV... I think you'll be okay," he said, a hint of amusement in his voice. With genuine concern, he added, "And don't worry about what those other people say. Being clean and detail-oriented is a good thing."

Violet couldn't help but smile. His compliment planted

deep in her heart and bloomed there. "Okay, well ... the main reason I called was ... I was wondering ... well, I've never visited a prison before. Can I ask where Derek is? How do I go talk to him?"

"Ah, well, he's not in prison yet—he's being detained for the time being. That is, until we get down there to question him some more."

"Oh okay, so where is that? Do I look up 'county jail' in Google Maps?" Violet asked.

"No, it's the military police, not the county sheriff."

Violet faltered. "Oh right, so ... military jail? Do they really call it the brig?"

"For now he's in the MP station," Whitehouse corrected.

"Is that on the base? Fort Sam, right? Will they let me in? Are the base gates open?" Violet said, then realized she was bombarding him with questions and her smile faded.

"Hey, um ... yeah," Whitehouse said as if resolving something. "How would you feel about driving over there with Donnelly and me? We are around the corner and headed there now."

"Oh, okay. That'd be great. As long as you're allowed to do that."

"Sure." Whitehouse's voice had a lightness that hadn't been there a moment ago. "You'll have to ride in the backseat, but we'll be right there."

Violet walked back to her apartment in a daze. *What am I doing?* she asked herself. *Am I really about to ride in the dirty back seat of a cop car? And for what, to see Derek? Why? For some kind of loyalty that he may or may not deserve?*

The thought came to her that she couldn't lean on Derek's

promises anymore, so why should she be keeping her promises to him?

Then that annoying corner of her brain interrupted her thoughts like it had last night. *Whether or not he can be trusted is yet to be seen. The real question is what kind of person do I want to be?*

Violet immediately knew the answer to that question. *I want to be the kind of person who is trustworthy. The kind of person that friends know they can rely on in any circumstance. So that's the kind of relationship I need to be establishing with Derek. I want us to get to a place where we have faith in each other. Where we rely on each other under any circumstances. Being loyal to each other under any circumstances. So I need to keep my promise and go see him.*

She stood with shaking knees outside her back door. She wasn't sure what to expect, but when the investigators pulled up in a shiny black sedan, she was taken aback. When Whitehouse jumped out of the passenger seat and opened the back door for her, a waft of fresh air-conditioning met her and she had no qualms about entering the car. It wasn't the beat-up and urine-soaked drunk tank that she'd imagined. Instead, it looked like a newer sedan with a back seat that had never been sat on.

"Sorry about this morning, Miss Davis," said Donnelly as she buckled her seatbelt. "I hope you understand we are under a lot of pressure to solve this case quickly. The victim being an officer and all."

Violet had not thought about that nuance of their job before, and it made her soften towards them. "Oh, um, I guess I understand. And call me Violet, please. It was a heck of a way to wake up though."

Donnelly smiled over at Whitehouse as he got back in the car, but Violet couldn't see his reaction. Only the back of his neck showed between the seat back and the headrest. Should she explain that nothing had happened with Derek last night and that he had slept alone on a couch in the spare bedroom? Not that it mattered, and it was not the time or place to talk about it. *I don't need to defend myself when we didn't do anything wrong.* she resolved.

Instead she asked, "Any updates on how the captain is fairing?"

"Nothing since we spoke last, but I can check in with the hospital." Whitehouse sounded more stern than necessary

Violet went on. "Look, I understand that you have to move quickly, I do, but I'm sorry to say that you're barking up the wrong tree. Derek didn't do this."

Donnelly shot a sideways glance at Whitehouse. The back of Whitehouse's neck bent down to look at his lap.

"I hope for his sake that you're right, Miss ... um, Violet," Whitehouse said.

Violet leaned forward to add, "After last night, I thought you would be arresting Suzanne Shoenthal."

"Alright, why's that?" Donnelly said.

"Well, it's no secret that she and the captain have had a few problems in their marriage lately," Violet said. "I guess they were having quite the adjustment period since he got back from Germany with the unit."

"Is that right?" Donnelly said, sounding impressed. "Sounds like you might have the inside scoop."

"I guess so, yeah," Violet said, realizing how much she knew about the people in the unit and their personal lives. "It's Derek's job to take care of the people in his battalion. And then he likes to, or used to like to, come home, have a drink, and tell me all about it."

"So he, and you by extension, would know a lot about these people. Where they work, what they do for fun, their personalities, their problems, their routines ..." Donnelly said, lifting a hand off the steering wheel to list all these on his fingers.

"Their motives," Whitehouse added.

And without anyone in the car saying it, Violet realized she was going to be hearing from these investigators a lot more than she'd planned.

After showing her driver's license at a gatehouse, Fort Sam Houston opened up to view in a surprisingly short time. Historic brick and limestone buildings with red tile roofs reminded Violet that this place had been around for a long time. She knew that the base was only about ten minutes from her apartment, but the drive was especially short today.

As Violet followed Donnelly into the low brick building, she read a sign that said, "2233 Wilson Way," but the rest of the sign was gibberish to her. "502d SFS BDOC."

That small snippet of military life reminded her that she was entering another world. *If I marry Derek, I'll be a military wife,* she thought. *Will I be expected to remember all these acronyms?*

Another sign that looked more temporary read, "502 SFS 2020, AETC Security Forces Annual Unit Award Winners."

Violet's chest tightened and her breaths quickened as she realized how little of that she understood. Thank goodness she wasn't navigating this alone. She stepped through the door and froze, staring at the room full of uniformed military police personnel. She took an involuntary step backward.

She bumped into Agent Whitehouse and he caught her back with a wide hand. "Are you okay?" he asked, and Violet realized that he might have thought she was fainting.

"I'm ... a little intimidated," she admitted.

Whitehouse surveyed the room, as if seeing it from her perspective, then turned to her with compassion and bent close enough that she could see the flecks of gray in his blue eyes. He curled his lips down to keep the smile off his face, whispering, "Don't worry, I–we will help you the whole way."

Soon Violet was seated at a wide metal desk and she couldn't help but be impressed by how clean it was. Every inch was polished and shiny—even the pencils in the cup looked dusted. She gazed at the only other thing on the surface: a hinged, double picture frame of two women. One looked to be in her early fifties with the same penetrating blue eyes as Agent Whitehouse, and one looked to be in her early twenties with a pretty, flirty smile that reminded Violet slightly of Josh's girlfriend.

Mom and girlfriend, Violet thought. *So why was Donnelly talking to Whitehouse about me?*

Before she could think of a solution, Derek stumbled into the chair next to her. He immediately launched into a long-winded explanation and her mind scrambled to catch up. "I wasn't even there! After I got this meringue with cream and sauce and stuff, I came back inside to see you, then left. I went home to sleep it off, but they are convinced it was me who beat up Captain Shoenthal! I even told them about that video that the captain posted online, but they won't listen to anything I say. You gotta help me, babe!"

"I'm here, I'm–I'm helping," Violet said and looked up to see Agent Whitehouse sitting at the next desk over and listening to every word that Derek said. "But the rest is up to you and the police. And a lawyer."

"No, I need you, Violet!" Derek leaned forward and took Violet's hands in his. Violet realized her hands must be especially cold because Derek's hands burned as if he had a fever. When her fingers touched the steel cuffs that shackled his wrists, even they didn't feel cold to her. "Yeah, a lawyer is coming, but only you can get me out of this."

"What?" Violet reeled. "What do you expect me to do?"

"Babe, I need you to find out who really did this," Derek pleaded.

"What?" Violet said again. "I can't do that! It's not my place to …"

"But you're my 'butter half', babe," Derek said, quoting her favorite mural from back home in Austin, where couples often posed with the cartoon toast and butter painting. She remembered the photo they took in front of it with him kissing her in a deep dip. He pulled her hands up to his lips and planted a delicate kiss on each. Violet watched the sinewy muscles in his forearms dance as he stroked his fingers over her hands. "I need you. I promise I'm still trying to make it up to you for … everything, but this is important. You're my girl. I'm royally f—" Derek looked at Whitehouse who returned a frown. "I'm … toast without your help."

"I can't get in the way of a police investigation. Besides, I wouldn't even know where to start. I–I …" Violet said.

"That's the problem, they're not even investigating anymore. They've decided that I'm guilty!"

Violet took Agent Whitehouse's silence as a confirmation of what Derek was saying.

"And I can help you get started," Derek wheedled. "I can

give you some leads, then you can take it from there."

Violet said nothing but stared at her hands as Derek squeezed them.

"I'm in trouble. I need you," Derek said again. "Without your help ... I mean, how else are we ever going to get back to normal?"

Chicken Tikka Masala for the Slow-Cooker

Serves 4-6

Prep time - 20 minutes

Total time with slow cooking - 6 hours

This recipe is glorious because it can be made with regular grocery store fare but still tastes amazing. The sauce is full of flavor—creamy and not too spicy so even kids love it! The chicken is best grilled separately, but it can also be thrown in with the sauce to slow cook all day. When I make this I marinate the chicken the night before, grill the chicken and start the sauce in the morning, then let it slow cook all day for dinner.

For the chicken:
 1 cup yogurt, whole or low-fat (not non-fat)
 2 teaspoons granulated garlic or garlic powder
 1 teaspoon salt
 4 boneless, skinless chicken thighs

For the sauce:
   1 teaspoon ground cumin
   ½ teaspoon ground coriander
   ½ teaspoon ground cardamom
   ½ teaspoon ground black pepper
   ¼ teaspoon ground cinnamon
   ⅛ teaspoon or 2 pinches ground cloves
   ⅛ teaspoon or 2 pinches ground nutmeg
   2 (15 ounce) cans crushed tomato
   2 tablespoons butter
   1 large onion, sliced or cut into crescents
   ½ green bell pepper, seeds removed and sliced
   3 garlic cloves, finely minced or crushed through a press
   1 tablespoon fresh ginger, grated or finely minced
   1 teaspoon sugar
   ½ teaspoon salt
   ½ cup heavy whipping cream
   ⅓ cup cilantro, roughly chopped

1. Stir together yogurt, garlic, and salt in a low bowl or pie plate. Nestle in chicken thighs, coating them with the yogurt mixture on all sides, cover plate, and refrigerate. Overnight marinating makes the chicken tender, but if you forgot to plan ahead you can let it marinate while you make the sauce.
2. Combine cumin, coriander, cardamom, black pepper, cinnamon, cloves and nutmeg in a small bowl and set aside. Open tomato cans and set aside. You will want to have both handy for the next step of cooking because it will go fast.

CHICKEN TIKKA MASALA FOR THE SLOW-COOKER

3. Saute onion and bell pepper in butter over medium heat until onions are caramelizing, then scoot all the onion and pepper to the outside edges of the pan. Add garlic and ginger to the middle, sauteing them until fragrant, then stir them into the onion mixture before they burn. Add spice mixture that you set aside.
4. When the spices have joined the fragrance party, cook for about 30 seconds, then mix in the cans of crushed tomato, sugar, and salt, then turn off the heat. With the residual heat in the pan, deglaze all the wonderful brown flavor on the bottom of the pan by scraping it up and mixing it into the sauce.
5. Now pour the whole spicy tomato-onion mixture into your slow cooker and set it to low heat for as long as you can stand to wait, at least 6 hours. You can start this in the morning or even the night before because the longer it sits in the slow cooker, the better.
6. At least an hour before serving, pull your chicken out of the marinade and get to grilling it. Mix excess yogurt into sauce in your slow cooker, but be sure that your sauce again reaches a simmer and is bubbling before you serve it (for food safety reasons.)
7. Grill your chicken thighs on the barbecue or under your oven's broiler. Cook chicken pieces for 5-7 minutes per side or until the yogurt coating is spotty and brown. Small black parts are okay, even wonderfully crispy. Let chicken rest for 10 minutes after coming off the heat, then slice against the grain into ½-inch thick pieces. Since you will be mixing this chicken into warm sauce, you can do this step way ahead and refrigerate your finished product, or wait till it's almost time to serve

and mix it into the simmering sauce right away.
8. Right before serving, and after mixing in your grilled chicken, turn off the heat to your slow cooker and mix in the heavy cream. Then mix in half of your cilantro and save the other half for garnishing. Serve over rice or with naan or flatbread.

Chapter 10

Derek had said the magic words. *Get back to normal.* The clouds in Violet's mind parted, the tension in her shoulders melted away, and if it had been a movie, she would've heard a choir of angels.

She thought of her first year of culinary school when she felt focused and assured. She thought of her company, thriving and blossoming. And she thought of her apartment, comfortable and feeling like home.

"Back to normal?" she said.

"Yeah, babe." Derek scooched forward on his chair. "Isn't that what you want?"

"Yeah, I think it is," Violet said to the far wall.

"We can get back to that. I know the deployment was rough. I'll make it all up to you, but first, I need you to do this for me. Can you do that?" Derek was shamelessly begging now.

"Yes, we can fix this. We can hang on. Okay, but … what would I even do? How would I start?" Violet felt her eyebrows knit together as she closed her eyes.

"We'll do it together. I can give you some ideas of who to talk to, then all you have to do is ask around. Go visit people while I can't. Until I can." Derek said, then kissed the back of her hand while his eyes lingered on her naked ring finger.

"Will you do that for me?"

Violet knew he was asking a lot, but she couldn't help but remember the many good times they had had. She pictured sitting quietly with Derek in a movie theater on their first date in high school. She remembered catching him measuring her finger one night as she slept, then surprising her a week before he was to ship out with a diamond that was so big it dazzled her. She imagined her future life with him as a Christmas card. Kids, a dog, matching sweaters, and Derek with a big grin. Hmm, maybe not the dog, unless she could get Derek to start helping with the cleaning.

The corner of her mind interrupted this moment, but she shoved it down. *He made a mistake. It's true that he was not loyal to me under extreme circumstances, but now if I am not loyal in trying to clear his name, does that make me any better? Is it just as bad if I leave him high and dry now? Wouldn't that be a kind of betrayal? What kind of person would I be if I betrayed him now in retaliation?*

"Okay," Violet said. "If we want to rebuild this, I'll take the first step."

"You'll ask around? You'll find who did this and get me out of here?" Derek asked with boyish enthusiasm.

Violet took a deep, slow breath to steady her nerves. "Yes. Well, I'll do my best. Now where do I start?"

"Sorry to interrupt, but time's up," Whitehouse said. He had walked up behind Violet and now stood with a frown directed at the linoleum flooring.

"Wait, um … it was about a month ago," Derek said in a rush. "On Facebook. On the Fort Sam Houston page."

"Which one?" Violet asked as Donnelly hoisted Derek up by the armpit.

CHAPTER 10

"I don't know, but one of the Fort Sam Houston pages on Facebook. The captain posted a video. Look it up. You have to find it."

"What am I looking for?" Violet pleaded as Whitehouse moved in front of her. She craned her neck, trying to look around his shoulder.

As Donnelly pulled Derek back and away, the hand that Violet had placed on Whitehouse's shoulder solidified into a desperate grip.

"It was a minor fender bender, but it turned into an argument. Please find it! I need you!" Derek called out as he disappeared through a doorway.

After Derek was gone, Violet realized she was still gripping Whitehouse's suit coat sleeve and breathing fast. She startled and released it in a flash, then looked at him, embarrassed.

He looked into her eyes with pity, the way someone might look at a hurt child. "Sorry."

He said it so sincerely that Violet couldn't decide if she wanted to slap him or hug him.

"Well—well, you will be," Violet stammered, then stormed out of the building.

Violet wasn't sure where she was going, but she stumbled through a maze of hallways and pushed open the first exit door she found. A fresh breeze brought instant relief to her burning cheeks. She fumbled in her purse for the travel-size hand sanitizer and felt the familiar sting of the alcohol on her chapped hands. She waved her hands to dry them and shake off her nerves, then put her hands to her face. She tried to even out the fire in her face and the tingling cold in her fingertips.

What did I agree to? Violet sighed. *Derek is always persuasive, but that was ridiculous. Am I really going to interfere with a police investigation?*

Not interfere, the corner of Violet's mind interjected, *just help. I won't get in the way, I'll pick up where they leave off. I can fix this. Like finding that video that Derek told me about.*

Violet took her hands off her cheeks and patted several of her pockets until she found her phone. She opened Facebook and typed in Fort Sam Houston.

At least ten groups and pages popped up. She felt safe scrolling past groups like "Fort Sam Houston Spouses" and "Buy/Sell at Fort Sam," but then slowed down when she reached the neighborhood pages. There were at least four pages that fit the bill for the kind of place a person would post a video of something that happened to them while on base.

Violet picked one and scrolled. At first, she looked at everything, then as her patience waned she scrolled faster until she reached dates that matched mid-January, or about a month ago as Derek had said.

Nothing.

She did the same on the next page. Nothing.

The third page had a video of two people having a heated discussion about a fender bender, but it was taken in the third person and neither one was Captain Shoenthal.

Violet took a moment to consider a different course, then realized she should be searching the text for 'Randy Shoenthal' on each page.

The first page had never even heard of him, but on the second page, she struck gold.

"Watch out for this clown!" the post from Shoenthal stated. "He'll hit your car, then yell at you. Even if you outrank him!"

CHAPTER 10

Violet blushed that Captain Shoenthal had posted such a video and that it had not been taken down by the moderators or admin. She watched the video with rapt attention as she brushed off a few pebbles off the curb and gingerly sat down.

"Say it again!" Captain Shoenthal's voice called from behind the camera. An extremely pale man in desert camo was walking away, shaking his head. "You want to yell at an officer, but you won't do it on camera? Say it again. Say it for the camera, and this time add 'sir!'"

"Please stop this," the other man said, turning around for a moment to reveal purple eyes. He was a Sergeant First Class, judging by his insignia. "I'll drop it. No problem."

"Oh, like you're doing me a favor?" The captain's harsh voice continued off-screen. "You hit me! Sure, you can leave. I've got all the info on you that I need!"

The video showed the license plate number of the other man's maroon Jaguar, then ended and replayed. Violet watched again, squinting her eyes to read the tiny name on the chest of the man's uniform. Violet watched over and over. She was able to write down the license plate number easily enough, but only the first half of the name was visible, no matter what she did.

"Pear something," Violet said to herself. "Maybe Pearson? Pearce?"

"It's just Pear," Whitehouse said as he came and sat beside her on the curb. "I looked it up by using his license plate."

"Wha—but I thought you were done investigating. Derek said..." Violet trailed off.

"Believe it or not," Whitehouse said with a smile, "we don't tell the suspects everything."

"Why are you telling me? You know I'm going to tell him."

"Well, he can find out eventually. We only needed him to only know what we wanted him to know during our questioning." Whitehouse looked directly into Violet's eyes. "Like with Josh, I'll do just enough to find out the truth."

"Well, good. You better." Violet yanked her coat tighter. "Because then you'll find out who did it. Because it wasn't Derek."

"You strike me as a very loyal person, Miss Davis, so I hope you're right. We'll see," said Whitehouse.

Violet felt a fire light inside her, both at the compliment and at the challenge. "I am very loyal, thank you very much. And we *will* see. I'll try not to rub your face in it too much when you're wrong."

Whitehouse slowly grinned at her and Violet couldn't help but smirk back.

"Can I take you home?" Whitehouse chuckled.

"What?" Violet's eyebrows shot up and she sat up straight.

"I mean ... uh ... your apartment," Whitehouse said as he shot to his feet. "I'll drive you. Are you ready for me to drive you home?"

"Yes, thanks. I, um," Violet said and tucked one side of her hair behind her ear. "I should get back. I might even be able to make it to my afternoon classes."

"Don has to stay here, but I'm headed out to check on the captain, so ... is it okay if it's just me?"

"Yes, please," Violet said, then realized she sounded too eager. "I mean, yes. Does that mean you are headed to talk to Sergeant Pear?"

"Nope," Whitehouse said. "Checking on the captain."

"What? But I thought you said you were investigating him," Violet said, feeling duped.

"Nope, I only said that I was still investigating."

"Then why not this Pear guy?"

"He has no motive," Whitehouse said as they returned to the dark sedan they had arrived in, Violet taking the front seat this time. "I didn't only look him up by his license plate. I also looked up the accident report and all the complaints and other paperwork from Captain Shoenthal after the accident."

"Does one accident create that much paperwork, or is that because it was military personnel?" Violet asked.

"It's because Shoenthal made a stink." Whitehouse stared out the windshield as he drove. "Pear left the scene of the accident when, according to him, Shoenthal was beyond all reasoning. So then Shoenthal reported Pear as a hit-and-run, but that fell through because they had exchanged information and taken pictures of the damage."

"So Shoenthal was mad because his hit-and-run charges didn't stick?"

"Definitely, because then he attacked from another angle. He blamed the accident on Pear, but based on the intersection and where it happened, that didn't work either."

"What do you mean?"

"I mean it happened where one road joins another at a tee," Whitehouse said. "Shoenthal had a stop, Pear didn't. So Pear did hit Shoenthal, but it was because Shoenthal shouldn't have been pulling out. The accident was Shoenthal's fault."

"Why was Shoenthal taking that video? And why was he so mad at Pear?"

"According to statements from both of them, Pear was raising his voice because he was upset about his car," Whitehouse said. "He didn't realize that he was yelling at an officer, and especially one that would ... go on such a power trip about it.

My words, not the report's."

Violet nodded. "Okay, that makes sense. So Shoenthal was making the video to get Pear in trouble for yelling at an officer?"

"Yep. And because he wanted to blame the whole thing on Pear. Maybe Shoenthal hadn't realized that the accident was his fault, or maybe he was going to condemn Pear in the court of popular opinion by posting it online and bad-mouthing him."

"That sounds pretty petty to me," Violet said with a frown.

"Yep," Whitehouse said again. "Army officers are like cops. Sure, there are rules, but some guys try to be understanding in tense situations and some guys will enforce every little thing if it makes them feel powerful."

Violet watched Whitehouse for a few seconds. He gripped the wheel with his hands at ten and two, and he kept his eyes on the road. She asked a question, even though she was pretty sure she already knew the answer. "So which guy are you?"

Whitehouse shrugged. "Trying to make the world a better place while building a career. I'm kinda the new guy. This is the first investigation that I have been in charge of."

"Oh, well then, congrats," Violet said, then felt her smile morph into a look of challenge. "And good luck!"

• • •

We had a great thing going. No one was getting hurt, we were making some extra money, and we controlled every step of the process. Nice and easy and clean. Until he had to ruin it. What did he think would happen?

...

Chapter 11

Violet stood by her back door and waved to Agent Whitehouse, but his car didn't pull away. Instead, he sat watching her with a piercing stare. She was reminded of her first date as a teenager when her mother had told her that a good man would walk you to your door, or at least wait until you got inside safely. At this moment, Violet wished Whitehouse was not such a good guy. Her key was in her hand and she put it next to the keyhole. No movement from the car. She was looking down at her door handle, but still he waited.

Why can't he be like Derek and get on with driving away? Violet thought as she planned her escape.

Finally, Violet unlocked her door and stepped inside, waving one more time for good measure. Through the window she watched the long, dark sedan pull away and drive down the street.

I suppose he has to be like that with people because he's police, Violet told herself, still picturing his lingering car and his face as he watched her at the door. *Probably his duty to be kind and protective, and all that.*

"Well, as long as I've had to come all the way inside anyway," Violet said out loud to herself as the relaxation of being home washed over her. "I guess my investigation can wait a minute

CHAPTER 11

while I refuel." She walked to the kitchen and opened a giant Tupperware with the maple, browned-butter blondies that she had made a few days before. "And talking to myself does not mean that I have a problem. Talking to myself is perfectly acceptable now that I live ... alone."

Violet looked around as she ate the soft cookie bar. The echoing space had not felt comfortable for a long time. For about a month, if she was honest with herself. Most of the furniture was packed away in the spare bedroom, along with the beautiful basket of bath salts that Derek had sent to her on her birthday while he was deployed, despite knowing that she hated baths. It had sat on the end of the island for months as Violet had deliberated on what to do with it. She didn't want to give it away, but it also wasn't right for her. At least it had brightened the apartment a little for about a week after she had hidden the furniture, but now even that was out of sight and out of mind. It left the apartment looking abandoned and cold. The only decoration left was a picture of her and Derek that she could not bring herself to pack away. She hadn't looked at it in a long time as it blended in with the scenery, but she gazed at it now and her heart melted. It was from the night they had gotten engaged.

It had been the June night before Derek left for his deployment to the big veteran's hospital in Germany. Violet had known it would be their last week together for a year and a half, so she'd bought a new emerald satin dress for their date and Derek had said it made her green eyes pop. They'd gone to dinner at Cured, the fancy restaurant near Violet's culinary school that she had always wanted to go to. Derek hadn't remembered that, but he had guessed correctly and Violet had awarded him all the imaginary brownie points as if he had remembered and taken her there specially.

The old, squat stone building was part of the same old brewery as The Stable and Violet's culinary school, but it stood alone in a courtyard in detailed yet understated charm. Violet and Derek had feasted on a decadent charcuterie board, foie gras, and rabbit prepared two different ways. Violet had etched every flavor into her memory and deconstructed how they had made everything, while Derek had taken selfies and posted about it all.

Afterward, they had walked over to Hotel Emma for drinks at Sternewirth, the tavern in the gorgeous hotel that used to be a room of tanks and hundred-year-old brewing equipment. Violet had indulged and gotten tipsy, for once, and noticed that the high stone ceilings were surprisingly clean as they partook of cleverly named cocktails like "Perfect Thyming" and "The Three Emmas."

When they were both deliriously happy, they walked out into the summer breeze and walked along the river that sparkled with the lights from the vibrant nightlife of San Antonio. They strolled to an outdoor amphitheater of grassy river banks that all faced a concrete island in the river. Violet clung to Derek's arm, uncomfortable with the lack of control that came with being drunk, but loving Derek's chiseled arms to hold onto. Derek somehow convinced Violet to follow his leaps out to the island that acted like a stage whenever a show was on. Then, there on the geometric, concrete island, Derek got down on one knee and brought out the ring box. Neither one of them could remember exactly what he had said in the moment, but Violet remembered being dazzled by the size of the ring, the enchanting scenery, and the people all around them cheering them on. Then she whispered yes and Derek yelled to the crowd with his arms up in triumph.

"She said yes!" he called out, then slipped the ring on her finger amid whoops, whistles, and wild applause. He had been so happy. From then, until deployment day, he'd worn that same wide smile. One that she hadn't seen since. Being deployed had changed him, but she could fix him.

Their engagement had made that summer and the holidays that year go by much easier. The assurance of his love, the news that she could share at every family function, and the beauty of the teardrop diamond made her miss having Derek there for beach trips, family reunions, Thanksgiving, and Christmas much less. She assumed that it would have been much harder to endure his absence without the fresh memory of a romantic proposal.

Not only the holidays but his entire deployment would have probably been agony if they had not gotten engaged before he left. The hard times during culinary school and the struggle to learn her knife skills, trying to work in a grueling traditional kitchen, and striking out on her own by getting an apartment far away from family would have been agonizing without the company and reassurance that that ring had afforded.

Violet took her last bite of cookie and remembered that the ring now sat buried in her pocket. She retrieved it, rinsed off the pocket lint, and slipped it back onto her left hand.

Derek's voice came back to her as he had yelled, "I need you!" and "How else are we ever going to get back to normal?" Then she thought of Agent Whitehouse and the tone he had used when he said, "We'll see."

Derek can depend on me, she thought. *I'll make this right, then it will be like none of this bad stuff ever happened. We'll get back to normal, then I can get back to focusing on culinary school and our business ... my business.*

Then Violet marched out the door and over to the parking garage and her own small white hatchback before any more memories could interrupt.

After seeing him yelling at a group of new recruits doing jumping jacks, Violet was surprised when the man from the video walked over with a gentle smile and an easy manner. Someone had told him that he had a visitor and immediately his stern exterior had softened.

Now that Violet stood facing the man from the video, it was obvious to her that he was a middle-aged man with albinism, which explained his pale skin and striking eyes. His violet eyes peered out from under his military-issue patrol cap's brim. His appearance had not helped her recover from her stunned silence.

"Yes, ma'am, I'm Sergeant Pear," he drawled. "How can I help you?"

"Hi, um," Violet said, shaking off her nerves. "I have a couple questions. Is now an okay time?"

"Any time is a good time for a lady, especially for the fiancée of an officer," he said and smiled down at her ring before she could ask how he had known. She grew self-conscious about the big diamond again.

"Oh, right," she said as she spun the ring around with her thumb. "But how did you know I'm engaged to an officer?"

"Well, the whole base is buzzing like a whole parking lot of street lamps about the captain and what happened last night. I knew someone would come to talk to me once they looked at his social media. It was a matter of time." Pear said and removed his hat out of respect and held it low in front of him with both hands. "I thought the police would be here before now, but I guess the record of the accident and all those darn complaints speak for themselves. Did I guess correctly that you are the fiancée of that XO who's getting blamed for this?"

"Yes, Lieutenant Valentine. Wow!" Violet exclaimed. "You're like Sherlock Holmes."

"Thank you, ma'am." He glowed with satisfaction.

"I guess I don't need to tell a lie about how I'm a reporter or something."

"No, ma'am," Pear said.

"Wait, then why are you agreeing to talk to me?" She squinted against the bright sun of the chilly day. "I would understand if you were angry at me for coming to see if you were actually the one to beat up the captain."

"No, ma'am, I was not and I have nothing to hide," Pear said and looked down, shaking his head. "You go right ahead and ask your questions. Or I might could tell you where I was last night?"

"Solid alibi for the time?"

"Rock solid and clear as crystal," he said.

"Alright, well now I'm even more curious," Violet said, trying to sound as friendly as the sergeant, but her heart was dipping down into her shoes.

"First of all, I was at Camp Bullis. See I live at Fort Sam but work at Bullis a lot. So the gate personnel can back me up on that. Then, to add insult to injury, I was even out doing a night land nav exercise in the woods on base. Two miles from anywhere. About a hundred of these maggots can swear to that," Pear said and gestured behind him with a thumb at the men that had stopped doing jumping jacks and were doing push-ups.

"Thanks. So you're a Sergeant First Class?" Violet asked as she looked away from the woman who had taken his place shouting orders and down at his BDU's insignia. "Like a drill sergeant?"

Pear gave her a patronizing smile. "Sort of."

Violet decided to cut her losses and leave before she said anything else that made her sound ignorant of the military's inner workings and before he noticed the blush that rose to her cheeks or the disappointment that stung her eyes.

Maple Browned Butter Blondies with Craisins and White Chocolate

Makes 12 bars, cut from 9x13 pan

Prep time - 1 hour

Ingredients:
- ½ cup or 1 stick butter
- 1 ⅓ cup packed brown sugar
- ½ cup maple syrup
- ½ teaspoon almond extract
- ½ teaspoon maple extract (optional)
- 2 large eggs
- 2 ¼ cups all purpose flour
- ½ teaspoon salt
- ¼ teaspoon baking soda
- 1 cup dried cranberries or chopped dried cherries
- 1 cup white chocolate chips

1. Put butter in a small saucepan over medium heat. You don't have to pay attention to the butter at the beginning,

but after it melts and gets foamy, then don't walk away. Keep cooking butter 5–8 minutes or until browned and nutty, then remove from the stove quickly before it burns. Set aside to cool slightly.
2. Preheat the oven to 350 degrees F and grease or spray a 9×13 pan and set aside.
3. In a big bowl, mix together cooled butter, brown sugar, maple syrup, and extracts. When smooth, mix in eggs.
4. In a separate bowl, mix together flour, salt, and baking soda.
5. Mix dry ingredients into wet ingredients until incorporated and fluffy.
6. Spread mixture flat in a 9×13 pan with spatula, then sprinkle fruit and chocolate chips evenly over surface while making sure they won't be touching the pan during baking. Bake for 30-40 minutes or until a toothpick inserted comes out clean.
7. Let cool for at least 10 minutes, then cut into 12 bars and serve. Store leftovers in an airtight container.

Chapter 12

Violet walked back to her car and a wave of hopelessness washed over her. She imagined Derek sitting in a prison cell, or rather standing at the bars and calling for help. With her limited experience with prisons and criminals, she could only picture a Hollywood dramatization of what he must be going through. Did they really wear orange jumpsuits? Did you really have to use a grimy toilet next to your pillow? She couldn't let him spend the night in there! She couldn't even imagine the horrors of having to spend the night in jail and she shivered as her stomach lurched.

But what else can I do? she demanded of herself. *Who else can I talk to?*

She unlocked her door and was about to get in her car when a voice came from the car next to hers and made her jump.

"So you really are investigating," Whitehouse said. He let a smile curve up on his left cheek as he spoke to her through the passenger side window. "And what did he say?"

"I thought you weren't investigating Pear," Violet said, rubbing hand sanitizer between her fingers and wincing from the pain of it stinging her raw knuckles. "So what are you doing here?"

"Well, checking on the captain took less time than I expected since he is still unconscious. And I didn't think Pear was a viable suspect, but I do need to chase down every lead and tie up every loose end before the trail goes cold," Whitehouse said.

"Makes sense," Violet said, then shivered. She had been on the verge of feeling cold, but the hand sanitizer had pushed her over the edge. "So how was the captain?"

Whitehouse leaned over, unlatching the passenger door and nudging it open. Violet took the cue and got in his car.

"Alright, but I can only talk for a minute. I have to get home," she added.

"The captain's doctors are hopeful that he'll make a full recovery, given time. So they are keeping him under a little longer. Giving him time," Whitehouse said, then gestured to Pear. "So what did he say?"

"You're not going to go ask him yourself?" Violet countered.

"I probably still will, but there is merit in hearing it from you," Whitehouse said. "And in hearing what he tells someone who isn't an MP."

"Do people tell civilians more or less than they do to cops?" Violet asked, shivering again.

"Depends on the person," Whitehouse said, starting the car and pointing the vents so that the heater would blow on Violet.

"Thanks. Okay, well..." Violet paused as the heater warmed her fingers. "He had a solid alibi. He was doing a night land nav exercise at Camp Bullis."

"Well, in that case, I can check into that," Whitehouse said.

"So I helped?" Violet asked with upturned eyebrows, imagining Derek's face pressed between prison bars.

"Yes," Whitehouse said, giving her a sideways glance. "Now

why does that make me think you are going to ask me for something in return?"

"Well ..." Violet gave a shaky smile. "Look, I've barely begun and I've already hit a wall. My one and best lead has the perfect alibi. Now what do I do? I have to get Derek free before he's stuck in jail for the night!"

"I would say 'Go home and leave it to the professionals,' but I think you have other ideas," Whitehouse said with a look of amusement in his eyes.

"Actually, yes, I do," Violet said. "Look, Whitehouse, since you said earlier that I have the inside scoop, I was thinking that my efforts might be put to best use by helping you."

Whitehouse and Violet looked at each other for a long time as he squinted at her with an assessing glare. When she scrunched her eyes and wrinkled her nose in a teasing imitation, his expression relaxed into a smile.

Finally, he chuckled and said, "Okay, I'm not supposed to talk to civilians about ongoing investigations, so I can't exactly work with you ..."

"That's okay, maybe we ... confer sometimes?"

"What if you tell me what you know and ... maybe I accidentally let some info slip sometimes?" Whitehouse said. "Cuz my hands are tied and I can't do a lot of things, but you're right, you probably have a lot of information that could help this investigation."

"Like what?" Violet asked.

"Like that information you gave us about the captain and his wife having had some marital troubles lately," Whitehouse said and gazed at her. "The wife didn't tell us that and no one else mentioned it either. I wonder if other people even knew. And I bet you have lots more info like that."

"I do," Violet said with a smile.

"Okay, so lay it on me," he said.

"Well ... like what?" Violet shrugged.

"Things like ... does the captain have any enemies?" Whitehouse said. He pursed his lips in thought. "Or maybe rivals or ... affairs?"

"He has a few professional rivals, but they're the other captains up for promotion," Violet said and stared out the windshield at the few clouds that moved swiftly across the sky like plastic bags caught in the wind. "I guess I should explain, but I don't know how much you know."

"Go ahead," he said, shifting his athletic frame in his seat to get comfortable. "As we've said, I guess we're both facing our own deadlines."

"So Captain Shoenthal was up for the rank of major once before, but he got passed over for the promotion. Now he's turned in his papers again, but the same problems that cost him his promotion last time are still there. So, it's like everyone but him knows that he's not going to get the promotion. Then, you know, if you get passed over twice for the promotion to major, that's when the Army says 'Okay, thank you. Next?' and encourages you to leave the Army."

"Right," Whitehouse said, nodding. "And you think that's going to happen?"

"Yeah, everybody does," Violet said. "He rubs a lot of people the wrong way. Not enough for charges or whatever, but enough to not win friends. Enough to alienate some people and to cost him the jump to major."

"So, the point is ... his rivals for the promotion wouldn't view him as a real threat?" Whitehouse asked.

"Exactly," Violet said and pointed at Whitehouse. "There

would be no need to take him out of the running. Instead, Shoenthal would have had reason to want the other guys taken out of the running."

"I see." Whitehouse pursed his lips again. "I'll look into whether any of the other candidates have had any attacks or close calls. What else? Any rumors about affairs?"

Violet considered, then said, "Well, no, not really. The captain did fraternize with the four nurses who worked for his wife's perfume business, but not ... *fraternize*, you know?"

"As far as we know," Whitehouse said with raised eyebrows.

"True," Violet said and felt a slight smile tug at her cheeks.

"Anyway, we already knew about that one," Whitehouse said. "That's why I was at the party."

Violet's train of thought screeched to a halt. She forgot that she had been wondering why he had come to that battalion's Dining Out if he was not in that unit. "What do you mean?"

Whitehouse pantomimed locking his lips closed with an invisible key and Violet answered with a bemused narrowing of her eyes.

"So no enemies?" Whitehouse asked again.

"No, none but that guy, maybe," Violet said and pointed out the windshield at Sergeant Pear as he led the group of recruits away on a jog. "But again, it looked like Shoenthal had more of a reason to be bitter than Pear did."

"Okay, so how about Taylor..." Whitehouse asked and looked down at some notes before saying her last name. "Williams?"

"What about her?" Violet said.

"Do you believe her story about him asking her to cook for him?"

"Yes, wha—" Violet balked. "What else could it have been?"

"That's what I'm asking you," Whitehouse said, searching her face as she thought. "Do they know each other?"

Violet answered, "No, well, I don't think so."

"They haven't spent time together before? Maybe you took her with you to visit Derek at work, and they met, and..."

"No, I–" Violet gulped and said, "I only visited Derek at work once. Taylor wasn't there, and it didn't go well, so I haven't been back."

Violet felt a heat rise up past her face as she remembered trying to visit Derek at work a month ago, finding his phone on his vacant desk, then the gentle notification dings that sounded as texts appeared from someone named Lieutenant Pfeiffer. *I miss you* and *Can you come over tonight* were the texts that had raised the tiny hairs on the back of Violet's neck, but then she had sent a racy picture that left no doubts or room for misinterpretation.

Violet rubbed her hands together as if washing them and it made the tiny cracks in her knuckles sting and the raw patch on the back of one hand glow red.

"Sorry, I didn't mean to ... bring up something unpleasant," he said as he watched her hands with knit eyebrows. "So Taylor and Captain Shoenthal have not had occasion to meet?"

"No."

"How about Josh?" Whitehouse asked.

"No. Again, not that I know of," Violet said.

"And you are friends with the RNs, aren't you?"

Violet sighed. "Well, kind of. I would say that I'm somewhere between acquaintances and friends with Eve Davis. No relation. Again, that I know of." Violet pointed to herself. "But then she has her nurse friends that I don't know well. She and the other nurses who work for Suzanne, or Mrs. Shoenthal,

CHAPTER 12

are a really tight group. They work together as nurses, as perfume salespeople, they hang out together ... I think that Josilyn Gibson and Reese Campos even live together."

"Do you know Eve's financial situation?"

"No, but how would that ...?"

"What about her boyfriend, Corporal Boggs?"

Violet felt her face pull into a frown. "I only know Pete by sight, but I know all I want to know about that guy."

"So, you're not a fan?" Whitehouse said with a chuckle.

"No way," Violet said. "From everything I know about him, I don't like him."

"It sounds like there's a story there ..." Whitehouse led.

"He's bad news. I probably shouldn't say anything though." Violet folded her arms.

Whitehouse perked up, then cleared his throat and fidgeted. "You should really report it if you know anything. Especially violence. Did he ever ... I mean do you have anything to report?"

"No, but I know he's not nice to Eve, and I suspect he's the one who gave her a bruise a couple weeks ago. But she's sticking by him, not saying it was him, saying she fell down some stairs ... you know, the classic story," Violet said.

Whitehouse bit his bottom lip and slowly nodded.

"You've probably seen this before as a cop," Violet said. "So why do girls stay with guys that aren't nice to them?"

When Whitehouse didn't answer, she glanced over at him and found that he was gazing at her with clear blue eyes that looked sad.

"Wait, you don't ... I mean ..." Violet said. Her words were barely audible, even to her own ears, but they tumbled over each other until Whitehouse's phone interrupted her.

"Excuse me a sec." He got out of the car and answered his phone, but then got stern and quiet.

Violet considered her current predicament. She was determined to help Derek out of loyalty and to build up the trust between them again, then he could prove how sorry he was, make it up to her, and their lives could get back to normal. She would clear him, prove Whitehouse wrong, even if it was with his help, and get her life back to even better than it was before. Solid, stable, and predictable. Derek would be so grateful that he would be eternally loyal and affectionately attentive. They would build a loyalty that could never be broken. However, she wasn't sure where to go from here on her way there. The one lead she had gotten from Derek had led nowhere and now she was in a maze, staring at a wall, and totally lost.

Violet jumped when her phone buzzed and wailed, "Since you been gone! I can breathe for the first time." She picked up her phone when she saw that it was Taylor calling.

"Are you alive?" Taylor cried. "You missed all our classes today and you've never missed. Are you okay?"

"I'm fine. I'm ... busy," Violet said.

"Is it Derek? Will he not get out of your apartment?" Taylor scolded.

"Oh, he's out of my apartment alright. He left early this morning ... when he was arrested."

"By Agent Sexy Shoulders?" Taylor asked and her voice went high.

"Um, yes, by Special Agents Whitehouse and Donnelly," Violet said in a hush.

"Are you okay?"

"Yeah, I–I'm helping with the investigation. I can't imagine how terrible it must be to be in Derek's shoes. And it feels good to be active instead of sitting around and waiting," Violet said.

"And to be spending time with Agent Whitehouse?" Taylor sang.

"Stop it!" Violet cried. She couldn't believe Taylor would choose this moment to tease her. "Are we still on for dinner? Despite all this craziness, we should still talk."

"Yeah, of course, and I know Josh was planning on it," Taylor said. "Ooh, I have to go. See you tonight!"

Whitehouse slid back into his seat behind the steering wheel as Violet hung up.

"Sorry to keep you waiting," Whitehouse said.

"It's okay, I needed a minute to think," said Violet.

"I thought of something too. About what we talked about a moment ago. Some people do talk to civilians more than MPs. And I think Eve and her boyfriend might be some of those people."

"Those people?" Violet raised her eyebrows.

"You know what I mean. People who don't like cops. Usually because they've had a bad experience with that one officer who was on a power trip or having a really bad day and was being ... well, an a-hole." Whitehouse said. "When the uniformed MPs spoke with Eve Davis and Pete Boggs last night, they got a distinct impression that they were nervous and holding something back. Or a lot of somethings."

"You want me to wear a wire, like in the movies?" Violet felt a thrill.

"Actually, I was going to ask you to meet us there," Whitehouse chuckled. "I have to check on lots of alibis and do a bunch of paperwork first. You know, law enforcement isn't like it is in the movies."

"I know, I know," Violet said with a smile. "But yes, I'll come. Especially if it makes Eve feel better."

"But we don't know the whole story, so don't go over there until Donnelly and I can join you, got it?" Whitehouse said.

"What? Like she's dangerous?" Violet guffawed.

Whitehouse tisked. "You never know what someone's going to do. Even when you think you know them."

"Sounds like someone's got trust issues," Violet said.

Whitehouse looked away. "Well, I've learned my lesson a few times."

Violet grew somehow suspicious and nervous. *Does he even suspect me?* she thought. *But I'm helping!*

"Do you trust anyone?" she asked, searching his face.

"Sure, I do," Whitehouse muttered and looked down at his lap, "but I'm cautious. I have to be. They have to show me they deserve it first."

Violet's mind kept playing that moment over and over as she drove home for her dinner with friends. *Does that mean that he suspects me or not?*

・・・

He made me commit the crimes, then he had to talk about them.

Why'd he do that? He had to open his big fat mouth, and then offer to say even more if he had a few drinks in him. What did he think was going to happen? He knew who was listening! It was really all his fault.

...

Chapter 13

Josh, Violet, and Taylor all stood in Violet's kitchen after their usual volley of greetings that doubled as compliments. They kept their heads down, hands flying, as they put the finishing touches on dinner. Josh fetched Violet's rice paddle from the drawer, ran it under water for a moment, then swung open the lid of the rice cooker. A plume of steam rose in a mushroom cloud, then he scooped fragrant basmati rice into three low bowls. Violet ladled creamy curry onto each bed of rice, then chopped cilantro into a fine chiffonade for garnish, but was embarrassed at how long it took her compared to Taylor. Taylor skinned a mango right in the palm of her hand before cutting into it and slicing off the halves by guiding her knife down both sides of the big, flat pit within. She threw the pieces into the blender with half a container of plain yogurt, like it was normal to have such daring with a blade, then blended it all together to make their dinner drinks.

"How have you guys gotten so far with your knife skills and I am still so ... beginner?" Violet scoffed at herself.

"I've watched you," Josh said. "You're good—you're only a little slow. I think you're scared."

"What he means is ... you are getting better. It'll come," Taylor said. "Besides, you're nervous for Derek tonight."

"Yeah, I guess so. But I'm not usually any faster," Violet muttered.

At Violet's folding table over a meal of curry, rice, store-bought naan, and mango-yogurt smoothies that Josh called Mango Lassi, they discussed what went well at their catering gig the night before.

"And I think people's favorite was the Italian pasta we made. The Rigatoni fra Diavolo," Josh said.

"Agreed. I think we had the least leftovers of that," Taylor said.

Violet made a note on a piece of paper that had started the meeting as perfectly clean and white, but now had half a page of notes.

"Now, what could we do better next time?" Violet asked the group.

Josh sighed. "Ugh! A lot."

Taylor rolled her eyes. "Have a vegetarian or vegan option, have a low-carb option, hire some help …"

Violet joined in, adding, "More trash cans, more coffee urns, less cake …"

Then Josh rattled off, "Plus, not to mention, avoiding getting hired by the twat who's going to ruin the party, not letting him point out any of us as knowing him while he's being said twat, and preventing the boss from getting attacked during dessert."

"None of that was our fault," Taylor said with sass. "I think Vi is asking us to think of what we can do better as regards the food."

Josh sighed. "Well, watch, we'll get blamed for all of it. If we're not careful we'll get a bad reputation that will stick to us like glitter. As soon as you think it's gone, it'll pop up and remind you that it's there again."

"Well, y'all won't get a bad reputation, but I will—and so will whatever is left of our catering company after y'all leave," Violet said, moping.

"Sorry, Vi," mumbled Taylor.

"Yeah, sorry," Josh grumbled. "But like I said, you don't have to buy me out."

"Ooh," Taylor grimaced. "I can't ... I mean my parents' loan ..."

Violet didn't make her finish the sentence after she trailed off. "No. Don't worry. I'll figure out something. I'll get a business loan, or ..."

Taylor suggested the path she had taken and said, "Ask your parents for a loan, or ..."

"Start selling on the black market," Josh said before Taylor punched his bicep. "Does that actually make good money?" Josh laughed as he rubbed his arm.

"Selling what? Like I learn some *different kinds* of cooking skills? Anyway, I'll figure out something," Violet joked, then sighed.

They all stayed quiet for a long moment as they scooted what food was left around in their bowls until Violet's phone buzzed from the couch and Kelly Clarkson's voice belted out from it.

"Is your business partner Taylor there with you?" Whitehouse asked after the opening pleasantries.

"Yeah, she's here. How did you know? Wait, why?" Violet said, exchanging nervous glances with Taylor.

"I'm here to see if you could come talk to Eve with me, but ... can I come in first?" Whitehouse cleared his throat. "I'd like to finish ... crossing her off my list."

CHAPTER 13

"Sure, c'mon in," Violet said as she gripped her phone with both hands.

"I knew it! I'm outta here," Josh hollered once Violet hung up. "Well, they're not pinning this on me. Good luck, rockstar. Stay strong, gorgeous."

With that, Josh slipped out the back door as a knock sounded at the front.

When Agent Whitehouse came in and took a folding chair, Taylor fidgeted on the edge of the mattress and Violet washed dishes in the background.

"So, Miss Williams," Whitehouse said, as both of them lasered strikingly blue eyes on each other. "I'd like to ask you more about your conversation with the captain."

"Okay," Taylor said.

"You were one of the last people he spoke to before he was assaulted," Whitehouse stated.

"Okay," she said again.

"What did you speak about?" Whitehouse cocked his head to one side.

Taylor gulped. "I told you, he wanted to hire me to cook dinner for him and his wife on Valentine's Day."

"Is that all you talked about?" he asked.

"Yes, sir."

"How did the topic come up?"

"He approached me after I brought something out to the buffet table. He said something like 'Hi, do you have plans for Valentine's Day?' At first, I thought he was hitting on me, but then he must have picked up on that because he spoke really fast. He was all 'Because I wanted to know if you could cook dinner for my wife and me. Like a personal chef for the evening. Do you do that?'"

"So he brought it up?" Whitehouse scribbled something on a small notepad.

"Yes, sir."

"How long did that conversation last?"

"Hmm, maybe ten minutes?" Taylor said.

"And you talked about Valentine's Day for ten minutes?" Whitehouse said with doubt in his voice.

"Yes, well, I had to ask him a lot of follow-up questions," Taylor said, rolling her hands in the air in front of her.

"Like when, where, and how much?" Whitehouse guessed.

"Yes, but also things like what they wanted to eat, how many courses, food allergies, food preferences, what their kitchen is like, the fact that I will not be able to work with kids or dogs under my feet ... that kind of stuff."

"Do they have a dog?" Whitehouse asked, surprising Violet into turning off the water and listening.

"Um, no. They don't," Taylor said with a squint.

"How about food allergies?" Whitehouse asked. Violet thought she was catching on to what he was doing.

"Only peanuts, for him," Taylor said, looking over at Violet. "I think I have the receipt that I wrote my notes on in my coat pocket."

Taylor returned from the entryway's coat rack and held the receipt out to them. Violet and Whitehouse stepped close to see the pen scribbles.

"See?" Taylor said. "I know some of it is hard to read, but this part right here says 'Allergic to peanuts, doesn't like broccoli.'"

"This is great. Thank you, ladies. I think I can move on, and I'll let you know if I have any more questions," Whitehouse said with a warm smile. "Miss Davis, I can go to that thing we were talking about. I don't need to trouble you while you have a guest over."

"No," Violet shot out, "please. I want to. I want to make sure things go smoothly. I haven't lost hope that we can get Derek out tonight."

"Uh, I was leaving anyway," Taylor said, picking up her bike messenger-style bag. "Thanks for dinner, Vi."

After a few pleasantries, Violet closed the back door behind Taylor and found Whitehouse with his gaze leveled on her.

A couple hundred thoughts flashed through her head in a split second and she became strangely aware that she was alone with him, with her bed about two feet away. She had never been happier that she had taken a moment to make her bed that morning.

"Are you ready?" Whitehouse said, speaking low.

Violet searched his eyes, getting lost. "What are you thinking?"

"I think we can carpool, as long as you want to."

"Oh, of course. Let's do that." Violet swallowed hard. "To Eve's, right?"

"If you're ready. It might get difficult to talk to a friend … the way we're going to need to."

"Like what?" Violet asked.

"Like in a way to get information, or get her to crack, but without making her so uncomfortable that she gets scared off or clams up. It's a delicate balance. It's maneuvering."

Violet smiled. "Meh, sounds to me like any other conversation between girls."

Mango Lassis

Serves 4

Prep time - 5-10 minutes

Ingredients:
 2 ripe mangoes, skinned, seeds removed, or about 4 cups frozen diced mango
 2 cups plain yogurt
 ¼ cup sugar or honey
 1 tablespoon lemon juice
 Dash of salt
 ¼ teaspoon mango extract (optional)

Add all ingredients to a blender, and blend until smooth. Serve alone or with Indian food.

Chapter 14

"Just a minute!" a woman's voice called out amid shuffling sounds. A toilet flushed somewhere far away, then Eve came to answer the door. "Violet? You're here with the police?"

Violet took in the view behind Eve, surmising that the noises had not been ones of rapid tidying up before guests came in. A pair of boxers lay as a figure eight on the kitchen floor and cereal bowls lined the coffee table. Pete sat sprawled in a recliner with a beer in his hand. His posture looked relaxed, but his eyes were keen and his chest was heaving, making Violet think he had been part of the scrambling noises. "I thought ... we thought you might feel more comfortable if I was here to help," she said.

Pete rolled his eyes and took a swig.

"Anyway, I want to help if I can," Violet said.

"That's nice of you, but ... what would I need help with?" Eve said, her eyes darting around the room. She perched on the edge of a brown couch.

Violet wasn't sure what to say, so she glanced over at Whitehouse.

Whitehouse cleared his throat. "Miss Davis, Miss Eve Davis, I needed to come to ask some more questions. Although the uniformed officers asked you a few things last night, I need to follow up. To keep crossing people off my list, you understand?"

"Of course," Eve said.

"So what? We're suspects now?" Pete honked. The light from the window behind him made him a dark shadow and accentuated the green-gray bags under his eyes.

"No, we—" Violet said.

Whitehouse said at the same time, "I'm trying to rule people out. You're no more suspect than anyone else at the party."

Violet noticed the gentle way he'd set the couple at ease, but appreciated that he hadn't lied to do it.

Whitehouse went on. "So Miss Davis, you were at the Dining Out event?"

"Yes, I was," Eve said, nodding.

"And so were you, Corporal Boggs?" Whitehouse asked.

"I sure was. Who else would Evie take?" said Pete.

Violet wanted to roll her eyes, but she restrained herself. *Does everything have to be an argument with this guy?*

She looked around the room again for a place to sit, but her scalp prickled when she noticed the brown stains on the armchair. Instead, she opted for a casual lean against the doorframe.

"Did either of you go outside at any point during the party?" Whitehouse asked.

"No, I didn't," Eve snapped.

"No. Why would I?" Pete said.

"Did either of you see or know of anyone else going outside?"

Eve shot a glance at Violet, then said, "No, I don't."

Violet realized Eve was probably lying. Her nurse friends may or may not have told her about Violet walking by to take out the trash, but based on her glance at Violet, she must have been told and was now nervously lying about it.

"I know about Valentine getting kicked out, but other than that I got nothin'," Pete said, then swilled his beer, leveling yellow-brown eyes on Violet. "Sorry, little lady. The only one who could have done it was your loser boyfriend."

Violet felt the hairs on the back of her neck raise and her breath quickened. There were so many problems with what he had said that she didn't know where to start.

Before she could find any words, Whitehouse defused the situation by saying, "Well, that remains to be seen. That is why I need to go back and talk to people who were interviewed by uniformed officers last night. They made notes, but I still need to hear all this from your own lips. So, do either of you know of anyone who has a problem with Captain Shoenthal?"

"No, no one," Eve burst out.

"Well, except his wife, right?" Pete leered. "It sounds like he has to learn how to keep that woman in line."

Violet felt the bile rise up in her throat. She wasn't sure how much longer she could tolerate Pete, or the bra that lay on the hallway floor in the corner of her vision.

"They were having some problems? Do you know of anything specific?" Whitehouse asked.

"Well, she doesn't want to move again, but that's nothing new for an Army wife," Eve said. She grinned at her own joke as sweat gathered at her hairline.

"She wants more money, she doesn't want to move, she thinks he's always wrong," Pete ticked off on his fingers. "It sounds like, from what Evie says, they can barely stand each other."

"It's true that they argue, but what couple doesn't? It's a part of real life, right?" Eve crossed her legs, then shook her foot at hummingbird speed.

"Did you talk to the Captain last night?" Whitehouse asked.

"No, I didn't," Eve said.

"Sure you did, babe," Pete scoffed.

Eve corrected herself. "Well, I was part of a group that was listening to him ... but I didn't ... I mean, I wasn't, like, talking to him."

"So he came to talk to you?" Whitehouse prodded.

"I guess so but not, like, *to me*," Eve said and wrung her hands around her braids. "It was in that milling-around time. You know, as people finished eating and mingled."

"So he came over to mingle?" Whitehouse clarified.

Eve blew out an attempt at a laugh. "He was mostly talking to the other people at my table."

"Who was at your table?"

"Me and Pete, Josilyn and her new boyfriend, Reese and her friend, and Heather with some guy I had never met before."

Whitehouse examined Eve, then Pete. "So basically, your friends and their dates?"

"Yes, me, my boyfriend," she said, glancing at Pete, "plus my friends and their guys."

"Who did the captain come over to talk to?" asked Whitehouse.

"I think all of us ... in general," Eve said.

Whitehouse answered with another question. "Did he know any of your dates?"

"No, he didn't. I mean, he fell into a loud conversation with Reese's friend, but it didn't seem like they had met before that."

Whitehouse jotted down a note. "What did he talk to Reese's

friend about? And what's his name?"

Eve looked at her crossed knees with knit eyebrows. "I think his name is ... Lincoln. I don't know if that's his first name or last name, but that's what she calls him. They've been friends since before our deployment, but I think they're just friends. And always will be."

Whitehouse looked at Eve in question.

"I mean I think he's gay. I don't know for sure because he's not public about it. Even though it's not supposed to matter anymore, it can still unofficially hurt your career in the Army. So he hasn't said anything to me, and neither has Reese, but I'm pretty sure. From things Reese has said about him, and also his mannerisms."

"So what did they talk about, Lincoln and the captain?" Whitehouse asked again.

"Just this and that." Eve spoke with a surprising finality that didn't match her words.

"Okay ... well, when was this?" said Whitehouse.

"About halfway through dinner. I was still finishing. Pete says I eat like a turtle in slow motion," Eve laughed.

"And where did he go after this conversation? Did you see where he went or who he spoke to?"

"He was talking really loud, so I heard him say he needed to go talk to the caterers," said Eve.

"And did he?"

"Yes, I watched him walk over to that half-black girl that Violet works with. I forget her name," Eve said, looking to Violet.

"Taylor," Violet said.

"Yeah, he went over to talk to Taylor by the buffet table, but

I didn't see where he went after that because I went to the bathroom," Eve said.

Whitehouse nodded and made another note, as Violet watched him and his process.

"And you work for both the captain and his wife, correct?" Whitehouse said.

Eve cleared her throat. "Yes, I do. I'm a nurse in Captain Shoenthal's unit and I have a second job selling perfume for Suzanne Shoenthal."

"So you both know them both pretty well?"

"Nah, I don't know them at all," Pete volunteered.

"Yes and no." Eve smiled, but her face was half sweat and half cardboard. Violet was reminded of varnished mahogany, slick and stiff, but she longed to commiserate with her friend and erase the tension. "I only know the captain professionally—we don't really chat. But I know Suzanne pretty well. She likes to talk any time we're together. Delivering orders, working the booth that she has inside one of the shops at Historic Market Square, stuff like that."

"Can each of you describe your movements during the event last night?" Whitehouse moved his gaze off Eve's vibrating foot and onto her face.

Pete broke in. "I was in that main room the whole time. I was enjoying not having to do everything, for once, and sitting and eating."

"Did you get up for the buffet?"

"Yeah, of course." Pete scoffed.

"Did you leave the room to use the restroom?"

"Well, yeah, what do you think?"

"I remember you walking by me and down the hall," Whitehouse said and tapped his pen on his chin.

CHAPTER 14

"That was you? Okay, yeah. I think I went twice."

"Hmm, yeah, that sounds right," Whitehouse agreed.

"What, you're doubting my answers now?" Pete barked.

"Nope, just agreeing with you," Whitehouse said without pausing to look up from his notepad, but Violet noticed the muscles in his jaw clench.

"Good," Pete said, puffing out his chest.

"And how about you, Miss Davis?"

Violet opened her mouth to answer, but realized he was still talking to Eve. Violet decided that the nervous tension oozing from Eve was infecting her too.

"She was in the bathroom half the time!" Pete hollered. "She went off with her friends and never came back."

"I, um…" Eve said. Her eyes darted around the room again and she fiddled with the long, dark braids draped over one shoulder. "Menstrual problems."

When Whitehouse kept his eyes on her expectantly, Eve elaborated. "My cup exploded and … my friends were helping me."

"And when was this?" Whitehouse asked.

"Halfway through dinner," Pete pouted.

Whitehouse pulled his gaze off Eve and leveled a glare at Pete. "Thank you. Now, Eve, can I call you Eve since we have two Miss Davises?"

"Ha!" Eve let out one nervous pop of laughter. "Sure."

"Eve, do you know what time you and your friends went into the restroom?"

"Who keeps track of the time during something like that?" Pete hooted.

This time Whitehouse kept his eyes on Eve, not bothering to acknowledge Corporal Boggs. "Eve?"

Eve blinked twice. "He's right, it was about halfway through. So maybe eight-thirty? We hurried by you—do you remember when that was?"

"No, ma'am. Sorry. But I would guess it was around eight-thirty too. I think an approximation is good enough."

"If it helps," Violet ventured, "I found them in the bathroom around nine because that's when the dessert course began. That's when I went to the back door ... the first time."

"Oh right," Eve said with a forced chuckle. "I heard you at the door. Yeah, we had already been in there for a few minutes, so yeah, about eight-thirty."

"So you went to the back door?" Pete shifted his jaw in smug satisfaction and raised his eyebrows. "Sounds to me like the questions should be going in the other direction."

Violet felt her nostrils flare and her teeth clench.

Whitehouse took one glance at Violet, then sprang to his feet. "I think we're done here. Thank you for your time. I'll get in touch if I need anything else."

Then he offered Violet a hand to her feet as if she were exiting a carriage in a Regency romance novel before ushering her out the door with a stiff hand on her shoulder blade like she was a suspect under arrest.

Chapter 15

"I'm sorry. I never should have brought you." Whitehouse looked down, shaking his head. "I didn't know he would start antagonizing you like that."

"It's okay. I'm okay," Violet said. She took a long, calming breath and rubbed hand sanitizer out to her fingertips, wincing when it stung her knuckles. "Did I help at all? Did we learn anything?"

"We had some things … confirmed," Whitehouse said, rubbing his buzz cut as they both got into his car. "They were definitely hiding something, and they are definitely involved in my original case."

"What original case? Is that what brought you to the Dining Out in the first place?" Violet turned in her seat.

"I … probably shouldn't say." Whitehouse didn't sound convinced.

"Well, how am I supposed to help you if I don't know what we're looking for?" Violet raised her eyebrows. "I mean, the two cases could be related, right? At least on TV, crime begets more crime."

"Okay, but maybe don't let on that you know," Whitehouse said, winking. "I was there to investigate a possible prescription drug ring that seems to be operating out of that unit."

"Oh wow!" Violet exclaimed and her eyes flew wide. "I don't know what I was expecting but not that!"

"There has been a lot of prescription drug abuse lately on the base and in the area around the base. Evidence from the bottles have led me to the patients being treated in the areas of the hospital where this unit works, but I haven't been able to narrow it down any more than that."

"Do you think Captain Shoenthal was involved?" Violet asked.

"On the surface it's unlikely, but you never know what someone is capable of."

"Do you think someone in the drug ring is responsible for beating up the captain?"

"No." Whitehouse glanced at Violet, then down at the diamond ring she wore. "Unfortunately, I still think your fiancé did that."

"No way! Wait, does that mean you think he's in on this prescription drug ring?"

"Actually no," Whitehouse sighed. "I checked his financial records and there haven't been any unexplained payments—in or out. He spends every cent he makes, but it's his normal Army pay. Nothing extra."

"Is he spending it on booze?" Violet winced.

He nodded. "There are some big receipts from various liquor stores, but also one very expensive trip to the jeweler's. I won't say more and spoil the surprise, but it looks like you're going to have a very happy Valentine's Day."

"Oh no," Violet sighed.

"What?"

"I ... I've told Derek a hundred times that I'm not a jewelry person, especially with how much I wash my hands, but he doesn't want to hear it." Violet shrugged. She tried to feel grateful at the prospect of receiving a fancy and expensive gift, but the corner of her brain had the intrusive thought: *But it's something Derek wants to get credit for giving, not something he knows I'd like to receive.*

"Maybe you can tell me—does Lieutenant Valentine ever act strangely?" Whitehouse said, watching Violet out of the corner of his eye. "Does he have a second job, go out at odd hours of the night, or frequently meet up with people in odd locations?"

"No, well, not that I know of," Violet said. "But if he has done any of those things in the last month, then I wouldn't know about it."

"Right. Because he has been sleeping at Lieutenant Costa's?"

"Yeah, for about a month. Ever since I found out that he was cheating on me." Violet wondered why she was revealing so much to Agent Whitehouse, but the words slipped out along with a long-held tension.

He let a respectful pause fill the space between them. "Sorry about that. I've seen how betrayal can tear relationships apart," Whitehouse muttered to the steering wheel as the sky outside darkened.

"As a cop?" Violet asked.

"As a kid. That's the reason my dad wasn't around for most of my childhood."

"I'm so sorry." Violet wasn't sure what else to say.

"So, you're still engaged?" Whitehouse asked the question in the same way he'd asked every other, but a sparkle in his eyes belied his interest.

"Y–well, kind of," Violet said. She felt a defensive wall come up. "We took a break, but he's making it up to me."

"And you're making it up to him by investigating even though you don't really want to?" Whitehouse asked.

"Who said I don't want to? I'm actually enjoying it a bit." Violet said, folding her arms. "And besides, what do I have to make up for? I'm not making it up to him by investigating!"

"Then what are you doing?" Whitehouse said. His eyes now bored into Violet's.

"I'm righting a wrong! Your wrong," Violet exclaimed. "I'm–I'm clearing Derek because he's innocent. I'm being a good person. A good girlfriend, or fiancée. I'm sticking by his side through thick and thin because that's the kind of person I want to be and the kind of relationship I want to have."

"Well, you are much more forgiving than I would be in the same circumstance." Whitehouse shook his head. "Cheating, then assaulting someone, then roping you into clearing him …"

"It sounds like cheating is a sore spot for you, but I believe in forgiveness."

"But is he doing anything to earn that forgiveness? Is he rebuilding the relationship, or is that you?" Whitehouse fired at her, knocking her back with his intensity.

"Stop it! He's innocent!" Violet cried as Whitehouse's phone rang.

"Sorry," he said and shook his head at his phone. "It's Don. Or, Agent Donnelly."

Violet was left fuming in the car as Whitehouse stood by the front fender to take the call. *Why does everyone ask me that?* she thought. *Why does everyone make such a big deal about Derek earning back my trust? Does that mean they don't like him? Do they think he's not trustworthy?*

CHAPTER 15

"You were right—partially," Whitehouse said as he slid back into his seat. "Derek is being released."

"Really? That's wonderful!" Violet cried. Her shoulders let go of a weight that she didn't realize she had been carrying and her thumb twisted her ring, then her stomach clenched. "Why partially right?"

"Well, Don checked into his alibis. The meringue shop and your apartment," Whitehouse said. "Turns out he was telling the truth. He really was eating a meringue dessert for most of the time, then he went back to your apartment after seeing you. His story was corroborated by the girl at the meringue shop, and the fact that he made several calls through your apartment's Wi-Fi after that. Looks like he probably didn't do it."

"That's great!" Violet swallowed hard. "But again, why does that make me only partially right? What's wrong?"

Whitehouse searched her eyes for a moment before answering. "Because he was hitting on the shop girl. And, I'm telling you this because I think it may help you in the long run, one of those phone calls through your Wi-Fi was to Lieutenant Pfeiffer—the woman who was found to be having an inappropriate relationship with him during their deployment."

Violet stood in her kitchen, punching down and beating up a big ball of bread dough as she stared at that big diamond lying in a little dish on the bar. Even in the dark, it still winked at her, and every time it did she punched the bread dough again. When the oven beeped to indicate it had reached temperature, the metallic clicking of someone trying to open her back door met her ears. She shook off most of the flour from her hands, tramped to the back door, and parted the blinds to peek out.

"What do you want, Derek?" Violet hollered through the door.

"I'm out! I wanted to celebrate with you. You fixed it, babe!" Derek called out.

Violet opened the door enough to glare at him. "Yeah, I did my part. But what really cleared you is the fact that you were hitting on two other women!"

"What? Who said that?"

"Your alibis were you hitting on the girl at the meringue shop, then coming back here and calling Pfeiffer again," Violet growled, "from my apartment!"

"Whoa, whoa, whoa," Derek said, holding up his hands. "I was not hitting on that girl at the dessert place. You know I get a little smooth when I've had a few, but I was not hitting on her, no matter what she thinks."

"And Pfeiffer? Did you call her or not?" Violet opened the door enough to feel the brisk evening wind that picked up as the sun went down. "Are you making booty calls from my bed?"

"No! No... no way!" Derek folded his arms against the cold. He was only wearing the t-shirt and tux pants that he had been arrested in, so Violet let him in the door. "Well, I did call her, but it's not what you think!"

"Explain!" Violet barked as she went back to the kitchen and punched her bread dough again.

"Is that your famous crusty bread? I didn't think it needed kneading."

"It doesn't need it. *I* needed it! Now explain!" Violet snapped.

"Okay, okay, I called her, but only to tell her to stop calling

CHAPTER 15

me!" Derek's eyebrows and shoulders raised. "She had called me earlier that day, so I called her back to tell her to stop calling me."

"What did she want?"

"I–she–I mean …" Derek said. He tried to look innocent, but a smug look crept up into his face.

"Ew, Derek! And you called her?" Violet slapped his arm.

"Only to tell her 'no'!" Derek raised a tentative hand to her cheek. When she didn't move away, he wrapped his sinewy arms around her waist. "You're the only one I want in my arms right now. I mean, the fact that she was asking me to come over and I told her no should earn me some points, right?"

Violet melted despite herself. "Yeah, that's definitely a point on the right side of the ledger. But no more calling her back if she calls you!"

"I promise," Derek cooed. "No more calling her back. Hey, is that your ring over there? Are you going to take it off every time you hear a crazy rumor about me?"

Violet wasn't sure how to answer that last part, mostly because it cut her deeply. She told herself that he was right—she was doing a dramatic amount of waffling regarding that ring. "I took it off to knead the dough."

Violet scrubbed the shards of dough from her hands, but realized she was taking longer than necessary and stared at the ring with a tightening throat. Her knuckles burned as the water got hotter and hotter. Finally, she slapped the faucet off and snatched up the ring, slipping it on her still-wet finger and forcing a smile. "See? I'd have to clean it with a toothbrush if I wore it while I'm baking."

Derek's eyes had glazed over, but he looked up at her."Hey, in the morning, will you come with me to visit the captain? I have to patch things up before my career is ruined."

"Yeah, good idea," Violet said as she let Derek kiss her on the cheek. "We can bring him some bread, but if he's still unconscious maybe we'll stick with flowers."

Crusty Dutch Oven Bread

Serves 6-8 people

Prep time - 5 minutes

Baking time - 1 hour

Total time including fermenting - 24 hours

Ingredients:
   6 cups all-purpose flour
   1 tablespoon salt
   1 teaspoon active dry yeast
   ½ teaspoon citric acid powder (optional)
   3 cups water, room temperature
   1 tablespoon butter

1. In a large bowl mix flour, salt, yeast, and citric acid. Then add water, and stir until roughly combined. Don't worry if there are still small dry pockets.
2. Cover and set aside at room temperature for several

hours, anywhere between 8 and 24 hours. I cover the bowl with a plate, but plastic wrap or a clean towel both work well too.

3. Place a cast iron Dutch oven inside your oven and heat to 450 degrees F. You want that Dutch oven to get screaming hot, so let it preheat for about a half hour.
4. Dump your dough out onto a well-floured surface, then squeeze and form it into a ball shape. I pull all corners around to one side, then put them on the bottom so that the top is pretty when cooked.
5. When your pan and your dough are ready, plop your dough into the pan with the prettiest side facing up. Spritz the dough with water, cover with the pan's lid, and bake for 30 minutes.
6. At the end of 30 minutes, remove the lid and bake for another 30 minutes until the top of the bread has dark brown edges and sounds hollow when tapped with your fingernail.
7. Pull the whole pan out of the oven and let it sit and cool for 5 minutes. Then, to remove the bread from the pan, tip the pan and dump it out. Rub the bottom of the loaf with butter to soften and let the bread sit for at least 30 minutes before slicing.

Chapter 16

Violet's knees shook when she saw him. She stood in the drab fluorescent lighting of the hospital's hallway, one hand holding a bouquet of pink Gerber daisies and white lilies. Her other hand was in Derek's as he spoke to the nurse behind the counter. Violet had been perfectly at ease until Agent Whitehouse emerged from what Violet presumed was the captain's hospital room.

"Hi" was all that Whitehouse said, but it made Violet coldly aware of the fact that she had not bothered to put on any makeup. She reflexively let go of Derek's hand and gripped both hands around the stems of the bouquet.

Before she could answer, Whitehouse's gaze shifted to the nurse behind the counter as she said to Derek, "I'm sorry, you can't go in there. You are listed specifically as someone who is not allowed to visit Captain Shoenthal."

"But I was released. I had an alibi. Two alibis," Derek said. "Surely you can make an exception for me. I really need to patch things up with him. See, he's my boss and—"

"I can take those to him," Whitehouse said, making Violet's knees wobble again.

"Or this lady can go in, maybe with your supervision, Agent?" the nurse volunteered.

Violet spoke to Derek, but she couldn't take her eyes off Agent Whitehouse. "I'll be right back, Derek."

The hospital room's beige walls, drop ceiling tiles, and smell of lemon-scent ammonia floor cleaner took Violet straight back to being a kid. It was exactly like the hospital room that she had had to stay in for a couple weeks as a tween.

"You okay?" Whitehouse asked as Violet backed into his outstretched hand like she had done at his office.

"Yeah, um, sorry," Violet gave a nervous chuckle. "I'm one of the few who actually like hospitals because they're so clean, but this one looks like the room I had to stay in for a while when I was ten."

"Oh sorry, getting a flashback? Was it painful?" Whitehouse produced a vase that he must have picked up at the nurse's station and filled it with water at the little sink in the corner.

Violet noticed that Captain Shoenthal was still unconscious. "The flashback or the hospital stay?"

"Both, I guess." Whitehouse pointed the mouth of the vase towards Violet as she inserted the flower stems. "Painful memory?"

"Yeah, I mean, it was one of those defining moments that only come a few times in your life. Those rare ones that you can point to and say 'That changed me.' I guess that sounds more dramatic than it was. It–it was a bad staph infection. Before that, I was always that kid who was covered in mud and refused to wash her hands."

Whitehouse set the vase on the small, rolling Formica table near the captain's elbow. "You? Really?" His eyes went huge and showed every facet of blue and gray. "I can't imagine that."

"Yep, it's true. Getting that infection is what taught me the importance of being clean, and the terrible hospital food is what taught me to appreciate fine dining and home cooking," said Violet.

"Wow! That really was life-changing!" Whitehouse chuckled as he stepped close to her. "Little Violet didn't care about food or being clean?"

"That's right," Violet said then gulped. She deflected the attention away from herself as she made use of the hand sanitizer dispenser on the wall. "But the captain? He, um, he's going through even more of an ordeal. Has he still not regained consciousness?"

"No, not yet." Whitehouse put his hands on his hips and stared at Shoenthal. "I guess they had him under on purpose. His stab wasn't too deep, but it was jagged and dirty. They were really worried about infection. But he's doing better and he should be coming out of it any time now. That's why I came down here—I'm hoping he will wake up and be able to shed some light on who attacked him."

"Right," Violet said, willing herself not to bring up the fact that Whitehouse had been wrong about Derek. "Well, good luck. If there is anything else I can help with, will you let me know?"

"You still want to be involved?" He peered into her eyes again.

"Absolutely," Violet said, feeling a blush rise up. "Even though Derek has now been cleared, kind of, I'm already waist-deep in this. And besides, you said that my inside information might be able to help."

"That's right. Well, I'll give you a call," Whitehouse said, then let a smile spread slowly across his face. "And you are pretty good at this."

Violet swallowed hard as she remembered Whitehouse's

quiet conversation with Donnelly. Was this him complimenting her to get some information out of her? Was this him testing the waters to see if she really was committed to Derek?

"I gotta go." Violet moved away before her eyes could betray anything. "Derek is waiting for me. Thank you for escorting me to deliver the flowers. Will you let me know when the captain wakes up?"

"Yes, ma'am," Whitehouse said in an official tone.

Violet rejoined Derek at the nurse's station as Whitehouse tapped on the shoulder of a uniformed man who sat outside the captain's door. The uniformed MP got up slowly from the chair as if he was stiff and walked over to a nearby bathroom and Whitehouse took his seat. Derek cleared his throat and suppressed a smile as the nurse behind the counter wiped the smile off her face.

"Are you ready to go?" Violet said. Her eyes darted between Derek and the young, pretty nurse with long legs and olive skin. "Or are you in the middle of something?"

Just then, Suzanne Shoenthal burst through the big double doors, wearing huge sunglasses and hoisting a floral bouquet in a mug that read 'Get Well Soon.'

"How is he?" she asked with an outstretched hand towards the counter of the nurse's station.

"The captain's the same as before, ma'am," the pretty nurse said with an empathetic head tilt.

"Oh good, well, at least he's no worse and he's getting his rest. Were you in there?" Suzanne pointed her sunglasses at Derek.

"Yes, ma'am, he's doing fine," Derek answered, making Violet think that he was trying a little too hard.

"Oh good, well, must go," Suzanne said, raising the bouquet

CHAPTER 16

in her hands and gliding down the hall. She nodded to Whitehouse as she went into the room.

"So ..." Violet looked between Derek and the nurse again.

"One more thing," Derek said. "Do we know why the captain hasn't regained consciousness? I really wanted to talk to him."

The nurse took almost five minutes to locate the captain's chart, then she nodded and pointed after Suzanne with a flat hand. "Yes, um, the doctor conferred with Mrs. Shoenthal. I guess they decided together to keep him in a medically-induced coma for a little longer."

"Why?" Violet interjected.

"For recovery, I guess," the nurse said. "It's up to the doctor if that kind of thing would help in a case like this."

"Was it the doctor's decision or Suzanne's?" Violet felt her eyes narrow.

"Well, it's not up to the family, so it was either the doctor's decision or maybe a joint decision if the family is very involved in the patient's care."

"Hmm," Violet said. "That's kinda weird."

"What?" said Derek.

"Wouldn't she want the captain to wake up and help us find his attacker?" Violet asked.

"Unless his recovery is more important to her than finding the killer!" Derek threw his hands out like the answer was obvious.

"Or unless she doesn't want us to find out who attacked him," Violet said, taking one step towards confronting Suzanne, when the woman herself ran out of the captain's hospital room.

"He's dead! He's dead! Someone help!" Suzanne screamed and flapped her hands.

Violet gasped and reeled back on her heels as several nurses ran into the room behind Suzanne. Whitehouse shot up from his chair. Violet felt a cold dread wash over her, making her shiver, while Derek behind her said, "Dead? The captain? But he was just …"

Violet finished his sentence after he trailed off. "He was fine a moment ago. I thought he was going to have a full recovery." She shook her head in confusion, trying to stop the rushing sound in her ears. "What happened? Did he have an infection? What killed him?"

Whitehouse walked forward with narrowed eyes and clenched fists.

"It was you! You killed him!" Suzanne yelled, shaking an exaggerated hand at Derek. "You had to come and finish him off, didn't you?"

"Ma'am," Whitehouse said.

She yelled again as she stomped towards them. "Murderer! Beating him up wasn't enough? Stabbing him wasn't enough?"

Violet gasped again. "Derek never assaulted anyone, especially not here in the hospital!"

Suzanne looked up at the ceiling with a dramatic sob. "You had to come and finish the job! And all because he threw you out of some party!"

"He didn't even go in the room," Violet said, mind whirring. Her thoughts ground to a halt. "The only one who went into the room after me was … you!"

"Then it was you!" Suzanne shrieked. "You killed my husband! For him? Really?"

"Agent Whitehouse and I know that it wasn't either of us, so there's only one person that could have done it—if it was murder."

CHAPTER 16

"What are you suggesting?" Suzanne leveled a fiery gaze on Violet.

"He didn't have a fever, he wasn't struggling to breathe, and his condition was stable," Violet forced herself to hold Suzanne's gaze. "I think you did something to your husband."

Whitehouse marched up behind Suzanne, but before he could lunge for her arm, Suzanne slapped Violet across the face, sending a sting down her spine.

Violet stumbled back and gingerly touched her cheekbone to find a bleeding slash. When she looked back Whitehouse was gripping Suzanne's hand, revealing a big diamond wedding ring twisted around so the diamond was facing Suzanne's palm. It was laced with Violet's blood. Whitehouse wrenched both of Suzanne's hands behind her back, then Violet heard the metallic clicking sounds of handcuffs.

Violet kept a hand pressed to her cheek and growled, "Lieutenant Valentine never entered the room, and I was with Whitehouse in that room when your husband was fine. If anyone killed Captain Shoenthal, it was you!"

Violet stood in her kitchen an hour later with the light streaming in through the big windows and one gray dove cooing on the railing that lined the steps at the apartment's back door. The nurse had meticulously cleaned the laceration on her face and determined it too shallow for butterfly bandages or stitches, but it felt worse than it looked. A block of frozen spinach thawed in the microwave, and she grated onion on a big box grater, which made her eyes sting too. Even her raw knuckles stung from the onion juice. She should have used a balm and slept with rubber gloves on, as she had meant to. She kicked herself for cuddling with Derek instead of taking care of herself like she should have.

Her mind kept wandering off to how Agent Whitehouse had rescued her from Suzanne, but she kept lassoing her thoughts back to the task at hand.

With a deep sigh, Violet reminded herself of her favorite quote about mindful cooking from Michael Pollan. "When chopping onions, just chop onions."

"What was that, babe?" Derek spouted from across the room, making Violet jump.

"Gosh, I forgot you were here!" Violet cried. "Well, any progress on getting in touch with someone at the office?"

"Nah, everything must be closed because it's Saturday, so I'm writing an email now. I have to assume that someone will check the captain's email once they go back into the office. I should start getting in good with the next guy."

"Well, have you heard anything about how the captain died? Was he really killed in the hospital or was it a result of his injuries?" Violet got out her cast iron pan with little cups specifically for making ebleskivers and sprayed it with oil.

"I don't know. Who cares?" Derek scoffed. "It wasn't me, so it's not my problem."

Violet stuttered as she finished grating and shook her hands over the bowl before moving to wash her hands. "You're–you're not curious? I mean we–we were right there when it happened, and he was your CO. And it could even come around to bite me in the butt because I had been in there!"

"No, not gonna happen. You went in there with that cop," Derek said, tossing his phone down on the table with a clatter.

Violet felt her stomach squeeze as she rang the excess moisture out of the thawed spinach. She stayed silent as she mixed the spinach and onion into the savory ebleskiver batter she had made and switched the heat on under her special pan.

"Well, whether you care or not, Whitehouse will know. I guess I can call him." Violet ladled the first batter into the little round cups.

"Hmm," Derek said. "Gettin' pretty friendly with that MP investigator, huh?"

"I guess we're friends. He's been really helpful. So what?" Violet stuck little cubes of cheese into each ebleskiver.

"Anything change while I was in jail?" Derek's expression grew dark as his eyes rested on the diamond ring that again sat on a little plate in the kitchen.

The blood rushed to Violet's face with both embarrassment and anger. She wiped her hands and wrapped her mind around everything that was wrong with him asking her that question. Before she could answer him, her phone rang.

"Speak of the devil," Derek said as he picked his phone up again, slumped in a chair, and retreated into texting.

She snatched up her phone, then fled to the other room for some much-needed hand lotion and quiet conversation.

Savory Green Ebleskivers or Ebleskivers Florentine

Makes about 36 minis or 24 regular

Prep time - 45 minutes

Since the process of cooking of ebleskivers has no downtime, make your dipping sauce ahead of time. This recipe requires a special ebleskiver pan, or, like me, you can use a Japanese takoyaki pan. You can use any heavy pan that can go on the stove with smooth round cups.

Ingredients:
　1 cup all-purpose flour
　½ teaspoon baking powder
　¼ teaspoon salt
　¼ teaspoon nutmeg
　2 eggs, separated
　½ cup milk
　½ onion, grated and squeezed in towel to remove moisture
　½ cup frozen or wilted spinach, thawed and squeezed in towel to remove moisture

SAVORY GREEN EBLESKIVERS OR EBLESKIVERS FLORENTINE

½ tablespoon fresh or ½ teaspoon dried thyme, or other herb

4 tablespoons butter, melted

½ lb. cheese in small cubes, such as Gruyere, Monterey jack, Swiss, or feta

1. In a medium bowl, whisk together flour, baking powder, salt, and nutmeg. Set aside.
2. In another bowl, whip egg whites until stiff, then set aside.
3. In a blender or food processor, whiz together egg yolks, milk, onion, spinach, and thyme, then blend in melted butter.
4. Take a moment to put your greased ebleskiver or takoyaki pan on the stovetop over medium-low heat so it can preheat while you finish mixing.
5. Now mix wet ingredients into dry ingredients until barely combined. There may still be some lumps, but that's okay.
6. Fold whipped egg whites into mixture until barely cohesive and uniform.
7. Cook in a preheated pan using about 1 tablespoon in each little round cup if you're using a takoyaki pan, or about 2 tablespoons in each if using an ebleskiver pan. (I use a cookie scoop for my takoyaki pan.) By the time you've filled each little cup, it's already time to turn them. If the cups were greased enough, you should be able to push down on one edge, which forces the whole thing to flip over. I do this with a chopstick in each hand, but a toothpick or fork works well too. Especially if you need

to pick and poke in order to flip them.

8. Flipping the ebleskivers should cause the inner batter to pour out into the little cup, creating a sphere and making them cook evenly. While flipping, cram a chunk of cheese into the little cavity created in the middle of each ebleskiver. If they get too brown, turn down the heat.

9. When both sides are cooked, move the ebleskivers to a plate, regrease the cups of the pan, and repeat the process until all the batter is used.

10. Serve immediately while the cheese in the middle is melty.

Chapter 17

"Are you okay?" Whitehouse asked, keeping his eyes on the road.

Violet let her hand trace the rough scab on her cheek. "Oh, yeah. Thanks. They said it shouldn't scar—it just stings."

"Well, thanks for coming with me." Whitehouse glanced sideways at her. "I'm glad to have your help."

"Yeah, no problem." Violet rubbed more hand lotion into the skin that was usually covered by her ring. "I've always wanted to go to Historic Market Square."

"Should be fun then," Whitehouse said, almost smiling, but he flexed the corners of his mouth down to keep it at bay.

"Wait, like ... a date?" Violet felt her face flush.

"Like undercover work but with some shopping to help us blend in."

A long silence stretched that made Violet pick at her nails. *Why did I say that? That was downright mortifying.* The intrusive thought came from that same corner of her mind that kept causing problems. *But he needs me! Squee!*

"Thanks," he said again. "I want to move fast on this before word of Suzanne's arrest spreads. Plus, you really do have a way of setting people at ease so they want to talk, and ... you'll help me not look like a cop."

"Okay ..." Violet drawled. "What exactly are you up to?"

"I need more information."

"Oh right, so what do we know about how the captain died? Was he killed in the hospital or was it an infection or what?"

Whitehouse sighed. "He was killed. Doctors think it was a pillow held over his face. It would have been quick and quiet."

"I'm so sorry," Violet muttered, reading the forlorn expression on his face. "It must be hard for you since you were right there. It's even creepy for me, and I was down the hall. What weirds me out is that she told us that he was still pretty touch and go, but everyone else was talking like he was out of the woods. And I ... believed her."

"Yeah," Whitehouse mumbled, "but it was my job to stand guard and make sure nothing happened to him. Uck!" Whitehouse slapped the steering wheel. "She snuck in right under my nose! I can't believe I didn't suspect her. You told me that I should but ... ack!"

"Sorry," Violet said again. "But you know this is not your fault, right?"

"I was so convinced she needed him for this other case that ..." Whitehouse trailed off and heaved a big sigh.

"Which other case?" Violet searched his face while he kept his eyes on the road. "You mean the prescription drugs or do you have a third case right now?"

"I don't know how much I'm supposed to say in a situation like this," Whitehouse said, then pulled up to a red light and peered at Violet. "I should only say what I absolutely have to about open investigations."

Violet raised her eyebrows at him. "If we are going in undercover, I think I should know what's going on."

Whitehouse sighed. "Alright. All I have are theories anyway," he said. "I haven't been able to prove it, but I think the prescription drug ring is, or was, mainly operating through Captain and Mrs. Shoenthal."

"Captain 'Straight-Arrow' Shoenthal? Really?" Violet balked. "He struck me as such a stickler for the rules!"

"Yeah, usually he is, but it goes to show you that you never know what someone is capable of."

"But what motive is there? Were they having money trouble or something?"

"Not that I have found yet," Whitehouse confessed. "But I think they have been at this for years, at several different duty stations. Anyway, when it comes to money, everyone always wants more."

"Yeah, I guess that's true. But the captain selling drugs? I assume he wouldn't support drug addiction if he was against public drunkenness."

"Well, it doesn't mean he was an addict. And it doesn't mean he likes or respects his customers or his business. It only means he wanted to exploit their addictions for profit."

"Ew." Violet's face curved down in disgust. "But still, how would that be possible? Where do the drugs come from, and where do they go?"

"I think Captain Shoenthal gets the prescription drugs in the hospital during his day job, then Suzanne moves and launders the drugs along with the money through her perfume business." Whitehouse raised a mischievous eyebrow.

"But how? Aren't there measures in place inside a hospital to prevent that kind of thing? At least on TV the meds are locked up and accounted for."

"That's true, but there are always ways. Like when medications are supposed to be disposed of," Whitehouse said, frowning. "That's why so many nurses still manage to develop substance abuse problems."

"They do?" Violet said, eyes popping.

A slight frown curled the edges of Whitehouse's lips. "Unfortunately, it's more common than you'd think."

Violet thought of the nurses she knew, which led her to think about Eve. "Do you think that's why Eve's toilet flushed before they opened the door to us?"

Whitehouse's frown deepened. "I hope not, but maybe."

Violet listed off the people involved. "So Captain Shoenthal, Suzanne, maybe Eve …"

"And maybe Pete."

"Yuck. Any way that Pete could be involved and not Eve?" Violet said, hopeful.

"I don't see how," Whitehouse confessed.

Violet sighed. "So back to Suzanne. You think she's involved in the original case that brought you sniffing around this unit?"

"Yep."

"And that made you believe that she was not the person who had assaulted him?"

Whitehouse considered for a moment. "Mm, let's say that if she was the assailant, I didn't think she would try to finish him off."

"Why?"

"Because people who are working together in a violent industry might want to work out their problems through violence, but they wouldn't want to lose that vital part of their thriving business," Jake explained.

"So because he was the one getting the drugs out of the hospital, she needed him?"

"Right," Jake confirmed. "And now that he's out of the business, she will have to find a new supplier—a new person to get the product."

"Oh right, that makes sense," Violet said. "Oh wait, I remember you saying something about … was the captain drugged?"

"Yeah, they did a tox screen and found a prescription sedative in his system," Whitehouse said as his arms whipped around the steering wheel to make a sharp left turn. "Why?"

"Because, to me, that opens it up to female suspects." Violet gazed out the window as she spoke. "As someone weaker and smaller than the captain, even if I was about the same height, I wouldn't want to face him in a dark alley unless I had sedated him first."

"I thought that too," Whitehouse said, sounding thoughtful. "So it really might have been Mrs. Shoenthal."

"So maybe she wanted to drug him and beat him up over something, but she wouldn't have wanted to kill him and tank her business. Unless he was about to ruin it?" Violet volunteered. "Was he ratting them out?"

"Nope," Whitehouse said and shook his head. "Everyone at the station knows I'm on this case, so they would have told me if he had become their informant. It also would have shown up when we entered his name into the computer system. Or else I would have gotten a call from the FBI or something."

"Well, how else could he have been about to ruin it? Or already ruining it?"

"Maybe he wasn't being discrete, but I still think that would mean a beating, not murder."

"So Suzanne drugged him and beat him up for some reason,

then decided to come and finish him off for a different reason?" Violet asked.

"I guess so," Whitehouse sighed. "That's the only thing that makes sense."

"But what about the twisted ankle and being at the table the whole time during the party? I thought you already cleared her for the assault."

"Did that supposed ankle injury look very real to you?" Whitehouse said, giving her a sideways glance and a hint of a smile. "I think she was playing it up. Maybe as an alibi, or for pity from her husband."

"And from Special Agent Donnelly," Violet giggled.

Whitehouse chuckled. "You saw that too?"

"Oh yeah! I've never seen her get like that." Violet grinned huge and batted her eyelashes, mocking Suzanne. "Of course. Anything to help, Special Agent."

Whitehouse guffawed.

"Is that what works on guys?" Violet laughed, then did her impression again. "I'll do anything to help, Super Special Agent Whitehouse!"

Whitehouse's laugh faded and Violet was left feeling like the floor had dropped out from under her.

She rushed to find something else to say. "And with her husband in the hospital, it was icky."

"Hmm, it makes me doubt her even more. Like maybe she was already shopping around for his replacement," he said.

"Aha," Violet agreed. "Maybe she already had a replacement supplier too?"

"Maybe," Whitehouse said, shrugging. "I guess that's one of the things that I hope will come up during this conversation."

"I don't like it, but you know who would probably be her

CHAPTER 17

replacement supplier of drugs from the hospital?"

Whitehouse gave her a pitying look. "One of your friends. The nurses that she already employs and who are probably already involved in the underground business."

"Oh no! Eve, what have you gotten yourself into?" Violet asked out the windshield. "But you were saying you don't have any evidence? Is that why we are going to Historic Market Square? I'm guessing it's not to buy the Mexican vanilla extract that I've heard such good things about."

"It is amazing, but no." Whitehouse pulled his shoulders back and narrowed his eyes. "With any luck, the counter will be attended by members of the ring that we haven't met yet, since we know our nurses spend most of their time at the hospital. Hopefully we'll be entering to shop for perfume but leaving with some hard evidence. Finally."

"So we're going undercover as a couple shopping for perfume?" Violet asked, blushing.

"Yes, at Suzanne's stand inside one of the shops," Whitehouse said and nodded. "You keep stalling and looking at the perfume, and I'll try asking about something extra special, or to see the stock they keep in the back, or whatever feels right."

Whitehouse pulled his car up to a parking meter outside the big square building with Dia de San Valentin decorations in all the windows. Violet got out and waited for Whitehouse on the curb.

After he paid for his parking, which Violet wasn't sure he even had to do as a member of law enforcement, Whitehouse stepped close to her and took her hand tenderly into his, saying, "We better sell it."

"Does that mean I can call you Jake again?" Violet said, beaming. "Since I met you first as Jake, it's felt funny calling you Whitehouse or Agent this whole time."

"Yes, please." Whitehouse grinned back. "I prefer Jake. Really anytime my bosses aren't in earshot."

"You got it, Jake," Violet said and tucked her hair behind her ear with her other hand. Then she remembered the cut on her face and put her hair back against her cheek to hide it. "Let's go pretend to shop for perfume."

After they entered through a door that squealed and drew attention from all the other shoppers, they saw the wilderness of trinkets, clothes, and candy in the big, concrete building. Violet noticed the exposed, grimy pipes of the ceiling and decided that she shouldn't look up anymore. Jake Whitehouse leaned close and tickled her ear with his breath. "We better not go straight there. Let's go blend in first."

Violet nodded and they took a left turn down the crowded aisle, walking by shops that overflowed with luchador masks, sombreros, and brightly painted pottery. They took a half lap around the inside of the building before Jake leaned close again and said, "I'll be right back."

Violet took the opportunity to shed her sweatshirt and wipe her sweaty palm down her tank top. She admired a rack of huge lollipops before realizing that she was a little frightened. Her hand longed to hold his again as it dawned on her that she was working undercover with an investigator in a place she had never been to before, working to uncover a drug ring, not to mention the person they were going to meet may or may not immediately recognize them or could even get violent.

Violet's breathing grew faster and faster and she used a dollop of the hand sanitizer she always carried in her pocket. She lost focus on the swirls of candy until warm, familiar fingers found hers, pressing into them a small glass bottle wrapped in beige paper. "Here," Whitehouse said.

"What's this?" Violet giggled as she unstuck a spot of tape and unwrapped the paper. Into her hand rolled a dark brown bottle with the name 'San Luis Rey' and a very Catholic picture of a saint printed on it. She peered up into his eyes. "Mexican vanilla?"

"Yeah, well," Jake said as he held a smile in his eyes. "I knew you wanted to try it, and you were saying you haven't been able to be adventurous with new foods yet …" He cleared his throat. "Plus, having a shopping bag will help us blend in."

"Well, thank you." Violet couldn't stop smiling. "Even if it's for the case, you are very thoughtful."

He flexed a smile, then attempted to keep it to a reserved smirk, but it didn't work. He beamed down at Violet and his cheeks went a blotchy pink. Violet smiled back and remembered what Donnelly had once said. It was true. One compliment could show you a lot and now it was written all over his face. For Jake, this wasn't all for show or all for the case.

Violet's heart felt like it was glowing from within and she interlaced her fingers into his again. They walked by an open door to the courtyard outside where a mariachi band was playing live and the accordion music slowed for a mournful ballad. Violet tried to untangle what she was feeling, but gave up and shoved it down, saying, "C'mon, Jake, let's go make some trouble for those dealers."

Chapter 18

Violet sighed, but she let it out slowly and with a shudder through her nose to keep it discreet.

"Okay, do you know her? Because I don't," Jake mumbled to Violet as they approached the glass case with a mirrored back, attended by a Latina teenager.

"No, she's new to me. This might actually work." Violet feigned an interest in all the other things in the shop, instead of zeroing in on the girl with the perfumes.

The little shop seemed to be carved out of the walls of Historic Market Square. The gray, metal walls make the space feel like a cave, except that it was full of colorful merchandise. The shop was well-tended, but the grime in the remote corners of the concrete floor showed how old this building really was. She stood looking at bright cotton dresses for little girls, beach towels, and the pinatas—as well as the red and white San Valentino papel picado banners that hung from the ceiling—before pretending to notice the perfume counter.

"Oh lovely!" Violet wondered if she was overacting. "They're so pretty!"

Violet bent over to look at the glass bottles through the lighted case. She really was captured by the plethora of tiny bottles, but not in the way that the shop girl probably thought.

CHAPTER 18

Violet bit her lip, wondering where a person would order gorgeous bottles like this. How was Suzanne buying big batches, as she had said, and rebottling them for retail sale? Was she watering them down? Was it all fake because it was really a front for drug sales? *Perhaps,* Violet thought. *It's the perfect business to hide the side hustle because of the huge markups on perfume.*

"Excuse me," Jake said with a smile to the girl behind the counter. "Is this all of your inventory?"

"Si ... yes," the girl said, revealing pink braces on her teeth and a cute, high voice.

"Do you ... have anything in the back?" he prodded.

"Um ..." The girl turned to look at a recessed, mirrored door in the corner.

"I was told by a friend to come and ask you. I'm looking for something extra special," Jake said and gave the girl a wry smile. "Maybe for this weekend."

The shop girl's expression fell as she assessed Jake, then Violet, taking in their street clothes, her shopping bag, and his sneakers. Then Violet saw her shoot a glance at the dark twenty-something man behind the main counter of the shop.

"¿Qué tal?" she asked, still looking at the man.

"Está bien," he said with a shrug as he rang up another customer.

"Only one person," the shop girl said in broken English. "Come with me."

"You okay here?" Jake asked with wide eyes as he walked away.

Violet nodded, struggling to look braver than she felt.

Jake disappeared with the girl through the doorway in the back corner.

Violet only had time to take one deep calming breath and sting her knuckles with another application of hand sanitizer before a voice behind her said, "Oh hey, Eve's friend, right?"

Violet whirled around to find Reese smiling behind her. "Oh, hi! Um, yeah, it's Violet. You're Reese, right?" Violet tried to sound conversational, but she could feel the pressure building behind her ears like a cartoon character shooting steam. *What will she do and what will happen when she sees Agent Whitehouse come out of that back door?* Violet screamed inside her head. But she only had a moment to wonder.

In a moment, Jake emerged from the mirrored door behind the teenage girl. Reese, Jake, and Violet all looked at each other with wide eyes as the girl picked up on the stunned silence and did the same.

"Reese, this is ..." Violet was going to attempt a lie, but was cut short by a sudden loud BANG!

Violet wouldn't have been sure it was a gunshot if the mirror on the door next to Jake hadn't broken, a jagged spider web of cracks snaking across it. Her heart jumped into her ears. She couldn't feel her hands. Gasping, she backed away from the mirror and stumbled toward the aisle of rushing shoppers. She looked at Reese's empty hands, surprised not to find the origin of the shot.

The teenage girl cashier split Violet's ears with a screech as she ran out of the shop and the man behind the counter yelled in Spanish as he hit the floor.

"Get down!" Jake yelled at Violet with wild eyes as he lunged towards her. He retrieved his gun from a holster that must have been hidden down the back of his jeans.

In the confusion of shoppers running and screaming, Reese fled too, and another shot cracked Violet's ears as the perfume

CHAPTER 18

case imploded and sent shattering glass flying.

Jake ran by Violet, sweeping her along with him to hit the wall opposite the perfume counter. Violet felt a cold, wet rivulet run down her back and she wondered if she had been hit. Jake's face fell and went ashen as he pulled his hand out from behind her. Clearly the same thought was on his mind until his hand emerged bathed in a thin brown liquid and a consuming smell of vanilla. He pushed her into a rack of cotton dresses and commanded, "Stay here!"

Jake, fully engaged in his role as Special Agent Whitehouse, looked briefly in the direction the shots were coming from, keeping his gun pointed at the ceiling in front of him, then darted out of the little shop.

The edges of Violet's vision dimmed and she thought she might pass out until she realized the shots had probably stopped. The first two had come only about one second apart, but now it had been about five seconds with no more shots or broken glass. Almost all the shoppers who had crowded the aisles between the shops were now gone, presumably outside, and only Violet and the twenty-something man, plus a sickeningly strong cloud of vanilla scent, were left in the shop.

"It's over. Get out now. Never come back!" the man said, his dark hooded eyes leveled at Violet.

She wasn't sure what she said, or if she even said anything, but she stumbled out to the aisle on wobbly legs, crunching over the glass of the broken vanilla bottle as she went. She stuck the top of her head out and looked one way. All she saw were some candy wrappers blowing in the breeze of an open door. She grew a little more acclimated and looked the other way. A sombrero lay upside down on the polished concrete floor as if it had been knocked off the wall in all the confusion, but there was no sign of any shooter. Or of Jake.

Violet wasn't sure what to do, so she scurried out of the shop, around the corner, and outside into the open air through the same squeaky door they had come in. With shuddering gasps, she found her way to Jake's dark sedan, crouched behind it, and broke down into sobs as the sounds of sirens grew in her ears.

She wasn't sure how long she cried there before she heard a familiar voice. "Violet!" Jake called. "Violet!"

She popped to her feet, realizing that he would not be able to see her as she squatted by the front bumper, but the sudden exertion made her shins and calves tingle and she lost her balance, grabbing the car for support.

She wasn't sure where he had come from, but Jake was there in a moment to scoop her up into a hug. Her toes barely touched the ground as he kept his strong arms wrapped around her, then ran one hand down the back of her head, along her hair, and onto her vanilla-soaked back for another squeeze.

Something else broke loose inside Violet and she cried again. She grabbed fistfuls of his shirt and buried her face into his shoulder.

"Don, or Agent Donnelly, got here. Can he drive you home?" Jake asked, muffled as his face was also buried in Violet's shoulder.

She grew aware of herself as her fingertips tingled and the cut on her cheek burned. She squeezed him tighter. "Do you have to stay?"

"I–um, okay," Jake muttered. "Give me ten minutes."

After Jake eased Violet into his car, he jogged away, then

CHAPTER 18

back again after a couple minutes. "Okay, Don is coming too, but it means we can get you home now."

Jake, Don, and Violet took the long drive back to Violet's house in silence. Violet had the front seat, but she didn't watch Jake as he drove this time. Don, as Violet realized later, must have been uncomfortably cramped in the back seat behind her with his long legs folded in behind her reclined seat.

"Don will get you inside and take your statement," Jake told Violet after he parked and was walking Violet up to her back door. "I'm sorry, I have to get back there and try to find out who was responsible."

"Yes, um, of course." Violet cleared her throat. "Sorry to pull you away. Definitely go … catch those bad guys. So you didn't see who it was that was shooting?"

"No," Jake said, so somber that he looked like he might be sick. "I'm so sorry. I never should have … that was way too risky and I take full responsibility. If you want to be mad, be mad at me, not my department. I think I broke several rules by taking you there and not organizing a task force … I'm so sorry."

"I'm okay." Violet squeezed Jake's hand, but then retracted it as soon as she remembered that Don was walking behind them and watching. "I'm not mad. I wanted to help. Don't worry about me." Violet smiled, but her eyes flinched with the foreign movement. "Donnelly will take good care of me and get my statement. Right, Don?"

"You got it, little lady," Don said in a bad John Wayne impression.

Jake forced a chuckle. "If you ask him to, he might even cook you his specialty, as long as you have pasta and sauce."

"Always. And I am always looking for good recipes," Violet

said. She already felt a little better. "You can't stay?"

Jake's eyes glittered between hers, hopeful and sad. "No, sorry. Duty calls."

"Will you let me know when you find out ... anything?" Violet said, brushing her hand down his forearm as he backed away.

"I probably shouldn't ..." Jake's sad eyes hardened into the cold ones of Agent Whitehouse. "I mean, yes, ma'am."

Violet thought about that transformation long after Jake had gotten back into his car and driven away. As she changed out of her vanilla-soaked shirt in her bedroom, she replayed the way his eyes had changed, put up an invisible wall, and how she hadn't been looking at the warm and approachable Jake anymore, but the professional and business-like Special Agent Whitehouse. Did he care about her or didn't he? If everything at Market Square had been an act to sell their undercover personas, then he was the best actor she had ever seen. He had made her truly believe that he cared, and now she was back to feeling like she didn't know who to believe, or how much.

Chapter 19

"Do you believe in people, Don? Oh wait, can I call you Don?" Violet asked.

"Please do. At least when my bosses can't hear you," Don said, staying at the stove, but with a smile in his voice.

"Ha," Violet laughed, then shuddered and relaxed by another degree, hugging her big sweatshirt closer. "That's exactly what Jake said."

"He got that from me," said Don, scooping a big spoonful of creamy, herbed penne pasta into a bowl. "This here's my specialty. You can have the recipe. It's perfect every time—easy too. I actually got it from Jake."

"Y'all are good friends?" Violet asked.

"Aw, Jake's the best," Don said, sliding the bowl in front of Violet and sitting down opposite her at her insistence.

Don and Violet sat staring at each other with a knowing look for a long time.

"But he has trust issues, doesn't he?" Violet finally asked.

"Eh, who doesn't? Some people trust too much, too fast, too slow, too little … whatever. Jake—and probably all investigators—have learned to be careful, you know? It's a good thing in our line of work. It makes him a good MP."

Violet nodded slowly, then took a bite. "Whoa! This is really good. You made this right now? That was really fast."

"Yup, It's Jake's mom's 'One Pan Penne.' Did you know he's a pretty good cook?" Don said, cocking his head and raising an eyebrow.

"You are one good wingman," Violet said, not knowing what else to say.

"So, is it working?"

"Oh, it's working, but I don't think it's gonna happen."

"Why not? Love conquers all, or whatever."

Violet pushed a noodle back and forth across her plate. "Cuz ... I'm ... in a committed relationship. Let's leave it at that."

Don's smile dropped. "Are you?"

The taste in Violet's mouth turned to ash. "Besides, Jake doesn't ... I mean ... Sometimes he might, but then he'll get all serious, and ... I even wonder sometimes if he suspects me."

"He might," Don admitted, wiping the smile off of Violet's face. "Or he might have before Mrs. Shoenthal showed her true colors. He definitely didn't suspect you today. If he had, he wouldn't have taken you to Market Square today."

"So you think Suzanne did it all?" Violet prodded.

"She is absolutely the one who killed him. What? You're not sure?" Don said, incredulous.

"I guess it had to be her. I'm both surprised and not, you know? Like, I had a bad feeling about her, but I thought I knew her! I've set up parties with her, organized a homecoming surprise for the unit with her, been in meetings together, worked side-by-side ... let her borrow my pen ... I guess it's still hard to believe even though I did suspect her after the party."

"Yeah, you never know what someone is capable of," Don said, frowning.

Violet thought long and hard. "I guess she is the only one who could have killed him in that hospital room, but I just don't see how she could have beaten him up."

"Wait, you believe that she could have killed him, but not that she could have beaten him up? You know killing your husband is worse, right?"

Violet chuckled, half annoyed and half amused. "I don't mean *how could she*, like *who does that*." No, I mean ... how could she? Like logistically. Wasn't she at the table the whole time when the captain was beaten up?"

"Well, no one has been able to confirm that. It looks like her complaints were actually justified. No one was indeed paying any attention to her," Don said.

"Well," Violet debated, "wouldn't Jake have seen her if she went outside or to the bathroom?"

"Maybe she went out the front door? It's hard but not impossible to get from the front door to that dumpster in the back." Don shrugged his rounded shoulders.

"Weren't you at the front door?"

"Unfortunately, not the whole time," Don said with a disappointed drawl.

"Wait, what were you doing during the party?" Violet said, then froze.

"Who's the detective here?" Don laughed. "Anyway, I was milling around and talking to people, like we had planned to do before Jake got put on back door duty."

"That was your plan—to mill around and talk to people?" Violet felt her eyebrows crawl up her forehead. "That's what brought you to that Dining Out?"

"Yeah, well, when you're trying to find a drug ring and you know your suspects are going to be at a certain party, Jake thought it was a good idea to try to get invited to said party, make some friends, and try to get invited to an after-party, if you know what I mean."

"Okay, I guess that makes sense," Violet conceded. "So how did it go?"

"Well, we kind of got distracted by other things," Don said, then gave her a pointed stare.

"Right," she chuckled. "So, did you ask Jake? Did we get anything today?"

"We caught a big break today. Several, actually. Thanks to you and Jake, we got a little bag of prescription pills distributed by the girl at Mrs. Shoenthal's perfume counter, *and* he was able to grab an empty pill bottle in the back room when the girl wasn't looking. Thanks to that, he might not get in as much trouble as he might have."

"Did he really break the rules? We were going where the evidence led us," Violet said around her last bite of noodles.

Don listed off the missteps. "He went in without backup, without permission, with a civilian ... he basically took you into a one-man sting. But at least no one got hurt, you hopefully aren't going to sue the department for the trauma of getting shot at, and he got his evidence to get warrants to search everywhere. He broke the rules to solve this case faster. This one has gotten inside his head. But you know why he wants to wrap up this case quickly, right?"

Violet and Don stared at each other with a knowing look again.

"I get it," Violet said, rolling her eyes. "You think he's into me, but ... I'm not sure."

Don folded his arms. "Not sure about which part—his feelings or yours?"

CHAPTER 19

Violet sulked. "Maybe both."

Don sighed. "I'm saying I think he would be super into you if he let himself. But he's in a tight spot. This is the first case he has been in charge of, you're a witness, everyone is still a possible suspect, he can't get personally involved with someone involved in an open investigation, *and* there's that ring that you're wearing sometimes and not other times."

"Yeah," Violet said, looking at the big diamond that she'd put on when she got home and washed her hands. She rolled it around her ring finger with her thumb. "I don't know if I should be wearing it or not. We've taken a step back, but I so desperately want it to be okay."

"Which part?" Don asked. "You, your relationship with Lieutenant Valentine, the case ..."

"All of it," Violet said, then rubbed her face with her hands. "I want it to all go away so it can feel like it did before."

"Yeah, I get that. I'm sorry," Don grumbled. "I guess I can do my part by getting your statement now. Are you ready to tell me what happened?"

Violet told him everything from the car ride over there, to Jake going in the back door, to the shooting, to crying on Jake's shoulder out on the street.

"Did you get a look at who the shooter was? Any idea?" Don asked.

"I have to assume it was someone who recognized Jake and didn't like that he was coming out of that back room, but I didn't ever see who it was, or even where the shots were coming from. It wasn't Reese though. She didn't have anything in her hands and she was scared too. Oh gosh, it felt like glass and sound were exploding all around me, I didn't know where the shots were coming from until Jake pushed me against one wall. So I took it for granted that he could tell where they were coming from."

"And I noticed that you're calling him Jake now," Don said, smiling.

Violet startled. "Oh, should I be calling him Agent Whitehouse in my statement?"

"Yeah, probably, but I already wrote it down," Don said, then closed his notebook. "I'll have you sign this later."

Violet took her bowl to the sink and rinsed it. "Did you want some pasta?"

"No, thanks, I gotta get going." Don checked his text messages. "Oh hey, Jake said they found the gun stuffed in a trash can at Historic Market Square. But it was wiped of prints."

"Any way to know whose it was?" Violet asked.

"Probably not. It's an M9 with the serial number filed off. A 9mm that was current-issue up until recently, so there are lots of them around. We'll keep going over it though," Don said as he scrolled farther down. "And he was able to trace that pill bottle back to who must have taken it out of the hospital."

"Who was it? The captain?" Violet said, hopeful.

"No." Don shook his head at his phone, then peeked up at Violet. "Sorry. It was your friend, Eve."

"What? She can't be our only lead! She's not ... I mean, she's so ..." Violet scrambled for anything else for her mind to grab hold of. "Wait, you said we got several big breaks today, but you didn't know about the gun yet and you hadn't found out about who took the bottle from the hospital yet, so what else?"

"I found something while you two were on your little hospital visit and unofficial sting operation," Don said, folding his arms. "You know, while I sifted through paper trails and did the real police work."

"What is it? What did you find out about this ring?"

"It wasn't about the ring. I thought it was another good lead on who might have beat up the captain, but now … now I don't know what to think," Don said, looking at her with sad eyes.

"Who?" Violet asked. "Does that mean you don't think it was Suzanne? Why are you looking at me like that?"

"It was definitely Suzanne, or Mrs. Shoenthal, but we need to run down this other lead in case the defense brings it up in her trial to get her off the hook. I need to question someone as if they did it, even though this person is very sensitive on that subject."

Violet crinkled her eyebrows at Don.

Don grimaced. "I found someone who was at the party that has a very old reason to hate Captain Shoenthal. Since I was coming up with nothing from the last few years, I looked farther back. I finally found something about ten years ago."

Violet suddenly thought of several people and what they must have been doing ten years ago. She and Taylor were the right age to have been in middle school at the time, still getting used to wearing bras and having acne. Violet had also been in the throes of some serious anxiety about dirt as she had been making a change from a dirty little kid to a young woman still recovering from a staph infection. Josh must have still been in elementary school, still adjusting from life in Scotland to life in Houston. Derek and Jake would have been thirteen, Don must have been in high school, and only the captain and his wife would have been old enough to be out in the world, earning and developing grudges that could last for ten years.

When Violet didn't respond, Don went on. "About ten years

ago, Captain Shoenthal was caught up in some investment scheme that went south. One of those "sure things" that ends up not being such a sure thing after all. I guess it was Randy Shoenthal who had spread the word about it. Anyway, I looked through the list of other burned investors, and I found a man named Joshua McLennan."

"Not possible!" Violet blurted. "Josh would have been a nine-year-old kid at the time. Besides, it can't be that uncommon of a name, so it's a different Joshua McLennan!"

Don shook his head. "I looked into it. The guy is, or was, Josh's dad. Small world, huh?"

"Yeah, small world." Violet sat stunned, then shook it off. "So, wait, you think Josh beat up the captain to, what, avenge his father's lost money?"

"Meh, I didn't say it was a sure thing. I said it was another lead that we have to cross off our list."

"Eve, is Pete here?" Violet asked, pushing her way past the door when Eve opened it. Violet had surmised that the investigators would probably think the Eve thread was more viable and time sensitive, so she had chosen to come here before going to see Josh.

Eve's apartment was even dirtier than last time. Cereal bowls lined the coffee table with bits of fermented yogurt in the bottoms of them, water glasses lined the kitchen counters, and the same pair of underwear in the kitchen haunted the corner of Violet's mind.

"No, he's out. What's going on?" Eve said with a growing squeak behind her words.

"Good, I need to talk to you, but he always gets in the way," Violet groaned, pacing around Eve's living room.

CHAPTER 19

"Violet, you're worrying me. What's wrong?"

"I know about your involvement with the prescription drugs, but I know you. You can't be the one hurting people. I wanna help you, so tell me. How did all this happen?" Violet asked.

"What? I'm not–I didn't ..." Eve stuttered.

"Agent Whitehouse was getting evidence in the form of a pill bottle that can be traced back to you at the perfume stand in Market Square this morning when someone took shots at us. Now, tell me that wasn't you!"

"Someone shot at you? Oh my gosh, are you okay?" Eve squealed.

"No one was hurt, but where were you around eleven this morning?"

"I was selling perfume—I was making deliveries to some customers. Why?" Eve said.

Violet made a face. "Does that mean little bags of pills?"

Eve opened her mouth and closed it several times.

"Eve, can you prove that you weren't at Market Square at that time?" Violet demanded.

"I think so," Eve said with tears gathering in her eyes.

Violet lunged at Eve, grabbing her hand and saying, "Then to save yourself, you have to tell the police who else is in your little operation. Who else do you work with?"

"Violet, I can't ..." Eve trailed off.

"You cannot rely on these people, Eve. Or whoever this person is. You have to tell them who you work with so they don't think that you took the shots at us!"

"But I can rely on the cops?" The venom in Eve's voice surprised Violet. "I've made the mistake of leaning on them before. Last time they came to talk to Pete, they messed him up pretty bad."

"Eve, you're making a mistake right now!" Violet waved around the apartment with her arms. "Trusting Pete instead of the cops? Really? Is he the one that got you into this mess? Does he have an M9?"

"Don't talk like you're better than me!" Eve spat. "You and I both know what it's like to have a boyfriend that isn't perfect, but you look past it because he's human. No one is perfect, but he's not shooting at cops! He's got his problems, who doesn't, but shooting people is not one of them. Pete has flaws I can deal with. You need to learn that. No one is perfect. You have to trust and accept someone's flaws or be alone!"

"You have to trust the police—and me!" Violet pleaded. "I can help you, but only if you tell the police everything."

"No way, I've tried that. Now I have to look out for myself. And my family."

"Pete is not your family!"

"I mean my mom," Eve said, oddly and suddenly serene. "But I've already said too much. I'm not saying anything."

"Your mom?" Violet squinted. "What do you mean?"

"Nothing." Eve stuck out her chin and let the tears shake down her cheeks. "I'm not saying another word without a lawyer."

A pounding on the door made them both jump.

"Police! Open up!" Jake's voice called through the door.

"Please, he's a good man," Violet pleaded again. "Tell him what you know!"

Eve didn't say a word but moved to the door, so Violet followed her.

When he spotted Violet standing behind Eve, the surprise

CHAPTER 19

on Jake's face was obvious. "Miss Eve Davis, I'm going to have to ask you to come with me for a few questions."

"Fine," Eve said in a defiant tone. "But you can start calling a public defender right now because I won't be saying anything until I have one in the room with me."

Jake handed Eve off to Don who was around the corner behind him, before coming to clasp Violet's elbow. "Violet, what are you doing here?"

"I warned Eve that you were coming and told her to tell you everything," Violet said, searching his eyes for a hint of familiarity but finding only suspicion.

"Didn't you think that could make her run? Or clam up?" Jake said. His eyes pierced hers. "Are you the reason she's asking for a lawyer before I can get anything out of her?"

"No, she said she doesn't have faith in cops, so I'm the reason you have any information at all," Violet said, whipping her elbow out of his grip. "Remember how you wanted my help in talking to her and getting her to open up?"

"Well, that was before." Jake clenched his jaw several times before quietly saying, "I don't think I should involve you anymore."

"Because of what happened at Market Square? I told you, I'm fine," Violet touched his forearm, but it was taut with frustration like his face.

"Because a lot has changed, okay?" Jake flexed his jaw again.

"Well, can I come down there with you? I still want to help," Violet said, swallowing around a dry throat.

"I can't stop you if you want to drive down to the station on your own," Jake grumbled, his eyes on her diamond ring.

"Okay … then I'll go it alone and check out what I can about her mom."

"What about her mom?"

"Look who wants my help now!" Violet said with a healthy dose of snark.

Jake said nothing but folded his arms.

"Okay, it's that Eve said she doesn't trust the cops because they messed up Pete the last time they came to ask questions and now she has to look out for herself and her mom."

"What, you think her mom is involved in this?" Jake said. His eyebrows knit together.

Violet grimaced. "I don't know, but I was thinking that Derek will probably know. It's part of his job to get involved in the personal lives of the people under him. He might know if her mom lives nearby, has a drug problem, is in prison, has escaped some drug charges, or whatever."

"I'll call him," Jake interjected.

Violet raised her eyebrows at him. "Do you really think he's going to talk to you?"

"Fine," Jake sighed as he spoke to the cut on Violet's cheek. "We can send Eve in one of the MP's cars so you can come with me. I guess I do still need you … but nothing dangerous."

"Yes, sir," Violet said, giving him a taste of his own medicine as she followed him out of Eve's front door.

One-Pan Penne

Serves 4-6

Prep time - 20-30 minutes

Crappy pasta sauce is surprisingly cheaper than plain tomato sauce, so I use that. If you don't want to, you can substitute any kind of crushed tomatoes or tomato sauce.

Ingredients:
  1 tablespoon olive oil
  4 cloves garlic, minced
  ¼ teaspoon red pepper flakes
  1 (28 ounce) can of cheap pasta sauce
  1 pound (16 ounces) dry penne, or some other short, small variety of pasta, like ziti or macaroni
  1 (14.5 ounce) can of petite diced tomatoes, including juice
  4 ¼ cups water
  ½ teaspoon salt
  Handful of fresh herbs like basil and rosemary, or 1 tablespoon dried herbs
  ½ cup sour cream

⅓ cup Parmesan cheese
Optional - more fresh herbs and Parmesan cheese

1. In a deep, wide, heavy-bottomed saucepan (I use a stainless steel casserole pan meant for the stove), heat the oil over medium heat. Fry the garlic and red pepper flakes for about 30 seconds until fragrant, then pour in the pasta sauce before the garlic turns brown.
2. Mix in pasta, tomatoes and their juice, water, salt, and herbs, then pat down any pasta that sticks up until it is submerged and bring the mixture to a gentle boil.
3. Cover and turn heat down to low. Simmer for 15 minutes, stirring occasionally and adjusting heat to keep it barely boiling.
4. When pasta is 'al dente' or firm-tender, turn off heat and stir in sour cream and Parmesan cheese. Serve immediately and garnish with more Parmesan cheese and fresh herbs.

...

But I swear I did not kill him. I hurt him. I made him hurt so he'd learn his lesson, but I did not kill him. Killing him wouldn't help me at all! I needed him to learn and do better. Now that he's gone, I'm no better off. I wonder what he did to get killed. He probably did something to deserve it.

...

Chapter 20

"Hey babe, when are you coming home?" Derek answered his phone with a purr, and Violet immediately regretted having her phone on speaker in Jake's car. Jake had asked her to let him listen in as she asked questions, so it was his own fault that he looked so stiff and sick now as he drove. "I've missed you," Derek continued.

The smell of vanilla was still overpowering from the last time she had been in Jake's car. Her heart sped up with embarrassment and the cut on her cheek burned.

"Does that mean you're in my apartment? I didn't say ..." Violet stopped herself from protesting so that she could get the information she wanted. "Listen, I need to talk to you about something else."

"Is it about the captain?"

Violet didn't answer but spun her engagement ring around and around with her thumb.

"C'mon, babycakes. You already got me off the hook!" Derek whined. "No need to think about that anymore."

"I don't think you are as free and clear as you think you are," Violet scoffed. "I need to ask you some questions about Eve."

"Your friend, the nurse? Alright," Derek said.

"What do you know about her personal life? Specifically,

has she ever talked to you about her mom or her family?" Violet asked.

"Um, lemme think," Derek said. "Oh right, yeah. She's one of lots of soldiers working to support their family, if I remember that right."

"Okay, do you remember anything about her mom?"

"Hmm, not off the top of my head." Derek sighed. "But I guess I can look up her file ... for you."

"Um, thanks," Violet muttered. "So I'll call you later?" Jake's phone buzzed, so Violet offered a rushed "Gotta go," then hung up her phone so that Jake could answer his.

"Special Agent Whitehouse," Jake said in an official tone through the car's speakerphone.

"Hey, it's Don," a voice said, amplified by the car's speakers.

"Is this something that Violet can hear? She's here in the car with me and you're on speaker," Jake said.

"Yeah, in fact, I was going to call her next about some of this." Don cleared his throat and announced, "So, first, Mrs. Shoenthal is ready to deal."

"That was fast!" Jake declared as he exited the freeway onto the frontage road.

At the same time, Violet said, "It really was her?"

"Yeah," Don said, "as soon as her lawyer got here and we talked about what we have against her, the lawyer kindly advised her to cut a deal."

"What does she want?" Jake asked.

"There's the reduced sentence and some other details, but mostly, she wants to set the record straight."

"About what?"

Don sighed. "She is insisting she didn't beat him up or stab him, only that she was seized by a momentary lapse in judgment in her husband's hospital room. She didn't plan it, it wasn't brutal, and she's even trying to say it was a mercy killing. But then a minute later she also talked about how her business didn't need him as a middleman anymore and he was about to be forced out of the military and therefore lose his life insurance, so it definitely wasn't the selfless act that she made it out to be during some parts of the conversation."

"Huh." Jake half grunted and half laughed. "Do you believe that she wasn't the one who beat him up?"

"Yeah, I do. That's why I was going to call Violet." Don sounded resigned. "You there, Violet? I think you were right."

"What? I can't believe this!" Violet squeaked.

"Wha–I'm saying you were right, Violet. She killed him, but she wasn't the one who beat him up," Don clarified.

Violet's head swam, confused with implications and suspects. "I didn't–I mean, I was just asking questions. I doubted at times, but then I was convinced ... Does this mean we have more than one murderer?"

"One assaulter and one murderer," Jake said.

"Plus at least a couple drug dealers," Don added.

Violet bent over and put her head between her knees to stop the tingling in her lips and fingers. "Sorry, guys. I need a minute. Maybe this is normal for you two, but I can't believe I have been surrounded by criminals and didn't know it this whole time!"

Jake set a reassuring hand on her back. "You seem more surprised to learn that it *wasn't* Mrs. Shoenthal that beat up the captain than when you found out that she killed her husband."

"I think I am," Violet chuckled despite herself. "It was so obvious and we were so sure that she'd killed him, that ... But

CHAPTER 20

now we have to keep looking for more criminals?"

"Are you going to be okay?" Jake gave her back a pat, then explained to Don. "She's kinda doubled over like she was feeling faint."

"Keep breathing, Violet," Don called through the phone.

Jake asked Don, "So what is Mrs. Shoenthal giving us in exchange?"

"The truth, as she put it. Plus a guilty plea on the understanding that we reduce the charges accordingly, and she's willing to name names. She's giving us her accomplices in distributing prescription drugs. But she also had some caveats about that."

"Yeah, alright. So who?" Jake said as he watched the road in front of them.

"It's those four nurses that work for her," Don said as Violet sat up.

"Reese, Josilyn, Heather … and Eve," Violet said, then shrank back in the passenger seat.

"That's them," Don confirmed.

"We were headed in to talk to Eve, but if we are bringing them all in …" Jake trailed off.

"Yeah, you better give them a minute to cool off. Maybe they'll turn on each other," Don said. "They are still on their way here for interrogations now."

"Nice going, partner." Jake whipped his arms around to make a U-turn. "But we have time to make a stop before coming in?"

"Yep," Don confirmed. "Are you stopping to talk to who I think you are?"

"That's right. We're going near his apartment anyway. And he's our only lead now that we are back to not knowing who assaulted our captain," Jake said, as Violet struggled to figure out who they were talking about based on where they were.

"You think that's wise with her there?" Don grumbled through the phone.

"Do you mean Josh?" Violet said with realization as Jake steered down Ashby Place in the wrong direction. "About the dad thing?"

Instead of answering her, Jake asked Don, "Did you talk to Mrs. Shoenthal about any of those nurses assaulting the captain, or shooting at us?"

"I asked her if she had said anything to them about planning to do away with her husband, or if they had been having the same thoughts as her about lifting him out of the chain, but she says no. She insists she was not planning to do away with him, none of them were planning to kill him or beat him up, and none of them would have any reason to want him gone."

"So she is insistent that none of them were responsible for beating him up either?" Jake asked.

"Pretty much, yeah," Don said.

"Well, at least our original drug case is wrapping up nicely. Plus the murder charge," Jake said. "But the person who shot at us and beat up Captain Shoenthal is still out there."

Jake pulled to a stop in front of the house that Josh rented with three other friends and Violet folded her arms.

"I told you!" Josh yelled, then took a deep breath and went on in a falsely even tone. "I only went between the kitchen and the main hall. I never went out the back door."

"And he never went out the front door either," Violet said, standing next to Josh as she was afraid to sit on his dog-hair-coated couch.

CHAPTER 20

"Right," Josh confirmed from his slumped position against the armrest.

"And he didn't hold a grudge against Captain Shoenthal for anything," Violet asserted.

"Nothing," Josh said, shaking his head.

"And he never even went in that back hallway," Violet said.

After the slightest of pauses, Josh said, "That's right."

Jake sat up a little straighter from his spot on the guitar stool opposite them, and he and Violet both leveled a stare at Josh.

"Well, I never went out the back door," Josh said again.

"Jooooosh?" Violet scolded and leaned onto one hip.

"Okay, I did go in the back hallway, but only to the bathroom."

"So, last time we questioned you and you said you never went to the restroom that night, you were lying?" Jake said and raised one eyebrow at Josh.

"No ... I forgot." Josh's eyes darted between Jake and Violet in the dark living room. His roommates had left "to give them some privacy," but the scuffling noises on the other side of the kitchen door told Violet that they had not gone far.

"Josh!" Violet burst out. "If I am going to come and try to help you, you can't be lying!"

"Well, I'm not now, am I?" Josh whined. "This is all really ..."

"I know, but that's why I'm here," she sighed. "I'm trying to help. I'm helping both of you by ... making this a smooth conversation. Now, no more lying!"

Josh looked down but said nothing.

Violet went on. "Josh, I can't help this get sorted out and make it go away if you lie about anything. Besides, can't you see that it makes you look guilty?"

"He's gonna make me look guilty either way," Josh pouted.

"No. No, he's not. We're friends now and I've seen him in action. He is very fair," Violet said.

Josh looked Jake up and down. "N'alright."

"Good," Violet said, taking a seat on the stool that she brought out from behind Josh's roommate's drum set. "So, you didn't go outside?"

"Definitely not," Josh said.

"And did you hold a grudge against Captain Shoenthal?" Jake asked.

Josh wrinkled his brow at both of them. "Why do you keep saying that? What am I supposed to have been mad at him about?"

Violet looked at Jake, unsure what she was allowed to say, and Jake looked at her and nodded. She surmised that he must have thought this information, if it was new, would be better coming from a friend.

"Josh, it turns out that the captain knew your dad," Violet said. "Like, about ten years ago, I guess he, your dad, Joshua McLennan, invested in some scheme with Captain Shoenthal before he was a captain, and he lost big."

Violet looked to Jake for approval, but his eyes were studying Josh's reaction.

"Which time?" Josh asked.

Violet was taken aback and had to blink several times before she could respond. "You mean, which time that he invested with the captain? So you remember his business dealings with Captain Shoenthal?"

"No, no, I didn't know anything about who he invested with or stole from or tricked or whatever. No, I mean, which time he lost big?"

"Oh, um," Violet said, then gulped. "Ten years ago? So you were like nine-ish. Maybe third or fourth grade?"

"Mm, nope," Josh said, then tisked. "No such luck. He was already long gone by then."

"You were not in contact with your father at the time?" Jake clarified.

"Nope, nor after that," Josh said, then slipped a hard look onto his face. "I only remember seeing my father twice, and the last time was when I was eight. Like, barely eight. In grade two. So I definitely don't know or care what he was up to when I was nine."

Jake said, "He, or your mother, didn't tell you about a bad business deal around that time? Maybe it affected her, or you."

"Nice try, but nope." Josh cracked into a smug smile. "I bet you can even find evidence that we weren't in contact. Phone records, child support payments, plane tickets, all that … or rather the lack of all that."

Jake let his head fall to his chest. "So you wouldn't, say, know about his bad dealings, hold a grudge against someone who had once cost him a big chunk of change, or want to beat them up ten years later."

"Mm, sorry. No such luck, Agent."

"And you ran away instead of staying and giving the police a statement after the party because …" Jake led.

"I told you. I don't like cops. I have narrowly escaped charges that cops have tried to pin on me a few times and I have no desire to spend another night in jail while you figure out that I'm innocent," Josh said. "So it wasn't me and you've got nothing. You have no idea how little idea I have of what my father did, even before he drank himself to death when I was twelve."

"Actually, I might have an idea," Jake said, then gave Josh a meaningful glance and they both gave each other a silent nod. "Sorry to interrupt your weekend."

"It looks like we're back to square one on the assault charge," Don groaned from his desk as he leaned back in his swivel chair with his hands on his head.

"So, you believed Josh?" Violet checked, leaning forward in Jake's chair towards him and fidgeting with her ring.

"Unfortunately, I do," Jake sighed as he sat on his big metal desk next to the double picture frame. "Why? Didn't you?"

"Definitely," Violet said. "And it hangs together with what I already knew about his family."

Jake nodded then slumped and sighed. "Drug case is going okay, and the shots fired are probably going to end up wrapped up in that, and the murder case is wrapping up, but how are we going to find any justice for the person that caused the captain so much pain ... which also led to his death?"

Violet had a glimmer of admiration for Jake's determination and how deeply he felt for the victim of his case.

"You gotta take the wins where you can find them, man," Don grumbled, clearly not taking his own advice. "We got several wins, and only one guy who's getting away with it."

"So you're giving up?" Violet cried.

"No, no, but ..." Don trailed off.

"We can't have nothing!"

"We have chased down every lead, but we haven't found anyone with motive, means, and opportunity," Jake said with a yawn. "We haven't even found anyone with a motive who went outside that party!"

"So no one went outside at all?" Violet asked.

CHAPTER 20

"Only Derek," said Don, "plus you and Jake."

"What about the front door?" Violet said.

"Some guy went outside for literally thirty seconds to throw up, then came back," Don said.

"Then how about when you were not watching the front door?"

"Yeah, it's possible," Don said. "It's still possible that someone went out the front door when I wasn't covering it and went through the maze it would have taken to get to that dumpster or that someone went out the back door without us noticing. Or that some roving psycho beat him up randomly. But none of those scenarios are very likely."

"Why not?" Violet argued. "It is possible."

"All of those scenarios are not very likely because of motive," Jake said, folding his arms. "Each person who did go outside or to the bathroom to possibly sneak outside, or could have gone outside or to the bathroom, didn't have a motive. And each person that had motive, didn't go outside or to the bathroom. Except for Derek."

Violet sighed. "Except for Derek. Why is it always 'except for Derek'?"

Jake frowned at her. "Sorry, all roads lead back to Derek."

"He's lucky he has a solid alibi," Violet said. She heaved an exasperated sigh and stared at the diamond on her finger.

"Hmm, it's time to check that alibi again," Jake said, still frowning. "After this, I think we need to go get some meringues. You know ... for the case."

Violet let a mischievous smile grow. "It's a delicious job, but somebody's gotta do it. That does remind me though—it's probably time to call him back."

Derek groused through the phone a moment later, "Babe,

did you actually hang up on me?"

Violet rolled her eyes, spun her diamond around to the inside, and clenched it in her fist. "Did I? I'm sorry. I was in a hurry, but I did say—"

"It's alright," Derek purred. "I know you'll make it up to me."

Violet's throat went dry and she forced herself to not look up at Jake or Don, who were listening to everything.

"Anyway, have you looked up Eve's file? Did you find out anything about her family or her mom?"

"What kind of thing were you hoping to find?" Derek scoffed.

"I'm not sure," Violet said, forcing a nonchalant tone. "Anything about her mom, like maybe her mom has a record, or gets into trouble, or is in prison, or anything at all."

"I don't know how much trouble she could get into from a hospital bed," Derek joked.

"She's in the hospital? C'mon, don't make me play twenty questions," Violet huffed. "What did you find out from her file?"

"It came up because Eve was picking up lots of extra shifts at the hospital," Derek conceded. "When asked about it, she said it was because of her sick mom."

"Sick how?" Violet pried.

"Cancer, I think," Derek said. "Yeah, it's right here. Her family was already on welfare and stuff, then her mom got sick with cancer and now they have spent all their money, every penny, on trying to get her well."

"So she was working hard to look out for her family?" Violet asked.

"Yeah, I guess she has a huge number of parents, siblings, and even grandparents who are depending on her income.

CHAPTER 20

That's why she was talking to me about what else she could do to earn money and picked up the second job. The one with Mrs. Shoenthal."

"Mm-hmm," Violet said and squinted at the framed pictures of two women on Jake's desk.

Jake whispered so Derek wouldn't hear him. "So her mom isn't involved but is her motive."

"Where are you?" Derek asked, picking up on the whispering. "Are you on your way back?"

"Um, yeah, eventually …" Violet said, then glanced at Jake. "But first I think I need to talk to Eve."

"I don't know anything," Eve moped.

"I think you're lying to me," Don answered.

"I can't," Eve squealed as Violet and Jake watched from the other side of the big two-way mirror. "I really can't!"

"Can't or won't?" Don demanded as he leaned against the table between him and Eve.

Violet watched Eve's lawyer whisper in her ear as Don waited for a response.

"I'm not saying anything," Eve said. "That's how the captain got hurt!"

Eve's lawyer leaned in quickly as if he urgently had to say something to her.

"So you do know something about how the captain got hurt? If you're afraid of getting hurt, we can protect you," Don said.

"In my experience, cops aren't the ones who protect people," Eve said. She folded her arms and set her mouth in a hard line.

"I did look into that incident with your boyfriend, Peter Boggs—the one you mentioned to your friend, Violet. There was no record of any charges of excessive force in that case," Don said.

"I was there. It was excessive. Just because the charges didn't stick doesn't mean it didn't happen."

"Alright, then you would know better than me about that case, but that wasn't me. I can promise you that I will protect you. You know I am friends with Violet? I don't want you to be afraid of the police, especially not me."

"That's just it," Eve said. "I'm not afraid of you, I'm afraid of them. Or—someone else."

Eve's lawyer looked down at his lap and sighed as he shook his head.

Don pressed for an answer. "The other police or someone you work with?"

Eve said nothing.

"We can protect you. What do you know about the other people who are distributing the prescription drugs?" Don insisted. "Is one of them willing to hurt people?"

"I wish I could tell you, but I've trusted the wrong people," Eve said.

"The other people you are selling the prescription drugs with? Are they the wrong people that you trusted?" Don said.

"I can't say," Eve whined.

Don shot another question. "Then do you know who fired the shots in Market Square?"

Eve shook her head hard as Jake left Violet's side. "I wasn't there!"

Jake slipped in the door of the interrogation room and asked, "Do you know who beat up Captain Shoenthal on the night of the Dining Out event?"

"I can't say," Eve said again. "I wish…"

CHAPTER 20

"Miss Davis is done talking." The lawyer sported a red face and a white-knuckled grip on his briefcase. "She has said too much already. I will be taking her home unless you are going to charge her."

"Not yet, but we do have more questions for her." Don stood up tall. "We'll be holding her for our full twenty-four hours. I'm sure I'll be able to find enough to charge you in that time. It also should be long enough for those dangerous friends of yours to figure out you're giving them up to us."

"You can't do this!" the lawyer yelled.

"And you think this is going to prove that I can depend on you to protect me?" Eve scoffed.

Don let a malicious smile spread over his face. "I guess you won't have any other choice."

...

My mom's the type of angel who would blame herself, even if I hadn't done it for her. I never told her where the extra money was coming from—I told her that I got a second job and that it was worth it to see her get better. I couldn't do nothing and let her wither away. I couldn't. I had to help as much as I could.
...

Chapter 21

"How well do you know Don?" Violet asked as she stood next to Jake at the counter in the meringue shop near The Stable after he had apologized again for the scare she had gotten that morning.

"Pretty darn. Why?" Jake said as he glanced around at the black and white striped wallpaper and hanging plants.

"I thought he was a good guy, but the way he was with Eve really freaked me out." She nervously tapped her ring, which she'd moved to her right hand and spun inward in case this deteriorated into another undercover operation. "He's trying to trick her and corner her into giving up what she knows!"

"Why is that bad?" Jake said. "Part of serving and protecting is getting people to give up what they know about the criminals. It's part of the job."

"I guess so, but it was so underhanded," Violet said, looking down into the glass dessert case. "You wouldn't do something so … icky."

"I don't think it's icky," Jake said, his eyebrows furrowing. "It's all part of being a good cop. How else are we supposed to catch the bad guys?"

"So Eve is a bad guy now?" Violet snapped. Her eyes grew unfocused as she stared at a pavlova.

"You have to admit that it looks bad for her," Jake muttered.

The silence stretched between them as they stood looking into the dessert case at meringue cookies, French macarons, baked Alaskas, and little meringue nests. Venomous and spiteful words threatened to bubble out of Violet until the woman behind the counter came up to them.

"One meringue nest, please," said Jake.

"With passion fruit pastry cream," Violet finished. After the woman walked away, she explained to Jake, "I'm working on my own recipe for passion fruit pastry cream, so I hope that's okay."

"Definitely," Jake said. "Better than standing around and hemming and hawing over which filling we should get while we're both being too polite."

Jake smirked at Violet, which made her melt and crack a smile back. Violet attempted to understand the rigors of his job, even if she didn't like them. She felt sure she couldn't be a police officer, but she softened and warmed at the feeling that she didn't have to because there were guys like Jake out there.

Jake and Violet sat opposite each other at a small white table as the waitress slid the decadent dessert between them—a pillowy confection cradling a dollop of passion fruit pastry cream and splashed with strawberry syrup. One plate, two forks. Violet blushed. How did this keep happening? Again she felt as if she were on a date with Jake, no matter how much they convinced themselves that it was for the case.

"What?" Jake asked and Violet realized that her feelings must be written all over her face.

"Nothing." Violet pursed her lips against a smile. "I'm excited to try it. I'm glad I got to come."

CHAPTER 21

"So pastry cream and meringue is the key to your happiness?" Jake laughed.

"I guess so," Violet said, smiling. "What about you?"

"What *about* me?"

"Tell me about yourself. Like, what's your favorite food? Thai food, right? Which dishes?"

"Yeah, I'm impressed you remembered," Jake said as his eyebrows shot up. "Any of the salads really. And there's this spicy soup with coconut milk called Tom Kha."

"What about dessert—what's your favorite?" Violet took a bite of meringue.

"Strawberry. Strawberry anything. But chocolate is a close second," Jake said, his eyes twinkling into hers.

"Aha! So this strawberry coulis is right up your alley," Violet said, smiling so hard that she had to close her eyes.

"Oh yeah." Jake took a big bite. "This is great."

"This *is* great," Violet said. She looked at him and he stared back at her, bemused.

"So, Agent, what's next?" Violet sighed. "How can I help?"

"Are you doing that Mrs. Shoenthal impression again?" Jake laughed. He put on a big fake smile and batted his eyelashes.

Violet swatted his arm and laughed. "No! I mean, I honestly still want to help with this case. What can I do?"

"Nothing," Jake said after she took a bite of meringue and couldn't argue for a moment. "I shouldn't have involved you in the first place. I'm sorry. It's too dangerous."

"Then what are we doing here?"

"I guess this is … goodbye." Jake avoided her gaze.

"But you wanted to check Derek's alibi, didn't you?" Violet felt a lump rise in her throat. "We're already here, so … at least let me help with that."

"Okay, I guess there's no harm in that. I don't think this waitress has an Uzi under her apron."

"Well, as you and Don have said, you never know what someone is capable of," Violet said, preferring to joke about it instead of facing her own feelings about that morning's shooting. Jake was probably doing the same.

Jake smiled at Violet as the waitress came back to refill their waters.

"Y'all are so cute," the waitress said. She beamed with big brown eyes from under blonde blunt-cut bangs. "Happy Valentine's Day Eve. Way to get the celebratin' in before the crowds tomorrow. You two make an adorable pair."

"Oh, um, no, we're here to ask you some questions," Violet said after gulping down her mouthful of water a little too fast and giving herself a shiver.

"Are you the woman who confirmed Lieutenant Valentine was here on Thursday night?" Agent Whitehouse asked.

"Derek? Oh yeah, he was here." She nodded with gusto.

"From about 7:45?" Violet said.

"Yep."

"Until about when?" Jake quizzed her.

"He was here until right before 9:00," the waitress said, then beamed and swished her long blonde hair behind her bare shoulder. "I know because that's when I had to get back to work."

Jake's eyebrows creased in calculation. "You mean you weren't working?"

"Yep. Well, I was, but then I took my break to, um, spend a little time with him, if you know what I mean," the waitress said, winking at Violet.

"Excuse me?" Jake asked.

CHAPTER 21

"We made out for a bit in my car..." The waitress sang it as if it were obvious and Jake shouldn't have needed to ask.

"We can't be talking about the same person!" Violet's voice cracked. "I mean, maybe ..."

"Hold on, I even took a selfie after I said he reminded me of someone I knew in high school." The waitress giggled and brought out a rhinestone-studded phone. "There. S'that him?"

Violet stared at a picture of Derek—her Derek—taken from a high angle with a flash as the waitress that stood before her kissed his cheek. He stared at the camera with bleary eyes and several lipstick kisses around his mouth.

"Alright, that's him," Jake confirmed as he laid his hand over the screen and dragged it down until Violet turned away. "Can you please send me that photo? And make sure you don't delete it."

Jake and the waitress exchanged a few more muted pleasantries as Violet stayed facing the wall. Her eyes stung and she struggled not to cry, but her chin quivered until she couldn't hold it back anymore. A tear fell from each eye and left dark spots on the lap of her jeans. The cafe felt oppressively stagnant and hot. She rushed outside the back door into something reminiscent of a wide alley or a skinny parking lot. She couldn't stand another one of Derek's girlfriends seeing her cry, so she shrank into an alcove where she found refuge from the wind with leaves and candy wrappers. She wrapped her arms around herself against the night breeze and something shiny caught the glow of the streetlight. That stupid diamond! She clenched her fist around the ring and jammed it into her pocket.

"You know what I realized in there?" Jake said, walking up behind her and folding his arms. "If you marry that guy, your name would be Violet Valentine." He wrinkled his nose at her, forcing her out of her torpor.

"So?" Violet let out.

"Okay, fine, I guess it's nothing. As long as you're okay with sounding like a stripper, or maybe a superhero's girlfriend."

Violet's mouth dropped open and she swatted his arm, trying not to laugh through her tears. "Shut up!"

Jake flashed a smile and rocked back, then looked down and grew somber. "I knew I shouldn't have brought you. I'm so sorry."

"No, no, it's okay," Violet sniffed. "I guess I should have seen that coming. You told me he had been flirting with the woman who alibied him. I thought … I don't know. Maybe she had been exaggerating, maybe it had been innocent flirty energy because he was drunk … I don't know."

"What are you going to do?" Jake rumbled.

"I don't know!" Violet cried. "I–I guess I need time to think. I…"

"Well, I'm done here. Can I drive you home?"

After buckling up, Violet took a hiccuping breath and vented. "I can't do this. I can't keep going on and trying to pretend that nothing is wrong. I so needed everything to be okay that … I don't know, I guess I thought I could fix it. Fix this. Maybe even fix him. I have to learn my lesson and change my expectations and move on. I have to … I can't rely on anyone. That must be what I am doing wrong. Taylor said I am too trusting. I guess she's right, but I can fix that. I shouldn't hang on other people."

"I have to disagree with you there," Jake muttered. "Leaning on people isn't bad, but you have to trust the right people."

"I can't … I mean, there's no one …" Violet trailed off.

CHAPTER 21

"I thought you were starting to believe in at least one person—someone who's been trying to earn it," Jake said. He kept his eyes pointedly on the road as Violet grasped his meaning and took a shuddering breath. "Plus yourself. It seemed like you were finally starting to trust yourself through all of this. Your judgment, your skills. If you can't trust yourself, then ..."

"Then who can I trust? Is that what you were going to say? Exactly. No one," Violet spat out the words.

"I was going to say that if you can't trust yourself, then you'll never be happy!" Jake insisted. "You'll keep making the wrong decisions and being with the wrong people. Or no one!"

"No one! Exactly. I guess my choice is to accept imperfect people I can't rely on or to be alone."

"True, no one is perfect ... and being alone is fine, but ..." Jake said, then paused for a long time. He hit the steering wheel with the heel of his hand and cried, "Look, I know you can tell that I ... I don't know ... that I ... would have feelings for you if I let myself, but ... It's–it's probably never going to happen between you and me, even if you weren't with Derek—who, by the way, does not deserve you."

Violet sat silent, stunned, with wide eyes and a gasp threatening.

Jake wasn't done. "But don't ... don't be alone, or lonely in a terrible relationship, if you want to be in a great relationship. Don't settle for someone you can't believe in. Someone who doesn't return your level of loyalty. Someone who isn't even trying! You know ... I mean, I told you that's what broke up my parents. My mom was lonely even when my abusive dad was around. Until he left for good because he found yet another someone else. That's what drove her into being yet another nurse with substance abuse problems for a while." Jake swiped at his eyes with the crook of his elbow. He was tearing up. "I learned the lesson early that a relationship has to be built on trust. Don't do that to yourself. Don't be with someone you can't rely on and feel secure with. I can't ... I mean, I want you to ... I hope you find someone ... I hope you find whatever it is you're looking for. Really looking for."

Violet was speechless, but she swallowed down the lump in her throat that threatened to burst out as a sob or as grabbing his face and kissing him. She wasn't sure which.

"I'll try to leave you alone tomorrow, so you can enjoy your Valentine's Day," Jake said, curbing his emotion. His next words were sullen and bitter. "Maybe you can still find someone to spend it with."

Almond Meringue Nests

Makes 12 smaller or 8 bigger nests

Prep time - 3 hours

Ingredients:
- ¾ cup granulated sugar
- ¼ teaspoon cream of tartar
- 3 egg whites
- ¼ teaspoon almond extract

1. In a small bowl, whisk together sugar and cream of tartar and set next to your excessively clean mixer.
2. In stand mixer or with handheld electric mixer, whip egg whites until frothy but still wet. While mixing, add sugar mixture a third at a time. When combined, add almond extract, then whisk for at least 5 more minutes until mixture reaches stiff peaks.
3. Take a minute to preheat the oven to 200 degrees F and put the oven rack in the middle.
4. Scoop batter into a piping bag or use a spoon to dollop

into shapes. On parchment paper or silicone mat-lined baking sheet, form little nest or bowl shapes that are 3- or 4-inch circles on the bottom, then giving them a raised edge.
5. Bake your nests at 200 degrees for 2 hours. Yes, 2 hours. Then, turn off the oven without opening the door! Let the nests sit in the closed oven another hour or more to cool off slowly so they don't crack.
6. Now remove them from the oven and store them in an airtight container at room temperature. They keep for a long time—maybe forever!

Passion Fruit Pastry Cream

Makes about 1 cup

Prep time - 10 minutes

Total time with chilling - 2 hours 10 minutes

This pastry cream looks sketchy during the cooking process, but finishes smooth and flavorful. The cream tends to be pale because of the egg yolks and juice, so I reinforce the color with a little food coloring for a richer yellow.

Ingredients:

3 egg yolks
  ⅓ cup (67 g) sugar
  2 tablespoons flour
  Dash of salt
  ½ cup (120 mL) whole milk
  ½ cup (120 mL) heavy whipping cream
  ½ cup (120 mL) passion fruit nectar (thick juice)
  4 drops yellow food coloring (optional)

1 tablespoon lemon juice

1. In a medium pot whisk to combine egg yolks and sugar. Whisk in flour and salt, then place on the stove, but don't turn it on yet.
2. To a large, liquid measuring cup, add milk, cream, and passion fruit juice. Microwave until hot but not boiling. It will start to look gross and separated, but it'll be great later. Don't worry.
3. Return to egg/sugar mixture and turn on heat to medium. Immediately start adding warm milk mixture very slowly and whisk vigorously the whole time. When completely combined, add food coloring and continue to cook until very thick. This takes like 5 minutes, but don't stop stirring!
4. Stir in lemon juice and pour into a clean bowl and cover with plastic wrap laying directly on top of the pastry cream. Refrigerate for at least 2 hours before using with your favorite dessert. Pastry cream will last in the refrigerator for at least 3 days, so save the headache and make it the night before.

Chapter 22

Violet wilted over the stove in her kitchen the next morning. It was a dark and cloudy morning which made it feel as if she had woken up very early. In reality, she had slept late, assured her friends over the phone that she was fine and wanted to be alone, then crawled back under her duvet. When she did emerge, cleaning had not taken her mind off of the fact that it was Valentine's Day so she resorted to cooking. Now she stirred and heated strawberries, sugar, and water together in a small saucepan. After having that coulis at the restaurant the evening before, she remembered that she had all the ingredients to make her own. Cooking made her feel better, but she moped when she thought about who she could eat it with, or what she would eat it on.

She could bake something, but why? There would be no one to share it with—Taylor was going out with her sister before she left town, Josh was with his girlfriend for Valentine's Day, Jake was keeping his distance, and Derek ...

Violet still wasn't sure what to do about Derek. He had already left her a message, but she had not listened to it yet. She needed to sort out her own thoughts first. He had cheated, but he had been drunk and upset from the dinner. And before that he had been in a high-stress situation for months on end.

When does it stop being forgiveness and start being justification? Violet wondered before shrugging it off.

Violet switched off the heat and dumped the whole mixture into the blender. It whizzed around and she watched it, mesmerized as if it were a lava lamp.

She resolved that she must be expecting too much from people. She had hung her future on Taylor and Josh, but now they were abandoning her. She had wrapped herself up in Derek, then he had cheated. Even Don had shown that he had an icky side, and Jake probably did too.

"I guess I just haven't seen it yet," she said to the empty apartment.

She stepped to the cutting board to cut a lemon in half and remembered to include herself in her dark rant.

"I can't even trust myself! If I cut my onions as fast as everyone else in the class, I'd probably lose a finger!" She retracted her hand and brought the knife down hard at the middle of the lemon, but instead of chopping it in half, the knife slipped sideways and the lemon skittered away into the corner of the counter. "Figures."

She poured the strawberry sauce into a clean squeeze bottle, deposited it in the fridge, then went back to her bed to mope.

She couldn't escape the thought that Captain Shoenthal had been too trusting as well. He had gone into business with criminals. He had met someone outside who had beaten him to within an inch of his life. He had married a woman who killed him at the first opportunity.

Violet threw the blankets over her head and called out to the empty apartment again. "The person that Captain Shoenthal probably relied on the most is the one who killed him!"

A knock sounded on the front door and Violet's first

CHAPTER 22

thought was that she had been talking to herself so much and so loudly that she was disturbing the neighbors.

"Violet!" Derek called out from down on his knees with a rose in his hand as she opened the door. She was still wrapped in her fluffy duvet and immediately felt silly as he said, "Baby, I miss you! I need you!"

"Derek, what are you doing here?" Violet squawked. "I haven't called you back yet because I needed time to think. Time to decide."

"C'mon, babycakes. You've been thinking for a month. If you haven't been able to let me go in that amount of time, then you don't want to! You love me!"

"That was before I knew that I still can't expect any loyalty from you!" Violet said. "Before I knew about–before you made out with that girl at the meringue shop!"

"I made out with someone?" Derek balked.

"Yes," Violet spat, folding her arms and wrapping her blanket tighter.

"Honestly, babe, I don't remember that," Derek said. "I was too drunk. I was upset because you were mad at me. So I've been making bad decisions."

"That's an understatement, Derek."

"Violet! I'm sorry! You're the one who kicked me out. I wasn't even sure if we were getting back together. But I know that if you forgive me—if you give me a chance—I would be inspired to do better. Please," Derek said.

"I've given you lots of chances already."

"I can do better. I will do better. And wait, you know you can't spend Valentine's without your Mr. Valentine!" Derek pleaded. "That brings me to my first Valentine's Day gift, besides the flower. Look!" Derek pulled out what looked like a yellow poker chip. "I went to AA. I got my first sobriety chip. That's for you, baby."

Violet accepted the rose with one hand, but kept her attention on the chip as she reached for it with her other. Her fingers trembled as she pushed the chip into her palm.

"Also," Derek said with excitement, reminding Violet that Jake had warned her about some incoming jewelry. "I got you something special."

Violet frowned down at the heart-shaped box of chocolates as he brought it out from behind his back.

"Since I know how much you like chocolate. Right?" Derek said.

"Yeah, but—" Violet debated how to frame her question, but he interrupted.

"There's more!" Derek cried. "Here."

Violet accepted an envelope from him, growing confused all over again, and pulled out a piece of paper.

"Lastly, reservations," Derek said before Violet could read the page. "To Cured. That place you love. Where we ate right before we got engaged. And they're for tonight. Valentine's Day. It's perfect, isn't it?"

"That's wonderful," Violet said, trying to convince herself. "It's all very thoughtful... The part that matters the most to me is that you're being honest with me and that you're really trying. Right?"

"Of course," Derek said. "I can't lose you, babycakes. So, can I come in? You wouldn't leave me hanging on Valentine's Day, would you?"

Violet stood staring unfocused at the piece of paper in her hands. This was great. This should be enough. His putting in some effort should be enough. She had to manage her own unrealistic expectations. Maybe Jake had been wrong about the big jewelry purchase, or maybe Derek had remembered that she wouldn't want jewelry and had returned it. She pushed her mind past what wasn't there and focused on what was there. As Eve had said, no one was perfect. Her options were to be alone forever or be realistic. Derek was human, but at least he was trying.

"Okay, I can do this," Violet said, "I mean yes, come in, come in."

It took twenty minutes for the two of them to maneuver Derek's couch onto its end and get it out of the spare room, to move it downstairs to the living room. Derek impressed her by not going back upstairs for the TV but cuddling up with her. Then he brought out his phone, starting his favorite YouTube show, *Super or Natural*, which was too scary for her taste.

When she hesitated on opening the box of chocolates, he made her close her eyes and pick blindly. She peeked but he held his hand over her eyes. He laughed when she'd gotten a coffee one and pulled a face. He put the half-eaten piece back in the box, checked the guide, picked out another one then held it to her lips. Caramel. Not her favorite but good enough. She sighed and melted against his arm. It was easy being with him. A call popped up on his phone and he didn't even look at it. He swiped it away and moved to put his arm around her shoulders.

She giggled and leaned into him but his breath as he kissed her cheek smelled yeasty and fermented. It was all familiar but ... *Why doesn't it feel like it used to?* Violet asked herself.

She brought out the Alcoholics Anonymous chip and her diamond ring from the pocket of her jeans and spun them between her fingers. He knew he had a problem, he was working to fix it, and he was finally making it up to her.

Violet frowned. His breath told her that he'd slipped up today and had some whiskey. He'd made a mistake but he was trying. She slipped the ring on and scrutinized the medallion, then noticed that the chip had the word 'month' under its big inscribed number 1.

"Derek," Violet said, leaning away from his lips so they no longer caressed her ear. "Derek! This is a one-month chip."

"No, it's not. It's a one-day chip," Derek laughed.

"No, it's a one-month chip," Violet said again, holding up the yellow medallion so that Derek could see it for himself.

"Oh ... well, they must have given me the wrong chip then," Derek said, smiling. He leaned in for a kiss.

"Which day was it?" Violet asked, shooting to her feet to look down at him.

Derek sighed then said, "What?"

"Which day did you decide to get sober? Which twenty-four hours was it that you went without having a drink?"

"I don't know ... it was–it was including the time I was arrested. So Friday. I went to an AA meeting after I got out."

"Did you have anything to drink when you left the party?" Violet quizzed him. "What did you have at the meringue place?"

"No, I only had two macaroons and some little, pink ... dollops. No booze."

"You promise?" Violet gulped.

"I promise," Derek purred.

Violet's knees shook. Her heart raced and her fist clenched around the sobriety chip. Waiting with patient fury, she let his own words pronounce his guilt before she did. "So you *do*

CHAPTER 22

remember what happened at the meringue shop."

Derek's mouth popped open twice without any words coming out like he was a baby asking for another bite of mush.

"And this is a fake AA chip," Violet said in a cold voice that she didn't even recognize as her own.

"Babe, like you said, I'm trying, okay?" Derek sounded hurt as if Violet was the one being insensitive.

"Oh, you're trying alright," Violet cried. "Trying to lie to me!"

"Look, I wasn't sure what to say about the girl at the meringue shop. Yes, I kissed her, but you were the one who wanted to take a break!"

"A break that you were trying to convince me to end!" Violet roared. "You were supposed to be ending it by making it up to me!"

"What more do you want from me? I'm trying, okay?" Derek said and threw his arms out wide. "Didn't I make it up to you?"

"How?" Violet was almost too bewildered to speak. "How did you make it up to me?"

"Come on, Violet!" Derek whined.

"No, really," Violet leaned in with intensity. "I want to know what you did that makes you think you had made it up to me."

"My monthly housing allowance still went towards this apartment, and I didn't say anything about how I didn't get to live here. I was a good boyfriend by being nice to you, trying to get back together, and waiting and giving you space …"

Violet couldn't believe what she was hearing. "You definitely did not give me space!" she hollered. "Plus, you were still unfaithful to me. Again! Then you lied to me about it. You tried to tell me you didn't remember making out with her. You might have even told me that you didn't kiss her if I didn't already know about it, seeing as how you definitely didn't tell me about it earlier!"

"Come on, Violet!" Derek said again.

"Are you lying to me about Lieutenant Pfeiffer too?" Violet said with realization. "You did call her. And is that who called a minute ago? You haven't ended it with her, have you?"

"This is crazy," Derek said and shook his head. "You're being paranoid."

Violet grew quiet. "Is that who you bought jewelry for?"

Derek froze. Clearly, he thought his big purchase was still a secret.

Tears gathered in Violet's eyes. "You lied to me about all of it. Loving me, ending it with Pfeiffer, the girl at the meringue shop, and about this chip. Did you even go to AA? Were you even sober for a day? You definitely weren't sober for a month because you were a total drunken mess on Thursday!"

"I did go to AA. I have committed to being sober." Derek said, folding his arms over his chest. "You can't stand the fact that I'm trying to do better. You want to lord my mistakes over me."

"You know, I really hope it's true. I hope you have committed to doing better," Violet pleaded. "But I have no way of knowing if that's true. I have no way of knowing what to believe. You lie, you cheat, and you lie about cheating. I cannot believe anything you say or do!"

"What do you want from me, Violet? I made a mistake!"

"This is not a mistake. A mistake is something very different. Something that you do over and over, and then deliberately lie about, and then ..." Violet held up the medallion and shook it. "And then go through the special effort to compound the lie by buying things online ... that's not a mistake, Derek. This

CHAPTER 22

... this is something very different."

Derek slowly stood up to look down on Violet. "I thought you believed in forgiveness." He bored into her with an icy stare, but she returned it.

"How dare you use that as a weapon! I am definitely sure now," Violet said, then swallowed hard, shaking. "I do not love you anymore. I cannot rely on you and you are not trying to earn back my love or make anything up to me. Not honestly at least."

Derek scoffed and put his hands on his hips.

"I don't believe anything you say and I might never be able to. And trust ... trust extends to everything. Every part of a relationship," Violet said. Her hands shook so hard that her fingers ached. "I don't think I've been in love with you for a long time, but I was holding on to the idea of you. I still thought I could help fix you, but I don't think you want the help. But if you think things can stay like this, you're wrong. Bottom line: I can't trust you and you don't want to do the work to change that." Violet drew a shuddering breath. "I don't think I can be with you and not be able to lean on you. I can't learn to accept that." Violet felt her eyes sting and angry tears shook down her cheeks. "Like Ja– like someone warned me, I actually feel more lonely with you than I do without you. Having you here, knowing that I can't let myself expect anything from you or give myself to you completely, feels lonely. More lonely than being alone. So ... it's over, Derek. For good."

Strawberry Coulis

Make about 1 ½ cups

Prep time - 15 minutes

Delicious on ice cream, over cakes, in drinks, or decoratively drizzled on a plate or pavlova!

Ingredients:
   1 lb. strawberries, quartered, fresh with top removed or frozen then thawed and drained
   ½ cup white granulated sugar
   Dash of salt
   ¼ cup water or fruit juice
   1 tablespoon lemon juice
   ¼ teaspoon strawberry extract (optional)

1. Combine berries, sugar, salt, and water or juice (sometimes I use the water from the frozen strawberries) in a medium saucepan over medium heat. Simmer, stirring occasionally until softened, thickened, and syrupy, about

5-8 minutes.
2. Turn off heat and let cool slightly before adding lemon juice and extract (if using). Blend until smooth using an immersion blender. (You can do this by pouring the mixture into a blender—remember to vent for the warm liquid and don't overfill.)
3. Now look at the consistency. If you want it to be thicker, return it to the pan and cook, stirring constantly, for up to another 5 minutes. If you want it to be thinner, add water 1 tablespoon at a time until you're in love.
4. You can put this through a fine mesh sieve, or not. I usually don't unless it needs to be absolutely smooth, like if you're putting the mixture into a squeeze bottle.
5. Coulis can be served immediately or stored in an airtight container in the fridge until showtime. Keeps for a week or more in the fridge, or even longer in the freezer.

...

I really thought I was helping. I was helping my mom and our clients. They told me that our clients were wounded veterans. Veterans who needed the meds but couldn't get them because of bureaucratic red tape and a lack of funding. Veterans who needed depression meds, pain killers, uppers, downers, everything that was hard to get because they were controlled substances. That's why they couldn't get them, but that was also why they needed them. We were solving a problem created by a broken system. So, it was illegal but it wasn't immoral. At least, that's what they told me, then what I kept telling myself.

...

Chapter 23

Violet stood in her kitchen again with tears streaming down her face as the afternoon sun warmed her tile floor. The light caught the diamond that lay in the little dish by the sink until Violet put it in a cupboard so it would stop glaring at her. The onions on her cutting board were only part of the reason for her tears. She was closing a long chapter of her life that had extended all the way back to high school, and she indulged in the catharsis of crying it out. She thought about what she had overheard Josh say, and she hated to admit that he had been right. She had lost and even let go of Derek himself long ago, but now she cried for what she had really lost—the idea of Derek. Of marriage. Of a perfect love story with her high school sweetheart. The idea of things getting back to normal and staying that way.

If Violet was honest with herself, this had been coming for a long time. Derek had slowly slipped from his pedestal from the day he'd graduated high school. Joining the Army had given him a solid career path, but he hadn't had the same guidance for his character. But he was so attractive, so familiar, so charismatic. Other people had always told her he was such a prize that she had never wanted to admit that she couldn't see it anymore.

Violet drew a deep sigh, curled back the fingers that held the onion against the cutting board and sliced the onion in front of her with short bursts of speed. If she went with her instincts, trusted her hands, and followed her training, she could finally picture herself getting as fast as her culinary school classmates if she kept practicing.

She dried her eyes on her apron and even cracked a wobbly smile as her phone sang the familiar breakup song from the couch. "I get what I want! Since you been gone."

"Sorry to interrupt your Valentine's Day," Jake said after Violet answered. "I know that Derek left work early, so..."

"No, no," Violet sniffled. "It's fine. He ... he left."

"Okaaay," Jake said, clearly not sure what to say. "Well, I'm sorry to call you when I said I wouldn't, but I think I might have to involve you again."

"Of course," Violet said and perked up. "What is it?"

"We're reaching the maximum amount of time we can hold Eve, and ... she wants to talk to you."

"Me?" Violet reeled.

"I think she has finally loosened up enough, or reasoned it out in her mind, or whatever. Anyway, she wants to talk, but ..."

"But she doesn't trust the police," Violet sighed. "Is her lawyer there?"

"Almost. He's headed back here now, but she is still insistent. I guess he hasn't earned her loyalty yet either." Jake heaved in exasperation. "Anyway, are you free for one more conversation?"

"Definitely!" Violet felt giddy.

Jake laughed. "So it's meringues, pastry cream ... and police interrogations."

CHAPTER 23

Eve sat at the same cold, metal table as before, but this time Violet was sitting across from her in the stark, gray room. Eve's lawyer sat next to her looking dejected and folding his arms in protest as if this was against all of his advice.

"Thanks for coming. I really need someone I can rely on," Eve said, leaning across the table towards Violet.

Violet glanced at her own reflection in the two-way mirror, knowing that the investigators must be listening in from the other side like they had been last time.

"Yeah, um, was Pete not available?" Violet squirmed in her chair.

"I said someone I can rely on, Violet," Eve said, rolling her eyes and folding her arms on the table. She was so petite that she could fit her arms between the two mounts for handcuffs that were welded to the table.

"Well, yeah, you can count on me. What's up?" Violet asked.

"First of all, do they think I beat up the captain?"

Violet glanced at the mirror again, but there was no way for her to receive any information about what she was allowed to tell Eve. She decided that the best way to get Eve to talk was with the truth. "They know that you were involved in distributing the drugs, but I don't know if they think that you beat up the captain. Are those two things related?"

Eve glanced over at her lawyer, so Violet added, "I mean, you said something about talking getting the captain into trouble. So, is that what someone got mad at him for talking about?"

"Okay, yeah." Eve looked down and nodded. "That's why he was beaten up in that alley during the Dining Out."

"For talking about the prescription drug ring?" Violet clarified.

"Look," Eve said, suddenly very loud. "If they already know, and have proof, that I'm involved, then I guess I can answer some questions and not make it worse for myself. Do they know who else is involved?"

"Yeah," Violet said slowly, hoping to be interrupted if she was saying something that she shouldn't. "They know about the captain and Suzanne, Josilyn, Heather, and Reese."

"Oh, wow," Eve confirmed with wide eyes. "The whole operation then. So what do they want me for?"

"Evidence, I think." Violet shrugged. "Testifying about the other people. Maybe answers?"

Agent Whitehouse came in the door and sat next to Violet but spoke to Eve. "Miss Davis, we need answers. Yes, we hope you will testify, especially in exchange for reduced charges, but we really need you to help us understand if, and how, all of this fits together."

Eve nodded and brought her knees up to her chest. "Can you offer me protection?"

"Absolutely," Jake said. "But we need to understand who and what we are protecting you from."

Eve nodded again.

"Eve, who is it?" Violet pleaded. "Which one of them is hurting people?"

Eve's face crumpled broke down crying, so Violet reached across the table to clasp her hand.

After a respectful pause, Jake asked, "What can you tell us about the drug ring?"

"I want you to know, I did it because I had to," Eve sobbed.

Violet's eyes flew wide and her hand drew back, believing that Eve was confessing to shooting at her and hurting the captain.

Eve sniffled. "I fell into the wrong crowd because of money

troubles. My mom is sick—lung cancer. I needed the money, and I didn't know what else to do! I worked more, asked for a raise, and got a second job, but it wasn't enough. And I only did it because we were delivering drugs to veterans who needed them but couldn't get them because of red tape and government funding ... At least that's what I thought. That's what they told me." Eve looked at both of them with frantic desperation in her eyes.

Violet forced herself to take a deep, shaky breath as she told herself over and over, *Oh! She's guilty of the drugs, not the shooting, not the assault. She's guilty of the drugs, not the shooting, not the assault.*

"But that wasn't the case?" Jake clarified.

"No, not at all," Eve said. Her eyes grew glassy with unshed tears.

Jake, or Whitehouse, said, "When did you find out that the operation wasn't as altruistic as you had hoped?"

Eve blinked and the tears broke free. "I found out that everyone else was in it for the money, or the drugs, and not to help people at all. All at that Dining Out."

"What happened?" Violet asked.

"When Captain Shoenthal was chit-chatting with our table, he got talking to Lincoln, Reese's friend. They got to talking about money and investing, then the captain said he had some money-making tips. Tips and strategies that he couldn't talk about there. He joked that he might be convinced to let a few things slip if they went out drinking together. He said it as a joke, or like he was bragging, but that's when I saw all the other girls' faces fall." Eve gulped hard.

"So you think he was talking about the selling of prescription drugs?" Violet prodded.

"I wasn't sure, but I could tell that that's what the other girls were thinking," Eve said. "They looked so ... furious and–and scared. That's when we all went to the bathroom and the whole truth came out."

"Please, go on," Jake said.

"I guess Heather is a user, but she hides it well. The other two were in it for the money. Reese said she needed a 'nest egg' as she put it, but Josilyn ... She's the scariest. I have no doubt she thinks she deserves more money than she makes in the Army, but I also think she likes the thrill. Like she likes being bad and getting away with it." Eve let out a loud sob, then slapped her hand over her mouth and clenched her eyes closed as if physically trying to hold it all in.

"Is that who you're afraid of? You're afraid of Josilyn?" Jake asked in a sympathetic murmur. "Is that who assaulted Captain Shoenthal?"

"We weren't helping anyone but ourselves!" Eve burst out. "The time I knew I needed to get out was the same time I realized I never could!"

"Because you were a witness to one of them assaulting Captain Shoenthal?" Jake prodded.

Eve sobbed into her hand with clenched eyelids again.

A light came on in the attic of Violet's mind. "You said you trusted the wrong people, and you said you were more afraid of them than the police." Her mind raced and all the events of the last few days strung together like beads on a wire. "It wasn't just one of them, was it?" Violet asked, her voice hovering above a whisper.

Eve shook her head, still keeping her face locked up tight.

Violet's chin quivered with the truth. "Did you do it? Did you hurt the captain too?"

Eve shuddered and nodded. "I had to!" she blurted. "We all took turns going out there from the bathroom. I had to do something to prove I was part of the group to not get beat up myself. All I could make myself do was kick him two times."

When Violet and Jake stayed quiet, Eve pushed the point.

"I had to or they would have probably taught me a lesson too!" Eve cried. "That's why I need protection. I mean, if they find out that I ratted them out to you …"

"They won't," Jake interrupted. "If anything, they'll find out that Mrs. Shoenthal gave them up on the drug trafficking charges. But we can protect both of you."

Eve took a long trembling breath, so Violet did the same.

"Where can we find them, Miss Davis?" Jake asked.

Eve leveled a stare at Jake, then said, "They are hiding somewhere that they know is empty, but it doesn't belong to any of them. They are hiding in the captain and Suzanne's house. I was supposed to meet them there by tonight to make a plan after Mrs. Shoenthal got arrested. We needed a new plan. We have no way to sell the drugs now, so we had to decide whether we were going to run, try to keep it going, stop and act natural, or what."

"They didn't think they could go home?" Jake folded his arms.

"No, they wanted to wait and see if anyone came looking for them first. They wanted to know if Mrs. Shoenthal would give them up. They wanted to see what happened before they made a decision."

"So they should still be there?" Jake said.

"Oh, they're still there alright," Eve said, then gulped. "But if you're going after them, be ready. They're armed."

"Well, whoever took those shots left their weapon in a trash can at the scene," Violet said.

"We may be nurses, but we're also soldiers," Eve said. She wiped her nose and muttered to the table. "That wasn't the only government-issued firearm being handed around the group."

"And we never recovered the knife used on the Captain," Jake said, staring at the wall. "Or maybe it was a shiv if it was short and jagged."

Eve scoffed. "She calls them shanks, but yeah, Josilyn is the one who took up improvised knife-making as a hobby. So bring your A-game."

...

I kept telling myself that I was helping—until it became too clear to ignore that we were all doing it for the money. At the beginning, I joined in to save my job and to earn extra money, and by the time I figured out everyone's real motivations, there was no leaving.
...

Chapter 24

"We figured it out!" Violet squealed to Jake from the back seat as Don sped through the streets of Fort Sam Houston toward the officers' houses. "We finally found someone, or rather several someones, who were behind you, close enough to the back door to slip out without you seeing them, and had the motive to beat up the captain."

Jake looked at Violet over the back of the passenger seat. "Mrs. Shoenthal thought they didn't have a motive, but that's only because she wasn't a part of that conversation during the Dining Out event. They got their motive, hatched a plan, and enacted it all in one evening, without even letting their boss in on the planning."

"And it was a group of people taking turns, not one person like I was thinking all along. And it really wasn't Derek!" Violet said, beaming.

Jake's face fell.

Violet winced. "Sorry, I didn't mean to be like 'I told you so.' I mean—"

"No, you were right. I was wrong," Jake said, offering the same flat-mouthed, polite smile that Violet had seen in the hallway at the Dining Out.

She was impressed that he could admit it so easily. "Thanks,

CHAPTER 24

but ... I mean, we cleared an innocent person but, you know, he's not totally innocent. Only of this."

Jake and Violet gave each other a wan smile.

"Say," Jake said as he squinted at her with the residue of his smile, "how did you convince Don to let you come with us? Where we're going might be dangerous."

"Me?" Don spoke for the first time as he came to a stop and put the car in park. "I thought you let her come!"

Violet grimaced. "I got in the car and no one stopped me. I thought it would be okay to see the resolution of this case."

"Fine." Jake put a bullet-proof vest over his head and Velcroed it at his side. "But don't come into the house."

"No problem," Violet said. "I'll help by staying out of the way."

"Good," Don said as he put his own Kevlar vest over his head. "Cuz we don't have a vest for you."

Violet offered a weak smile, her stomach fluttering with nerves.

"We'll be back with the bad guys," Jake said. He smiled and drew a handgun as he threw the sedan's door closed and walked over to meet up with other MPs. They congregated and Violet lost Jake in a forest of dark Kevlar vests that read 'POLICE' and shortened black pump shotguns.

Violet held her breath as the MPs flowed quickly down the block of cookie-cutter 80s houses that stood side by side. With smooth, rolling steps and their shotguns pointed at the ground as they crouched, they slid into place at the front and back doors of the house. She got a sick feeling as she watched, but she also couldn't look away. Don was the one who finally pounded on the door and Violet stood outside the car to hear what was going on.

"Police! Open up!" Don bellowed. "We know you are in there, so come out with your hands up!"

At first, Violet was hopeful that they could arrest Reese, Josilyn, and Heather without incident, but when Don had to knock a second time her heart fell. Keeping the police waiting at the door could never be a good sign. Had they left? Were they hatching a plan? Were they hoping to pull a 'Butch Cassidy and the Sundance Kid' and fight their way out?

Violet picked at her fingernails and couldn't stand the tension until it exploded.

BANG! BANG!

Violet heard the pops of handguns and instinctively crouched next to the car as she saw a blonde mop stick out a side window. She couldn't tell what it was until a set of shoulders followed, then her brain put it together. A person—Josilyn by her coloring—was crawling out the side window head first. The body curled as it finally fell from the window and Josilyn landed softly on the back of her shoulders, easily rolling with a combat roll to her feet.

BANG! The shots continued. BANG!

Violet's feet almost stepped forward, but she was frozen in disbelief. Was no one else seeing this? All looked like organized chaos to Violet. The main body of MPs were amassed at the front door, ducking to the sides to avoid being shot. They were too distracted by the gunshots to look down the side yard. A battering ram appeared and the MPs stood aside to let the thick man with the battering ram through. A second group stood, barely visible, on the back porch and yelling into radios, but no one was watching the windows as Josilyn scrambled into a matching side window on the neighboring house.

CHAPTER 24

BANG! BANG!

Don and another officer were knocked backward, away from the front door as the other officers rushed in after the battering ram shredded the front door into splinters.

Violet ran over to Don. He was grasping at his shoulder and the navy blue fabric around his hand seeped dark and wet. The other officer was sitting up and gasping as if he'd been hit square in the vest, but Don was growing pale. Violet took off her sweatshirt and balled it up over his wound, but it lay barely to the side of, and almost under, his Kevlar vest. She wedged the fabric of her sweatshirt under the edge of his vest as the other officer who had been hit in the vest spoke over his radio.

"We have an officer down. Special Agent Sean Donnelly has been hit. We need a bus here," the MP hollered at his own shoulder radio.

"Don, it's gonna be okay," Violet spoke with more assurance than she felt. "An ambulance is on its way."

Violet shook so hard that it hurt in the joints of her spine.

"Take that sweater back," Don mumbled. "We don't need you getting hypothermia."

Violet gave a wobbly smile. "No, it's okay, they're almost here."

The other MP, disguised by his helmet, gently pushed Violet aside. "It's alright, I've got him." He pulled out a packet of QuikClot from a pocket along his belt and broke off a small piece, wedging it into Don's wound, then pressing his hand hard over the area with Violet's sweatshirt.

Violet pried her mind off of Don and back to the event at hand. "Well, did you see that someone got away? Someone made it into the next house over!"

"Tell the other men—I'm not leaving Agent Donnelly."

Violet stumbled to the front door of the Shoenthal house and called to the men inside the front door. She called out, but Jake was already inside, surrounded by yelling.

"Get down! Down on the ground!" and "Police, Don't move!" volleyed around the group as they stormed in the interior doors.

Violet's cries of "Wait! Help!" from the front yard fell unheeded by all but one very junior, small officer in the back who finally looked at Violet. She realized, despite the helmet and vest, that it was a woman. Violet jumped and waved, pointing to the house next door, but the woman officer still disappeared deeper into the house as a scream burst out of the neighbor's window that Josilyn had disappeared into.

Someone is in danger in there! Violet's mind blared. *Even if I'm only a distraction so Josilyn leaves those people alone, I have to do something!*

Violet knew she didn't have a choice. She ran over to the front door of the neighboring house and walked in the unlocked front door.

Everything was silent for a moment, but then Violet heard a woman growl, "Car keys!"

When another woman whimpered and cried, "I don't–I can't find them!" Violet felt words bubble out of her involuntarily.

"Hey!" Violet called out but then clenched, unsure of what to say. "Hey, Josilyn!"

"Who's there?" Josilyn's voice called from down the narrow hallway.

Violet moved from the living room to the kitchen, looking for people—innocent or otherwise. She said, "It's Violet. Eve's friend."

CHAPTER 24

"What are you doing here, Violet?" Josilyn said. Her voice was agitated, and the other woman whimpered again.

"I–um," Violet said as she admired the knife block of German high-carbon stainless steel blades that sat on the kitchen counter. "I'm hoping I can help you."

"You can't help me!" Josilyn spat. "You're working with the cops!"

Violet's stomach twisted. She hadn't been sure that Josilyn knew that, but Violet reasoned that it did make sense that that news would travel fast. Her fingers grew cold and she shivered.

"You can't stop me," Josilyn said. Her words came out with such venom that Violet felt a rock of terror settle in her stomach. "I'm getting out of here with that car out there, whether I need to take a hostage with me or not!"

The woman who presumably lived here let out one piercing sob and Violet grabbed the long chef's knife from the knife block. A soft SSSHING met her ears as she drew the blade, but she hoped Josilyn had not heard it.

"Josilynnn," Violet said, drawing out her words to give herself time to think. "You don't … you don't want to do that. You don't want to hurt anyone else. Things–things can still get a lot worse."

"I'm taking that car and the whole Army can't stop me!" Josilyn screamed.

Violet stood frozen again. Should she go down the hallway to help the woman that Josilyn was probably holding captive? Should she go outside to block her eventual escape in the car? Should she try to find the car keys before Josilyn and her hostage could?

Violet settled on distracting and stalling her until the

military police came looking in the surrounding area for their lost suspect. Surely they would find the open window, then see the front door on the neighbor's house that Violet had left open, right?

"They already know everything, Josilyn," Violet called down the hall as she moved from the kitchen back to the living room that held the entrance to the hall. "They know about the prescription drugs, the beating of the captain ... and they know that you were not the person that killed Captain Shoenthal. You don't have to worry about that."

That's when Violet noticed a drop of blood on the carpet by the entrance to the hallway. Violet deflated. Did that mean that Josilyn had already hurt her hostage? She thought back to what Eve had said about Josilyn liking improvised knives and she gripped the chef's knife a little tighter.

"Of course I wasn't!" Josilyn flung out her words. "But I wasn't sorry to hear that he was dead. Now he's not my problem anymore!"

Violet came closer and found another drop of blood, then realized there was a slight trail leading from the front door, past the hallway, and into the kitchen.

Am I bleeding? Violet thought before a big pair of hands seized her from behind.

...

I was doing it to make money for my mom's treatments, but Heather is a user. She might have been doing it for the drugs. And the thrill. Reese was like Suzanne. They both thought that they would not be able to live forever on a military salary, so they were "laying away a nest egg" as they put it. But Josilyn, she was the one who scared me. She was burning through the money as fast as she could make it. She always wanted more, needed more, and thought she deserved more. It was never enough. She even threatened Heather with a shiv once when they disagreed over some money. That's when I learned to never get between Josilyn and money.

...

Chapter 25

"Shh shh, it's okay," Jake breathed into Violet's ear, then took his hand off of her mouth. "I didn't mean to sneak up on you. But Josilyn can't know that I'm here."

He unwrapped his arm from around her waist and she faced him as her breath caught in her throat. One of his arms had red rivulets going down its length.

"Oh my goodness, did you get shot?" Violet whispered.

"Just a graze. It's fine."

"I'm so glad you're here," she said close to his ear. "I didn't know what to do, but I knew I couldn't let her ..." Violet gestured with her arm down the hallway.

"It's okay. I have a plan but ..." Jake said then searched her face with wide bloodshot eyes. He whispered, "But, you have to trust me. I won't let anything happen to you, okay?"

Violet nodded, then Jake leaned into her hair and whispered his plan to her ear. He held her arms steady and she rested her hands on his biceps. Their bodies almost touched as they steadied each other barely out of sight of the hall. Violet struggled to keep her head clear for the task at hand, despite the questions and fears that loomed.

"Josilyn," Violet called down the hall a moment later. "I've been thinking ... I'm worried about that lady with you."

CHAPTER 25

"She's fine. What's it to you?" Josilyn grunted.

"I–I was thinking you should take me instead," Violet said and gulped. "I'm not a cop, so I'm no more dangerous to you than she is, but I know the cops on this case, so I might even be a more valuable hostage."

Josilyn paused. "You would come with me if I let her go?"

"Yeah, I'd rather you hurt me if something goes wrong. I know I'd never be able to live with myself if you hurt someone when I could have, you know, taken their place."

When Josilyn didn't respond Violet decided she needed to be more persuasive.

"It's my fault!" Violet called. "I made Suzanne–I tricked Suzanne into talking to the cops. I–I regret that and I want to make it up to her, and you, by helping you now. I can help you escape!"

Violet was so stiff that her whole body was shaking when Josilyn came out of the bedroom door down the hall. She had a small, dark-haired woman around the neck with one arm as her other hand held a short shiv that looked like it had been made from duct tape and broken glass.

"You'll come with me?" Josilyn said. She looked haggard with dark circles under her eyes and a limp. "Only you and me? No tricks?"

Violet took a moment to nod and say, "I–I even found some car keys that probably belong to the car outside."

"Show 'em to me!" Josilyn barked.

"I don't–I'm sorry, I left them in a kitchen drawer," Violet lied.

Josilyn came a few steps closer, almost to the end of the hall, and Violet felt like a little kid playing hide-and-seek again. Her knees shook and she wanted to cry out as if the person who was 'it' lurked just outside of her hiding spot. She took a deep breath and reminded herself, *I can trust Jake, and I can trust myself. I can do this. And I'm not alone.*

Josilyn took two more steps, but Violet's eyes flitted to Jake a moment too soon. Jake lunged out from the corner where he hid, but Violet's eyes had already unwittingly warned Josilyn. Instead of Jake being able to grab Josilyn and control the knife as he had planned, Josilyn was already in a whirl of motion. The dark-haired woman was knocked to the floor and Josilyn struck out with the improvised knife. Her hand met Jake somewhere on his side, making him cry out and stunning him long enough to give Josilyn the time she needed to kick out, sending him sprawling on the floor.

Josilyn zeroed in on Violet.

Jake was already popping to his feet, but there was no way he could get to them in time as Josilyn ran at her, shiv raised.

Violet had no thoughts but moved on instinct. She drew the chef's knife that she had hidden in her boot and swung it toward the jagged glass that was coming at her. The shiv and Josilyn's thumb tumbled to the floor. Violet had sliced off the digit without realizing it, so she stood gaping at the mess she had created as Jake reached them, only half a second too late.

Josilyn crumpled to her knees and screamed, "Ah! My thumb!" She cradled it and wrapped it in the hem of her shirt.

Jake growled in pain and clicked one end of his handcuffs around Josilyn's uninjured hand and the other end around the banister of the nearby stairway. Then he fell to his knees to put pressure on Josilyn's thumb since she no longer could. "Violet, can I trouble you for another towel? Actually, better make that two. One for her and … one for me."

CHAPTER 25

Violet ran to the kitchen, snatched at three dish towels, and darted back. The red had wicked up Josilyn's shirt and down Jake's arm, but there was a new splotch of crimson on Jake's side. She tossed one towel as a shroud over the gruesome thumb, shoved one towel into Jake's hands, and kept one for herself, thinking that she would have to be the one to wrap up Josilyn's hand as Jake tended to his new stab wound. Instead, Jake bent to wrap Josilyn's hand, so Violet ripped her towel in half at a frayed spot and pressed half to Jake's ribs and half to his bicep.

"Thanks," Jake said. "I know it's gross, especially for you, but ... thanks."

With a fresh flood of emotions, Violet wanted to throw herself into Jake's arms, but she kept each of her hands firmly on one of his wounds. He finished tying the towel around Josilyn's hand as she leaned against the banister, panting. Only then did he let himself crumble into a sitting position against the wall. Violet followed him and covered both wounds again as Jake got on his police radio. "Whitehouse here. When you get a chance, some of y'all better come next door."

"Tell them you need an ambulance!" Violet cried. "You were stabbed!"

"I'm okay. I promise. Neither one is deep."

"Still. You left a trail on the floor. You need some stitches, gauze, something," she said, leaning in.

"I'll get some stitches if you say so." Jake gave her a pale smile. "They won't be my first, and they definitely won't be my last."

Violet took his joke as a sign that he was going to be okay. She tied the one half-towel around his arm and kept the other towel pressed to his ribs as she scooted closer on her knees and kissed his stubbled cheek.

She didn't let go of his ribs as his hands wrapped around her free hand and pulled her to him. He slumped onto her shoulder and Violet wasn't sure if it was from exhaustion or affection. He leaned in farther and buried his face in her hair, making her heart shift gears.

As the dark-haired woman got up and asked questions, Violet came out of the cloud that had settled in her brain. She pulled back from the hug and moved her hand up to rest on Jake's shoulder, but he didn't budge. Jake kept leaning on her, and Violet even thought she felt a tear fall onto her neck.

"What are you going to do about it?" The tiny dark-haired woman was still talking, but Violet had no idea what about.

"Jake," Violet whispered, "I think it's time to be Agent Whitehouse again."

"I can't let go of you," he said. "Not yet. When I let go, it will probably be goodbye."

Over the next hour, things were a blur. Violet remembered sitting dazed in Jake's car contemplating the blood stains on that strange house's carpet. She fixated on them. She hoped that the carpet was Scotchguarded. She hoped the towels would not be missed by the woman who had been held hostage. Anything to avoid the real, deep thoughts that loomed.

Would Don be okay? Would Jake be okay? Would they be able to reattach Josilyn's thumb? Would this case, or these cases, ever get closed? Had they apprehended Reese and Heather? Was the hostage lady going to be okay? Would anything ever be able to happen between her and Jake?

Only when Jake opened his door and slid into the driver's

seat did Violet feel the breeze hit her cheeks and realize that she was crying.

"Are you okay?" Jake asked first.

"Yeah, I think I'll be okay," Violet said, trying to smile. "But how are you?"

"Good enough to drive myself to get a couple stitches. But, worried about you," Jake said simply. "I know I let you down in there …"

"You were hurt. Twice!" Violet cried.

"Yeah, but … I promised you …"

"You still saved me, even if it didn't go as planned." She watched Jake from the passenger seat. "We just had to work together more than we anticipated. But you didn't let me down. If anything, I'm sorry that I gave away your location by looking at you, like you told me not to."

"You did great," Jake said.

"So did you," Violet said.

They smiled at each other until Jake's expression hardened to cardboard, then fell into a mournful distance. "I better drive you home."

He navigated the streets of Fort Sam Houston, then the streets of San Antonio, moving towards the Pearl district. They were halfway to Violet's apartment before they spoke again.

"So what were you thinking about right now?" Jake finally asked.

"Dumb stuff. Maybe I shouldn't say," Violet admitted.

Jake looked at her expectantly. "Try me."

"Okay, I hope it doesn't sound … insensitive, but I was thinking about the mess we left in that lady's house," Violet said, grimacing.

"It's alright. Sometimes the brain turns to subjects that it can handle rather than thinking about trauma."

"Yeah, that sounds about right." Violet frowned. "There are too many big questions. Important ones. Like how is Don?"

Jake turned a mournful gaze on Violet and for a moment she was afraid that he had bad news until he said, "I guess it was touch and go for a little bit there, but they got him to the hospital and they think he should be okay."

"What a relief! And are you okay?"

Jake flapped his arm like a chicken wing. It was roughly bandaged by the medics who had taken Don away. "Yeah. I think it looked worse than it was. Maybe a couple stitches but I'll be fine."

"It could have been a lot worse," Violet muttered, thinking of the stab wound at his side that he didn't think was even worth mentioning.

"Yes, it definitely could have."

"I mean ... the trauma of all this," Violet clarified.

Jake gave her a sideways glance and said again, "I'll be fine."

"And Josilyn? Will her thumb be okay?" Violet felt her throat tighten. "Are they able to reattach it or do I have to live with that guilt forever?"

Jake's lips curved up in a tiny smile. "Chances for the thumb's survival are also really good."

"Good. And how about Reese and Heather? Did we get them?"

Jake inhaled, gripping the steering wheel and kept his eyes fixed on the road. "We got Reese, but Heather was shot and killed. She was the one who opened fire on my men. When we got in, she didn't stop firing, so ..."

Violet wilted. "Suicide-by-cop rather than going to prison?"

"Probably. Essentially."

"Was she the one who fired the shots at us at Market Square?"

"I'd put good money on it. Since her weapon of choice is a handgun."

"Like Josilyn's is improvised knives. So she was probably the one that stabbed the captain," Violet said with a queasy feeling. "And how about the hostage? Is she okay?"

"Medically, yes. EMTs checked her out and she was fine, but it sounds like she is laying the groundwork for a lawsuit against the department or the Army. She's not totally wrong though. We did neglect the side yard when we stormed the house."

"Does that mean you will get in trouble?" Violet asked.

"Maybe. But I might have already been, so what's one more slap on the wrist?" Jake said. He attempted to smile at Violet, but his eyes still looked sad.

"Does all this mean that this case is going to take even longer to close?" Violet locked her eyes on Jake's.

"Yes," Jake rumbled. "Probably. Even after the long process of getting it to trial, and even if we get a conviction, then there's more time for sentencing ... then years of appeals ..."

"Years?" Violet squeaked.

Jake nodded with a frown as he pulled to a stop next to Violet's apartment. "Sorry that I ruined your Valentine's Day."

"It's really okay," Violet said, sweeping her hair behind her ear and peering at Jake. "I think I ended up spending it with who I really wanted to be with."

Jake looked into her eyes and slowly leaned in as his breathing quickened. His slate gray eyes and the smell of his shaving cream were intoxicating. This was the closest they had ever been. Violet followed his lead and leaned over the center console of the car. Her heart was pounding as Jake looked at her lips and slipped his hand around the nape of her neck. Violet closed her eyes, but instead of the kiss that she was expecting, Jake's hand fell and he said, "I'm sorry, I shouldn't have ... We can't. Not during an open investigation. I wish ... I–I am already in a lot of trouble."

Violet opened her eyes and zipped her backbone straight, embarrassed that she had been left hanging and leaning. She cleared her throat. "Right, I'm ... sorry too. I–I understand."

Her heart pounded in her throat. If only she had met Jake under different circumstances. She pictured their first meeting, then her figuring out some other way that Derek wasn't for her, then finding Jake by going to his department and tracking him down. She would have found him, surprised him at work, then asked him out in some way that was worthy of a rom-com. But none of that would ever be possible because some captain had opened his big fat mouth, incurred the wrath of his co-conspirators, and then been smothered by his wife. Violet puffed a frustrated sigh.

Jake sighed too. "Well, it was nice knowing you, Miss Davis."

"You too, Special Agent Whitehouse." Violet kept on a brave face, but inside it felt like her heart was oozing down into her stomach. His phone buzzed with a text message, but she went on. "Can you let me know when I can visit Don though? Maybe I can bring him some brownies or something. They work miracles in the healing process."

"Actually, this text from my captain says he got out of surgery and can receive guests now. And I was headed to the hospital anyway." Jake pierced Violet with a keen look. "Want to prolong the inevitable a little longer?"

Chapter 26

...

That night at the Dining Out, when I did it, was when I learned that it was all about the money for the other ladies. We weren't helping anyone but ourselves. That was when I wanted to leave but also when I realized that I couldn't. Ever.

The captain came over to our table and we were all chatting like we didn't all know each other already, so it all started off great. He was playing it perfectly—like we weren't all committing crimes together—until he got too comfortable talking to Reese's friend. They talked about how they both have a hobby of investing, then they spoke about their stock market investments, then about how they wanted to invest in owning businesses. When Captain Shoenthal hinted that he already partially owned a business, the side chatter around the table died down.

I looked around and saw that it was because all four of us were riveted to every word that the captain said. He was already flirting with the line of what it was okay to say about our organization and what wasn't, but then he hinted that he would say more.

He said something like, "Well, I do have some tips and strategies that I can't talk about here. But I might be convinced to let a few things slip if I were plied with some good company and a single malt." He was smiling like he was bragging, or fishing for an invitation, or maybe joking, but that's when I saw all the other girls' faces get hard and angry.

As soon as he was gone Josilyn pulled us aside and insisted we needed to teach Captain Shoenthal to keep his mouth shut. I wasn't sure what she meant at first. She said we needed to make sure he never talked about our setup.

That's when Heather gasped and asked if Josilyn was going to kill him. But she said no. I know from that that she also didn't mean to kill him, okay? But she said that we needed to hurt him and teach him not to rat us out. She even had a plan for all of us to do it, have an alibi, and not get caught.

When she said that we were going to beat him up and that we all had to do it, that's when I freaked out. I think I was sweating and breathing fast. I can't remember if I said anything out loud, but the other girls caught on and started on me. They worked to convince me that we had to do it and we had to do it together, but I wasn't convinced until they threatened me. They said if I didn't help them beat up the captain then I would be as bad as him. They said things like 'traitor,' and 'not part of the family,' and then they said that maybe I needed to be taught a lesson too. That's when I said that I'd help them. I convinced them that I wasn't trying to get out of helping them, but that I was nervous that we would get caught.

They seemed to be satisfied with that, so they went back to planning.

First, we needed him to be compliant. Heather had some sedative in her purse, which was when it came out that she's a user, so we decided to slip that into his drink right then, in the big group of people. Then, either he would excuse himself when he couldn't keep it together in front of his men, or we would lead him out the front door and around to the back and dump him there.

CHAPTER 26

After he was safely knocked out, we would all go back in the front door while no one was watching, then go to the bathroom under the pretext of woman's problems, then we could stay in there for a while and deadbolt the door, saying that it was a big mess and we were trying to clean up. We also used our trips out to search for supplies as a disguise for us opening the bathroom door and sneaking out the back since the bathroom door made a noise every time we opened it.

Someone would go out towards the party and distract the guard, Agent Whitehouse, while someone else went out the back door and did a little more damage to Captain Shoenthal. The idea was that we would all take turns going out to kick and punch him a few times each—even me, but I didn't want to. I had to!

Anyway, the plan was that when we were done we would hide one of our purses, Reese's I think, say we couldn't find it and that it might have fallen from this one specific spot and into the trash. Then we would get someone to go out to the trash to look either for us or with us, then they would find the captain and call him an ambulance.

See? We did not want to, did not plan to, and did not kill him! It was definitely Suzanne, but I guess you already know that. She asked me once if I thought our operation could do without him. I said yes, thinking that she meant he might have wanted out or be leaving for another deployment or something. I guess she was already thinking about it and waiting for the perfect opportunity to get rid of him.

I said we could perfectly go on without Captain Shoenthal. The four of us nurses would continue to schedule shifts together, pocket the drugs that we were supposed to be disposing of, and get another one of us to vouch that we had actually disposed of the meds. Then we'd bring them back and sell them through Suzanne's perfume business. That way the money was made and laundered at the same time. It was perfect because if anyone asked about where all the money was coming from, or looked at Suzanne's books, it was all explained by the huge markups on perfume.

We had the perfect system, but it could have run fine without Captain Shoenthal. I guess I shouldn't have told that to Suzanne though. I guess that, mixed with the ticking clock of the captain probably leaving the Army and losing his life insurance, was too much temptation. And he had faith in the wrong person.

I've had faith in the wrong people too. I know what that's like. There's the usual stuff like boyfriends and authority figures that have let me down, but I was thinking of my nurse friends. I joined the group so then we were all loyal to each other to keep quiet about our crimes, but we found out that we couldn't trust the captain to keep our secret. Then I found out that I couldn't trust the other ladies to not turn on me if I stepped out of line.

Anyway, it was the captain that ruined the setup because he was an idiot and talked in front of us. Then, it was my friend Violet and the MP that I think she has a crush on that ruined the new plan by finding him out by the dumpster too early, but it sounds like it was good that they did. I mean, the captain was much worse off than he was supposed to be. Josilyn was the only one that went after me, so it could only have been her that stabbed the captain.

I only kicked him two or three times, you know, and he was not that bad when I left him. Josilyn went last. I don't think she was trying to kill him, I mean she said not to, but I also wouldn't put anything past her. Her and those stupid knives she makes. You can protect me and Pete from her, right?

No, Pete wasn't involved at all. He didn't even know that I was making extra money. He probably would have insisted on us keeping some of it if he had. But no, it all went straight home to

CHAPTER 26

my mom. Ugh, is there any way she doesn't have to find out about this?

Or maybe she should. Can you protect my family too? I'll help you with anything. I guess that's how I can protect my family. Josilyn needs to be put away for a long time. She is scary—that's why I had to do it, but it's also why I have to help you put her away now.

Signature : Eve Davis

Chapter 27

Violet followed Jake down the same hospital hallway that she had walked through the day before. She marveled at everything that had happened in the last few days. Had the captain really only died the morning before? Now it was Sunday evening and each hospital room had reminders that it was Valentine's Day. Paper hearts were stuck to the walls with tape, balloons stood suspended in doorways, and some doors had cards and pictures from children plastered on them. The nurse's station had two tall bouquets of red roses. Even Don, who didn't have any romantic influences in his life and had barely been admitted, had a room that boasted store-bought glittery die-cut hearts on the empty spaces of the wall and a pink sunset glowing in the window.

"Did we get 'em?" Don asked before Violet or Jake could even say hello.

"We got 'em," Jake said. "I'll tell you more as we find out more, but you can rest easy. We're gonna nail them to the wall."

Don let out a long sigh and leaned back, revealing his left arm in a sling with a fat wad of gauze in the spot where Violet had wedged her sweatshirt.

"How are you?" Violet asked and came to sit by Don's feet.

CHAPTER 27

"At the moment, great because the drugs from my surgery are still working, but they say I'll hurt later. And that I have a long road to recovery ahead of me."

"We were worried about you," Violet said, pulling the table with Don's water cup closer.

"It sounds like I should have been worried about y'all!" Don raised his eyebrows at Jake. "Shot and stabbed?"

"Just scratches. And they've stopped bleeding. I'll go get someone to stitch them up after this."

"And you!" Don looked at Violet. "Did you really go after one of the suspects?"

"Well, I was the only one who could see her getting away. And with all the confusion I couldn't get anyone's attention," Violet said. "Then I really knew I had to do something when I heard the lady inside scream."

"Wow!" Don said, shaking his head. "Even after we tell you to stay out of the house …"

"I did!" Violet protested. "I stayed out of *that* house. Oh, I meant to ask … How did you know to come into that house? Was it the missing suspect and the open door?"

"That should have clued me in," Jake said, "but actually the new officer on our team came and got my attention. She clued me in that there was a woman outside hopping, waving, and pointing to the house next door."

Violet glowed, embarrassed but vindicated. "Oh, yeah, that crazy lady was me, but I thought my signaling hadn't worked."

"Officially I'm telling you that you should have waited for the authorities and stayed outside," Jake said with a rare, wide smile that spread across his whole face. "But unofficially and off the record, I'm glad you believed in yourself and helped someone in distress."

When Violet pried her eyes off of Jake to sweep her hair back behind her ear and look back towards the patient, Don was switching a bemused smile between the two of them.

"Anyway, we thought we could come to check on you and see if you need anything," Violet sighed with the remnant of a smile.

"So is it 'we' now?" Don smiled.

"Shh, here comes my captain," Jake said quickly, then a tall, muscular man with a white-blonde buzz cut trudged in the door to Don's room.

The captain wore a pristine, updated dress uniform, as if he were going to a Dining Out, with a dark green jacket and pressed brown pants.

"As you were," he said before even clearing the door as if Don had been thinking about getting up to greet him.

"Thank you for coming, sir," Don said in a staccato tone.

"I wanted to come to tell you, Special Agent Donnelly, and you too, Special Agent Whitehouse, that this case is progressing nicely ..." Jake's captain said, then leveled a gaze on Violet, making her feel as though she had interrupted their conversation.

"Uh, Captain Crocker, this is Miss Violet Davis. She has been very helpful, and I would even say instrumental in bringing this case to a satisfactory close," Jake said, making Violet blush.

"Ah, a pleasure to meet you, Miss Davis," Crocker said.

"The pleasure is all mine, sir. I've heard wonderful things about you from Agents Donnelly and Whitehouse," Violet lied, prompting a smile from all three of the Army officers.

"I have news, but I suppose I can speak in front of Miss Davis, since she has been so heavily involved," Captain Crocker said,

CHAPTER 27

exactly as Violet had hoped.

"Yes, please, sir," Jake said.

"First of all, they are all turning on each other. All of our witnesses and suspects are telling us everything. With the evidence we are getting from one, we can hang the other, and vice versa," Crocker said with a look at Violet. "Figuratively speaking, of course."

"Of course ... sir," Violet said.

Captain Crocker nodded. "Plus there's the evidence that we collected from the back room where our dealers were doing business. Pill bottles are tracing back, fingerprints are matching up, and all the loose ends are getting tied up like a dang Valentine's Day gift—the gift of lots of irrefutable evidence of their guilt, and a notch in my investigators' belts. Maybe even an award or two."

"Thank you, sir," Don said, sitting up a little straighter.

"Plus, Eve Davis, oh, uh ..." The captain looked at Violet as if realizing something.

"No relation," Violet said, winking.

The captain continued. "Oh, uh, Miss *Eve* Davis has fully committed to our side. She comes with emails, texts, dates, a veritable chocolate box of evidence."

"Sounds perfect, sir," Jake said with a light in his eyes.

"It *is* perfect," Crocker bellowed to Jake. "This is the best-case scenario in situations like this. Now, don't get cocky because this was the first case you were in charge of. It's definitely a feather in your cap, but ... well, it never works out this well. So enjoy it, celebrate it, try for it next time but don't get used to it!"

With that, Captain Crocker saluted the room in general, then marched out without another word as Jake's eyes sparkled at Violet. After they said their goodbyes to Don and promised to come back and see him the next day, they made their way to the emergency room.

Only after they were deep inside the bowels of the hospital's hallways and Violet had ignored a call from Derek did she ask, "What? Now it's your turn to be giddy? Is it because this case is going so well?"

"Indirectly," Jake said, prompting a questioning look from Violet. "This case is closing. Like actually closing."

Jake's eyes twinkled into Violet's in the fluorescent lights, then she finally grasped his meaning.

"Oh!" Violet said. She beamed and twirled a piece of her hair around a finger. "Like no appeals?"

"Probably not," Jake said.

"No digging up how evidence was acquired and arguing that it was obtained without proper paperwork, or something like that?"

"Already the Army has less of that than regular courts."

"So, case closed, move on with your life?" Violet said as her smile widened.

"I–I didn't let myself hope until now, but I might actually get to take you to Thai food someday soon," Jake said, beaming. "If you're interested, that is."

"Want to come over after this?" Violet said. She wrung her hands together and she smiled so hard that she had to close her eyes. "I already started on dinner for tonight." She thought of how she had prepped ingredients before Derek had surprised her with reservations. Reservations that she had missed because of their official breakup. It seemed like ages ago. "I can make the mapo tofu that I already had planned."

"You make mapo tofu? That's pretty adventurous for

CHAPTER 27

someone who says they haven't explored the world's food much." Jake laughed.

"It's Taylor's recipe again," Violet admitted with a blush. "And I'm ... getting started." They arrived through a pair of double doors into an empty waiting room. "And you're pretty leisurely for someone that's headed to the ER."

"Meh, why rush?" Jake said with a grin. "Looks like there's no line, so if you don't mind waiting, then ... yeah, I think I can come over for some innocent mapo. Besides, I have something that I've been meaning to give you all day."

The interval in the waiting room and then the drive home meant ignoring another two calls from Derek, plus noticing that he had left several messages, but Violet was finally at ease. Sitting in Jake's car felt right and comfortable now. Ignoring calls from Derek gave her a pang of guilt, but it also felt good to have finally made a decision and be sticking to it—especially one that she knew would bring her even more peace, as opposed to betrayal, in the future.

Jake parked the car outside Violet's apartment and they walked and talked all the way inside, not noticing the lights that were already on in her apartment.

"You really grew up on a ranch near here? That's so cool!" Jake said, continuing their conversation.

"Yeah, my parents still live there. It's outside Austin, so they are only a couple hours away. I even went to UT, so I'm an Austinite born and bred."

"Do they not have a culinary school up there?"

"Oh, they do, arguably the better one, but ... well, like an idiot I came to this school to follow Derek."

"Speak of the devil," said a familiar drawl.

Derek sauntered down the stairs and folded his arms at

them. "So now it's idiotic to be loyal to your boyfriend?"

When she recovered from her surprise, Violet fired back, "When he's not loyal to you? Yeah, I think it is."

"Now, hold on." Jake put up his hands. "Have you two reached an understanding? Should I be getting out of the way or asking him to leave?"

"Getting out of the way!" Derek yelled.

At the same time, Violet said, "Asking him to leave," but her voice was drowned out by Derek's outburst, so Jake was left looking from one to the other.

"Violet?" Jake stepped closer to her.

"I guess I need to change the locks because I already made it very clear to Derek that I cannot trust him and that I do not wish to speak to him anymore," Violet said. She folded her arms and she felt her nostrils flare.

"But you can trust this clown?" Derek groused.

"He doesn't lie to me, Derek!" Violet spat.

"You think not?" Derek balked. "You know he suspected you of the assault, right?"

Violet shifted her weight as she thought about what to say, then settled on "Well, he had to suspect everyone."

"No, I mean he really suspected you!" Derek yelled into Jake's face. "Tell her, Whitehouse!"

"There were times … that I thought …" Jake said slowly as if he were choosing his words carefully.

"See? I told you!" Derek hollered. "He was playing you the whole time. Seeing if he could get what he needed from you. And maybe even what he wanted!"

Jake clenched his fist by his side and his face hardened. "I had to … I had to do just enough to find out what I needed to know. But I wasn't …"

CHAPTER 27

Violet felt her fingers go cold and numb. She stepped away from Jake. "You kept me around so that you could keep an eye on me? You really suspected me?"

"It's not that–I mean, that was part of it but—" He took a step towards Violet, but she took another step back.

"He was playing you the whole time," Derek said.

"No, I was—" Jake argued.

"That's not loyalty! If you can't expect loyalty from me, then you can't expect loyalty from him either," Derek said. He let a malicious smile crack his face in half. "He was lying to you. He was playing you. And he just wanted to solve his case. He wasn't looking out for you, no matter what it looked like. Or maybe felt like. He was manipulating you."

"No, you're the one manipulating the situation," Jake raised his voice to Derek, then turned to Violet. "I wasn't–I mean I didn't—"

"Did you actually suspect me?" Violet whispered as tears gathered in her eyes.

"I told–I told you that I—" Jake stumbled over his words.

"And you were keeping me close. Playing me." She could hardly see for the tears that filled her vision.

Jake was breathing hard. "This is all too fast. I–It wasn't like that. He's making it sound ..."

"Icky," Violet said as she blinked the tears back and leveled a stare at Jake.

"If you can't trust me, then you can't trust him either," Derek said again.

After they all stood silent and shaking with tension for a long moment, Violet said, "You're right. Both of you have said it now. I need to build a relationship of trust. And if that's a required ingredient ... then I have to ask both of you to get out ... and leave me alone."

Jake drew a sharp breath as if he was going to protest but then thought the better of it. "Okay, I can respect that."

"Fine," Derek said. "But you'll be back, baby."

Violet closed her eyes, deciding and determining that no matter how hard it got, she must never go crawling back to Derek. Violet stood stiff in the middle of the room and hugged herself as Derek stomped out the back door, slamming it behind him.

"I—" Jake said. He swallowed hard, then forced something wrapped in brown paper into her hand. "Well, I hope you find what you're looking for."

Jake strode toward the back door, pausing for a long time with his hand on the doorknob as if deciding what to say, then he too disappeared.

Violet decided it was safe to melt now that both men were gone, so she leaned against the wall and slid down it until she sat with her legs sprawled on the living room floor. For once, she didn't care if she had vacuumed. She didn't think about when the rug was last steam cleaned. She let the tears run down her face, and when she moved to wipe them she remembered that her numb hands still clasped the cylinder of brown paper.

She slipped her finger under a spot of tape and let the contents roll out into her palm. When she saw San Luis Rey's face and the fresh bottle of Mexican vanilla, she dissolved into hopeless tears.

Mapo Tofu

Serves 4-6

Prep time - 15 minutes

This zingy Sichuan dish requires a trip to the foreign market but it's worth it. Even tofu-haters love mapo. You can get creative with the substitutions, but do not bother making it without the Sichuan pepper (a.k.a. prickly ash, Chinese pepper, Timut pepper, or mala pepper).

Ingredients:
- 16 ounce package soft tofu (or firm but not silken)
- 1 cup chicken stock (or beef, or vegetable)
- 2 tablespoons soy sauce
- 1 teaspoon granulated sugar
- 1 tablespoon Shaoxing wine
- 2 tablespoons cornstarch
- 3 tablespoons Chinese black vinegar
- 4 tablespoons vegetable oil
- 8 ounces ground pork or beef (½ lb.)
- 2 tablespoons fermented chili garlic paste or chili bean paste

(toban jian, douban jiang, or sambal)
   4 large garlic cloves, minced or grated
   2 tablespoons ginger, minced or grated
   1 teaspoon ground Sichuan pepper
   1 teaspoon sesame oil
   3 spring onions, finely sliced
   Optional - serve with steamed rice

1. Cut slit in tofu container, drain off liquid, then cut tofu into 1-inch pieces and set aside in a paper towel lined bowl to drain a bit more.
2. In a small bowl, combine stock, soy sauce, sugar, and wine, then set aside for later.
3. In a second small bowl, mix 2 tablespoons of the vinegar with the cornstarch. Set next to your stove, with everything else, for later.
4. Now it's time for the stove. Have everything within reach because everything comes together quickly. Take a deep breath, then put oil in a wok or nonstick pan over very high heat.
5. Brown meat in your hot oil while breaking up with your spoon for about three minutes, then add chili garlic paste or chili bean paste and cook for one more minute.
6. Scoot meat to the outside edges of the pan, then dump garlic and ginger into the middle of the pan so it makes contact with the pan. Jab at the ginger and garlic in the middle for about 30 seconds, then mix all ingredients in the pan together. Pour stock mixture over your meat mixture, turn heat down to medium and let cook

for about 5 minutes until sauce is reduced and getting thicker.
7. Remix vinegar mixture, then add to your pan. Mix in. When the pan bubbles again and your sauce is thick, add tofu and Sichuan pepper, then gently stir or fold in.
8. When mixed, turn off your heat. Drizzle in your sesame oil and the last tablespoon of vinegar, sprinkle on half your green onions, mix, and serve.
9. Enjoy immediately over steamed rice with the rest of your green onions as garnish.

Chapter 28

It had been almost a month since Violet had cried herself to sleep on the living room floor on Valentine's Day. She had visited Don once more in the hospital, and Don had called her twice to update her on the progression of the case, but she had avoided seeing Jake. She'd convinced her friends that she was fine by punctually attending all of her classes. Derek had moved out all his belongings into a place of his own, and she was even starting to believe what she had told Taylor and Josh about being fine and enjoying being alone. Violet had even gone out and gotten a great deal on a beautiful new dining room table. Now, as her friends were coming over to talk about their latest catering gig, a bar mitzvah that had taken place the night before, she doused cellophane noodles in hot water and whisked up a marinade for another of Taylor's recipes, a Chinese noodle dish called 'Ants Climbing Trees,' with lightning speed.

"Hey, gorgeous!" Josh called as the back door closed behind him and he made his boisterous entrance.

"Hey, handsome!" Violet responded and raked back her hair. She felt a wistful smile play on her lips as she thought of Jake for probably the thousandth time since Valentine's Day. She pursed her lips to chase away the smile. "You're late."

"Only five minutes. I keep getting better. For you." He called to Taylor as she emerged from the bathroom, "Hey, rockstar!"

"Hey, handsome," Taylor played along, zeroing her piercing gaze on Josh, then shifting it to Violet. "Whoa, girl! When did you get so fast?"

Violet was blazing her way down the length of some green onions, slicing them with record-breaking speed and uniformity. "Oh, I've been practicing."

"And she finally learned to trust the money makers!" Josh said, holding up his hands and twiddling his fingers.

"Yeah, trusting myself was also a big part of it." Violet laughed and shrugged. "But, to be honest, it was also demystifying to see the worst that could happen and how even that is fixable."

"You mean getting run at and almost stabbed?" Taylor said sarcastically.

"No, she means seeing someone lose a finger and having it stitched back on!" Josh said with boyish intrigue. "It gave her the confidence to slice and dice things other than thumbs."

"Ew! But, actually, yeah," Violet blushed. "I mean, that's what you have to be afraid of while you're cutting, or keep a healthy respect for. It used to be all I could think about while I was cutting, but now that I've seen how even a severed finger can be mended, I think it helped me take a chance on myself and forge ahead."

"Well, good job! Now you really are unstoppable! It seems like you're starting to believe in yourself, so I guess it's paying off," Taylor said as she squished ground meat into and through the marinade.

Another pang of missing Jake twitched at Violet's lips.

"Speaking of paying off," Violet piped in as she washed

her hands, then laid her accordion-style file folder full of meticulously organized receipts on the table, "I finally pawned my old ring. Really I can't believe that I kept it for so long. I think y'all were right. As much as it's embarrassing to admit, I think I was clinging to that ring and the idea of Derek more than the actual douche-bag himself. Maybe I was in denial, I don't know. Anyway, after that chunk of change, I talked to my parents and they are going to give me a loan for the rest. Now I can buy y'all out of your parts of the business."

"Congrats! And ... thanks," Josh said as he lit the stove and heated a wok.

"And sorry," said Taylor. "Sorry again that we're leaving but I hope you know that we still love you."

"No, I'm sorry. Sorry that I made such a big deal out of y'all leaving and took it so personally. I'm glad y'all are moving on to amazing jobs. And you never promised that you would stay forever. I shouldn't have put so much emotional stock into our ... business arrangement. I think I was wallowing because of all that not-being-able-to-trust-Derek stuff, so I transferred that over but I know y'all are nothing like him. I love y'all."

"You too," Josh said and beamed. "So we can still be friends after graduation?"

"Definitely," Violet said with a smile at both of them.

Taylor screwed up her mouth. "Well, still ... Sorry we let you down on the business side, but I hope you can still trust people in your personal life. I know you were talking about ... Anyway, I hope you find someone to build a healthy relationship with."

"Jake said the same thing," Violet muttered. "Y'all keep saying the same things he used to say."

"Well, I guess he was right, then," Taylor said. She brought all the prep bowls over to the wok as Josh added the oil and grabbed a wide bamboo utensil. "I mean, business and personal ... Those two situations are very different."

"Anyway, yeah, I'm fine. I'm okay with waiting for someone to build a real and healthy relationship with." Violet watched and grew mesmerized by the steam as Josh stir-fried the ground pork in its marinade. She mentally patted herself on the back for emptying out the room where Derek had let his stuff linger in the back of her life for too long. She had even scrubbed the baseboards and vacuumed the room twice.

"I've been trying not to ask but ... what happened to Agent Sexy Shoulders?" Taylor asked Violet with a sideways glance.

"I–I found out that I couldn't trust him," Violet mumbled.

She saw Taylor and Josh look at each other, then grow silent as Josh squeezed her shoulder.

Over dinner at Violet's new oiled beech wood table, they talked about the bar mitzvah, the drunk uncle who had made a scene, the mom who wouldn't stop crying and hovering, and what they would do differently next time.

"I will look more into what's kosher and what's not," Josh said as he tapped his pen on the table.

Taylor went to open a bottle of wine that she had brought. "I mean, lobster! Who knew that half the people there wouldn't eat lobster!"

"I should have known, but I forgot," Violet said, covering her face with one hand. "My Jewish friend in high school wasn't very orthodox, but her parents were."

"You know what we should do for the St. Patrick's Day party this week?" Taylor said with excitement. "You're gonna think it's crazy but ..."

"Try me," Josh said.

Violet's eyes grew unfocused as she spaced out, thinking about Jake again. Josh had even said it in exactly the same way that Jake had about a month ago.

"Violet?" Taylor asked, holding out a glass of wine, snapping her out of her reflections. "Do you want one?"

"Oh, uh, no thanks."

"What's up with you? You're smiling but ... not," Josh said, taking a glass from Taylor.

Taylor spoke before Violet could. "Uh-oh, she's relapsed. Is it Derek or Agent Sexy Shoulders? Are you sure you're okay?"

"I thought I had finally convinced you!" Violet groaned. "I will be, okay? I'm happy to finally be done with Derek, but there are a lot of little things that remind me of Ja– I mean, Agent Whitehouse."

"You're still thinking about him a lot?" Taylor let down one side of her twisted-out curls, then the other side. "Are you sure it wasn't ... the real thing?"

"I do still think about him," Violet admitted, "But like Derek said on Valentine's Day—if I can't believe in Derek then I shouldn't believe in Jake either."

"Why? What happened?" Taylor asked between sips.

"Derek confronted Jake and it came out that ... Jake suspected me of the assault and he was playing me the whole time."

"Did he, Jake I mean, ever say that he liked you, or make a move?" Josh asked.

"Yeah, we almost kissed once. And we talked about being interested in each other right towards the end," Violet said, then let her eyes phase out again. "We had been talking about how we could go on a date soon when the case was wrapped up. That was the first thing he said after he found out that the case would end sooner than he had expected."

Taylor and Josh looked at each other again.

"And ... how exactly did he play you?" Taylor asked into her wine glass.

Violet rolled her eyes. "I don't know, like he only told me barely enough, was careful about sharing information with me, stuff like that. He could have even been faking being into me to string me along and get me to admit things, or make a mistake if I was guilty, or whatever."

"Do you know that he was faking?" Taylor asked.

At the same time, Josh said, "As much as I'm skeptical of cops, no. As a guy, that's not the reaction of a guy who's faking being into you. Sorry. Nope."

Violet blinked twice, then looked at Josh for more.

"If he had been faking feelings, he would have lost interest in you when he found out that you definitely weren't his suspect, right?" Josh said, frowning. "And when he found out that the case would stop stopping him from dating you, he wouldn't have gotten more interested in you if he was faking. He would have gotten distant or quiet or something."

"That's true," Taylor said, tipping her glass at Violet.

"So, I guess he was only careful about sharing information with me. Like telling me 'just enough,' like he always said," Violet said, her breath quickening.

"So he was doing his job?" Taylor said.

"Sounds like he already got into trouble for sharing and doing too much with you, or would have if it hadn't been the Army or had such a happy ending, so what did you want him to do?" Josh said, taking Violet down a notch with every question.

When Violet opened her mouth twice without uttering any words, Taylor drove the point home. "Sorry, honey. It sounds like he was being a cop during a murder investigation. I mean, he didn't know you. It's not like he could believe you right away. So, did he keep a safe distance from you to not get too involved with you or did he actively suspect you enough to come after you?"

Violet considered Taylor's logic and muttered, "I guess he kept a safe distance, and even that didn't really work. We kept drifting together, despite trying to stay apart. And I thought he really trusted me by the end."

"Okay, I have a question," Taylor said, shifting in her seat. "Now, forget anything that the douche-bag said and really think about this. Did you, before Derek said anything, feel like you could rely on Jake?"

Violet took a moment to answer. "I have to say yes. Everything that I learned about him told me that I could, until Derek…"

"Until Derek twisted the truth around to vindictively ruin your chance at happiness!"

Violet gulped through a dry throat, then said, "Do you really think he was only being a good cop?"

Josh and Taylor looked at each other again, this time with raised, snarky eyebrows.

"But didn't Derek have a point? If I can't believe Derek because he lied, then I can't believe Jake because he … omitted the truth. Right?"

"Again, those two situations are totally different," Taylor sighed, looking like she pitied Violet. "It's being careful with someone you just met and not saying too much because it's your job. That is not the same as getting engaged to someone,

CHAPTER 28

essentially making promises, then repeatedly breaking those promises, with several different people, then lying about breaking those promises, then—"

Josh interrupted with his own rant. "Yeah. One was being cautious before jumping in and one was sleeping around behind your back. It's totally different."

Violet looked between the two of them as she felt her face drain of color.

"Oh no," Violet cried. "I've made the wrong decision! Do you think it's too late?"

Ants Climbing Trees (a Chinese noodle dish)

Serves 4-6 people

Prep time - 20 minutes

Ingredients:
7 or 8 ounces cellophane noodles (also known as mung bean noodles or bean thread)
⅓ cup soy sauce
1 tablespoon Shaoxing wine
2 tablespoons chile paste (sambal or toban jian)
2 teaspoons cornstarch
1 lb. ground beef or pork
1 ½ tablespoons vegetable oil
4 to 6 green onions, chopped, divided
½ cup chicken or beef stock

1. Boil 2 quarts of water and place dry noodles in big heatproof bowl. Pour hot water over dry noodles and soak for 10 minutes. Then drain and set aside.

2. While noodles soak, prep other ingredients. In a medium bowl, whisk together soy sauce, Shaoxing wine, and chile paste until smooth. Add cornstarch and whisk until combined. Now add the ground meat and squish it all together with your super clean hands.
3. Heat a large wok or saute pan over high heat and add vegetable oil. When oil is hot (after 1 or 2 minutes) add ground meat mixture and cook for 2 more minutes while you stir and break up any chunks.
4. Add half of your chopped green onions and finish cooking the meat until browned, about another 2 minutes.
5. Turn heat down to medium, add stock, and cook until reduced and thicker, about 5 minutes.
6. Turn heat to low and toss in noodles, breaking up clumps, until well combined. Sauce should be absorbed and meat should be clinging to noodles. Serve immediately and garnish with the remaining green onions.

Chapter 29

"The Secretary of the Army of the United States of America has granted this award for unique achievement..." A man was reading a script as Captain Crocker, Jake, and Don stood at the front of the room at attention when Violet rushed in the door to the station. He went on as Violet noticed the crowd that was gathered, taking pictures and smiling. "... To Special Agent Sean Cathal Donnelly and Special Agent Jacob Collin Whitehouse for exceptional valor and project management in action on February 14th..."

Violet shrank back against the beige wall, suddenly sheepish about bursting in with a bag of takeout. Don had confirmed that Jake would be at the station, but had he known that this awards ceremony would be taking place when he had told her when to show up?

A discrete smile crept into Don's eyes across the room as Jake moved his eyes between him and Violet, then let his gaze linger on her. She had agonized over every detail of her appearance—from her violet sundress to her low heels and blown-out hair, but she still grew self-conscious as he stared at her without a trace of emotion. She smiled at Jake, but his face remained chiseled out of stone.

"Signed, Christine Wormuth, Secretary of Army," the announcer finished, then Captain Crocker pinned the ribbon to Don's BDUs, then Jake's, among a torrent of applause and camera flashes.

Violet deposited her bag on the ground and joined in the applause, but a heat grew in her cheeks and her throat grew tight as Jake's face continued to look cold and immovable.

He doesn't want to see me, she thought. *I'm too late. That door has closed. Maybe he even got together, or maybe back together, with that girl whose picture he keeps on his desk.*

As people milled around and Violet lost sight of Don and Jake in the hustle and bustle, she grabbed her bag and looked back the way she had come. She assessed how quickly she could get out the door and away from there.

I wish I hadn't come! Violet agonized. *I should have called him or asked Don to talk to him. Why did I think this was a good idea?*

"S'cuse me," she said to a wide civilian woman as her eyes stung and threatened to tear up. "Can I ..."

"Hey, gorgeous!" Violet heard an excited voice some distance behind her. She spun and her embarrassed tears melted to ones of joy. In one moment her throat loosened and her shoulders eased. Jake was also trapped by the crowd of people that milled around the room, but he stood tall above them and waved his arm. "Where you going?"

Violet let the tears shake down her cheeks as a laugh made her bend forward and cover her mouth.

"You're not here to see Don, are you?" Jake called as he fought the crowd.

Violet laughed again as she wiped her cheeks and fought the crowd in the opposite direction, toward Jake. "Not exactly. But that joker did tell me when to come and see you. I think he tricked me into coming to your medal ceremony."

Jake finally broke through the last line of people that separated them and brushed his thumb along her cheekbone where her laceration had been a month before.

"That sounds like something he would do," Jake said, beaming. "You know, he hasn't stopped talking you up since ... Well, he's been doing it for almost a month."

"My friends have been talking about you too. When I finally opened up to them and talked it out ... that's when I realized I needed to see you." She searched his face and took a step closer.

"The look on your face during the ceremony ... well, it gave me some hope," Jake said with a smile.

"The look on your face took away mine!" Violet exclaimed.

"Sorry, you know I have to do my job," Jake said, then grew somber.

"I know, I'm so sorry." Violet squeezed his hand. "I'm sorry it took me so long to realize that. You really were just doing your job, and ... I'm sorry I ever lumped you in with Derek. You two are worlds apart. No matter what he said to muddy the water."

"Thanks, yeah, I admit that hurt," Jake said. He peered down at his beige boots. "But hearing that you wanted me to leave you alone hurt more."

Violet felt a heavy weight on her chest. "I was so wrong to listen to him ... again. I think you were right. I must have been in denial about a lot of things."

"So you two aren't ..." Jake led and looked down at her left ring finger.

"No. Oh goodness, no," Violet scoffed. "No, Derek is gone for good and has been since that night. The ring's gone too. He has moved his stuff out, changed his address on official

CHAPTER 29

paperwork, and is even dating that Lieutenant Pfeiffer."

"Yikes, are you okay?" Jake asked.

For the first time in a month, Violet didn't mind being asked that. "Yeah, I'm good. I know I made the right decision to cut him out of my life."

"Good. Good," Jake said, nodding, then stayed quiet and kept looking down.

Violet took another step closer until the only thing separating them was the hand that she laid on his chest. "Am I too late? Did I take too long to realize that I made the wrong decision about you? Too long to realize that you are nothing like Derek? Now I know that you … You, I can trust. You were just … doing your job."

"I tried … I tried to get over you for the last month," Jake said to the floor and Violet's heart fell, until he went on. "But it didn't work."

Violet's heart felt like an ember flickering back to life, and heat radiated from her chest. "So you didn't start dating that girl that you have a picture of on your desk?"

Jake's face twisted up in confusion, then relaxed into a smile. "Oh! I have pictures of my mom and my sister on my desk. Which one did you think was your competition?"

Violet laughed, then let her head fall forward onto Jake's chest. "Oops. I guess … your sister," she said.

"Yep, she is a heart-breaker… at least, that's what I've heard from her prom date," Jake grimaced.

Violet continued to bury her face in Jake's chest and laughed harder. She wrapped her arms around his ribcage, and he chuckled and interlocked his fingers behind her back.

"I'm sorry," Violet said and raised her face to him. "I do know how important fidelity and trust are to you, and I promise that's the last time I'll be jealous. I know I can rely on you if you want to ... stop leaving me alone?"

"Absolutely," Jake said, squeezing her. "I'm sorry about something too."

"What?" Violet's face fell as she searched his eyes that stayed jovial.

"I'm sorry I did leave you alone. This whole time I didn't know if I should chase you and fight for this, like I wanted to, or give you your space."

Violet thought her heart might burst. "You made the right decision since that's what I asked for, but ... from now on ... let's fight for this." Violet shot her arms around his neck and kissed him.

Before Violet could grow self-conscious about pouncing on him, Jake's lips responded and his arms tightened around her, lifting her up, despite the crowd that pressed in all around them.

"It's about time!" Don called out and clapped from a few feet away, prompting the rest of the room to clap along with him.

When Jake bent enough for Violet's toes to touch the floor again, she drew back to find that both of them were blushing and the applause died down.

"I wish I could keep kissing you, but I think we should get out of here."

"Me too," Violet said with a grin and tucked one side of her hair behind an ear.

Jake had a twinkle in his eye as he went on. "Hey, could I ask, what are you doing for lunch?"

Violet bent and retrieved the bag from the floor, then said, "I'm having a date with you!"

CHAPTER 29

"This isn't our first date—the last time we had Thai food was," Violet protested as she slid into the booth across the tiny table from Jake. She grabbed a napkin and wiped the table compulsively. "You know, when I brought the picnic after your award ceremony."

"That was an amazing gesture, but we were eating out of a Styrofoam box and sitting on a curb, not a real restaurant and ... not a date," Jake argued with a smile and set his hands over hers to stop her wiping motions. "I want to treat my girl right, and that means *real* dates."

"Well, I'm not picky," Violet said with a frown at the table. Jake raised his eyebrows at her.

"I'm not! Especially when a restaurant is like this and about as clean as eating outside. I mean, is there much difference?" She looked at the cloudy fish tank and the matted brown trails worn in the carpet by the people who only came in for takeout.

"Okay, next time I'll take you somewhere cleaner, but this little hole in the wall has the best food," Jake chuckled. "Violet, I'm glad we got to do this. This is great."

"This *is* great," Violet agreed. "For a long time, I thought I would have to always wonder about you, you know, because I think we make a great team."

"We do," Jake said as a smile curled up one cheek. "But next time we investigate something, I'll have to be more careful about involving you. Or keep you out of danger altogether."

"I know it didn't always go to plan, but you came through in the end. We can get through whatever it is together. Oh, and now you know I'm not a dangerous criminal," Violet said and beamed. "Besides, there probably won't even be a next time. I mean, how many crimes do regular people like me really get tangled up with?"

"I hope you're right. We'll see," said Jake.

"We *will* see," Violet said with a sharp nod.

When the tiny waitress brought out a giant plate of beef salad and a hot, tart coconut soup, Violet felt her eyes go wide and a tingling in her cheeks brought a flood of salivation. The first bite was a show-stopping revelation. Violet felt time slow down and she froze staring at Jake. His smile washed over her and she grabbed his hand across the table. He clasped her hand and laughed, showing a wide and carefree grin. She wasn't sure how, but she knew then and there that her life would never be the same. For two reasons.

"The best," Jake said. "Believe me now?"

Tom Kha (Thai Coconut Milk Soup)

Serves 4-6

Prep time - 15 minutes

For the paste-
    1 teaspoon chile flakes or hot pepper powder
    2 cloves garlic
    ¼ red or sweet onion
    2 tablespoons vegetable oil

For the soup-
    3 tablespoons tamarind paste
    2 cups chicken stock or broth
    1 (15 ounce) can coconut milk
    2 tablespoons fish sauce
    1 teaspoon palm sugar, or granulated sugar
    3-6 ounces raw meat, thinly sliced, like chicken breast, steak, pork chop, or maybe a handful of shrimp
    2 cups sliced vegetables, whatever you have, like onion, mushrooms, tomatoes, bamboo shoots, baby corn, etc.
    ¼ cup cilantro, chopped

2 tablespoons lime juice

Optional garnishes-
1 stalk lemongrass, bruised and cut into 2 inch lengths
2 thin slices galangal, or ginger
4 leaves kaffir or makrut lime leaves

1. In a blender, mini chopper, food processor, or a mortar and pestle, grind together chile, garlic, onion, and oil into a paste.
2. Over high heat, saute paste in the bottom of a big pot, stirring occasionally, until it starts to brown and stick to the bottom. Add tamarind, stock or broth, coconut milk, fish sauce, and sugar. Bring to a gentle boil, then lower heat to medium low. If you are using the optional garnishes like lemongrass, galangal, and lime leaves, throw those in now.
3. Let simmer for 5 minutes. Stir in raw meat, then let soup come up to boiling again. Add vegetables, then let soup come back up to boiling again.
4. Right before serving, add cilantro and lime juice. Serve hot and garnish with extra cilantro, but instruct diners not to chew and swallow the lemongrass, galangal, and lime leaves. They are harmless but unpleasantly woody.

Thank You!

Thank you so much for reading the first book in my series!

Please enjoy my other culinary cozy mysteries featuring Violet and Jake by looking up my "Caterer's Guide to Crime" series on Amazon, or go to:

https://jessicathompsonauthor.com/CGSeries

To get more recipes or to sign up my newsletter, head to my website at:

https://jessicathompsonauthor.com/

Enjoy!

Jessica Thompson - Mystery Author

About the Author

When Jessica discovered mystery novels with recipes, she knew she had found her niche.

Now Jessica is the author of the Amazon best-selling "Caterer's Guide to Crime" culinary cozy mystery series and the classic mystery, "Shoot Shovel and Shut Up." Her first book was a finalist in the Wishing Shelf Awards and her other books were Whitney Award nominees in the mystery category. She has also curated two anthologies and has been included in many others. She is active in her local writing community and volunteers on the Board of Directors of the Storymakers Guild.

As an avid home chef and food science geek, Jessica has won cooking competitions and been featured in the online Taste of Home recipe collection. She also tends to be the go-to source for recipes, taste-testing, and food advice among her peers.

Jessica lives outside Austin, Texas with her husband and

two children. When she's not writing or cooking, she likes getting her boots dirty with the family at her parents' nearby Longhorn cattle ranch.

You can connect with me on:
- https://jessicathompsonauthor.com
- https://www.facebook.com/jessicathauthor
- https://www.instagram.com/jessicathauthor2

Subscribe to my newsletter:
- https://jessicathompsonauthor.com/email-list-1

Also by Jessica Thompson

Mysteries that are clean, exciting, and delicious!

A Caterer's Guide to Love and Murder
Book 2 in the Series
   A wedding caterer, a florist...and a dash of poison.
   "Wow, this dough is sexy!"
   As their wedded bliss starts to show signs of serious strain, Violet and her new husband, Jake, put their feelings aside to focus on catering a wedding that could make or break her career.

When murder ruins the rehearsal dinner, and her sister, Greta, the florist, becomes the prime suspect, Violet risks everything to clear her – and still deliver the beautiful wedding her new friend deserves.

But will she be in time before the killer dishes out seconds?

A Caterer's Guide to Love and Murder takes you on a culinary journey you won't forget!

A Caterer's Guide to Holidays and Homicide
Book 3 in the series

Deck the halls...with a personal chef, a snowed-in lodge, and a sprinkling of murder!

"Watch the knives!"

While acting as personal chef for a friend's mountain retreat, Violet and her husband, Jake, must set aside their stress over infertility and create a magical and delicious holiday – until tragedy crashes the party.

Being snowed in and unreachable from town, Violet and Jake end up hired for a different kind of job – finding out which of the guests committed murder and why they're trying to frame their hostess.

Violet must find a balance between following her gut and keeping it all under control until the police can reach them, while still managing the kitchen. But can she sniff out the killer before anyone else bites the big one?

A Caterer's Guide to Holidays and Homicide will give you a culinary holiday you won't forget!

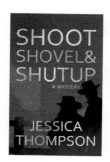

Shoot Shovel and Shut Up
"**Suspenseful, shocking, and sweet! A riveting mystery set in the heart of Texas.**"

-J.R. Lancaster, author of *Someone's Always Watching*

After a fight over the family ranch, Dad's young fiancée is found dead. Bria risks her family's disapproval to sneak around and investigate as the tragedies pile up. Luckily, she has help from her childhood crush and from the handsome new deputy.

When new love blooms in two directions and her suspect dies, she must face her grief and discover the family's secrets before she loses everyone she loves.

Made in the USA
Columbia, SC
11 October 2024

43434157R00178